Office 2003 XML
for Power Users

MATTHEW MACDONALD

APress Media, LLC

Office 2003 XML for Power Users

Copyright ©2004 by Matthew MacDonald

Originally published by Apress in 2004.

ISBN 978-1-59059-264-9   ISBN 978-1-4302-0707-8

DOI 10.1007/978-1-4302-0707-8

Trademarked names may appear in this book. Rather than use a trademark symbol with every occurrence of a trademarked name, we use the names only in an editorial fashion and to the benefit of the trademark owner, with no intention of infringement of the trademark.

Technical Reviewer: John Paul Mueller

Editorial Board: Dan Appleman, Craig Berry, Gary Cornell, Tony Davis, Steven Rycroft, Julian Skinner, Martin Streicher, Jim Sumser, Karen Watterson, Gavin Wray, John Zukowski

Assistant Publisher: Grace Wong

Project Manager: Beth Christmas

Copy Editor: Ami Knox

Production Manager: Kari Brooks

Production Editor: Laura Cheu

Proofreader: Linda Seifert

Compositor: Diana Van Winkle, Van Winkle Design Group

Indexer: James Minkin

Artist: Diana Van Winkle, Van Winkle Design Group

Cover Designer: Kurt Krames

Manufacturing Manager: Tom Debolski

Distributed to the book trade in the United States by Springer-Verlag New York, Inc., 233 Spring Street, 6th Floor, New York, NY, 10013 and outside the United States by Springer-Verlag GmbH & Co. KG, Tiergartenstr. 17, 69112 Heidelberg, Germany.

In the United States: phone 1-800-SPRINGER, email orders@springer-ny.com, or visit http://www.springer-ny.com. Outside the United States: fax +49 6221 345229, email orders@springer.de, or visit http://www.springer.de.

For information on translations, please contact Apress directly at 2855 Telegraph Avenue, Suite 600, Berkeley, CA 94706. Phone 510-549-5930, fax 510-549-5939, email info@apress.com, or visit http://www.apress.com.

The companion content for this book is available to readers at http://www.apress.com in the Source Code/Downloads section.

For Faria

Contents at a Glance

Contents

About the Author

Matthew MacDonald is an author, educator, and MCSD developer. He's a regular contributor to programming journals such as *Inside Visual Basic*, and the author of several books about .NET programming, including *The Book of VB .NET* (No Starch), *ASP.NET: The Complete Reference* (Osborne McGraw-Hill), and *Microsoft .NET Distributed Applications* (Microsoft Press). In a dimly remembered past life, he studied English literature and theoretical physics.

About the Technical Reviewer

John Paul Mueller is a hands-on programmer/author who has written 61 books and over 200 articles to date on topics that range from networking to artificial intelligence; from database management to heads-down programming. His current books include *Web Matrix Developer's Guide* from Apress, several C# developer guides, a small business and home office networking guide, a book on SOAP, and Windows XP user guides. John has provided technical editing services to more than 30 authors, as well as both *Database Advisor* and *Coast Compute* magazines. He has additionally contributed articles to *SQL Server Professional, Visual C++ Developer,* and *Visual Basic Developer.* He currently edits the .NET electronic newsletter for Pinnacle Publishing. Sign up for John's free newsletter, *.NET Developer eXTRA,* at http://www.freeenewsletters.com/. For updates and other book information, visit John's web site at http://www.mwt.net/~jmueller/.

Acknowledgments

No **AUTHOR COULD** complete a book without a small army of helpful individuals. I'm deeply indebted to the whole Apress team, including Laura Cheu and Beth Christmas, who helped everything move swiftly and smoothly; John Mueller, who performed expert tech review; Ami Knox, who performed the copy edit with an unerring light touch; and many other individuals who worked behind the scenes indexing pages, drawing figures, and proofreading the final copy. I owe a special thanks to Gary Cornell, who always offers invaluable advice about projects and the publishing world. He's helped to build a truly unique company with Apress.

Finally, I'd never write *any* book without the support of my wife and these special individuals: Nora, Razia, Paul, and Hamid. Thanks everyone!

Introduction

SINCE ITS INTRODUCTION in the late 1990s, XML has revolutionized the way data is stored, manipulated, and shared. XML has made it possible for applications written in different programming languages (and running on different operating systems) to exchange any type of information. XML also allows different organizations to "glue" together their business processes, so that a purchase order from one company can flow seamlessly into the inventory management system of another. At the same time, a host of XML-related standards has sprung up, defining standards for everything from real estate listings to vector graphics.

Of course, along with all these remarkable developments is one significant catch. If you want to harness the full features of XML, you need to write your own software. For example, if you want to funnel an expense report into an automated payment system, you need to create an application that can read the original format of the expense report (which might be Microsoft Excel or Word), and manually convert it into the appropriate XML representation. This type of application is difficult to create and even more difficult to maintain. It's also extremely fragile, meaning that minor changes in the layout of the source document can easily lead to conversion errors.

Life becomes even trickier if you want to create a workflow that sends data through several different people. For example, if an expense report needs to be created by an employee, verified by a team leader, and authorized by a supervisor, you'll need to convert the document to XML and then back to its original Office format several times. The current generation of Office applications just isn't designed with this type of scenario in mind. Every time you convert Office data to XML, you lose important formatting details, versioning information, macro code, and other Office-specific features. The result is that XML, which is widely touted as a universal language, is used mostly by application programmers—not by knowledge workers and business professionals.

Office 2003 promises to change all this, and bring XML to a whole new audience: Word and Excel power users. These users can now harness the benefits of XML without needing to write conversion macros or full-fledged applications. Of course, you'll still need to understand the fundamentals of XML, and how they are implemented in Office, which is where this book fits into the picture. In this book, you'll find a complete introduction to XML and related standards like XML Schema and XML Transformations. You'll also learn how XML technology is embedded into the Office 2003 application family.

As you'll discover throughout this book, the new XML features in Office 2003 are nothing short of revolutionary. Here are a few things that the new XML support in Office 2003 allows you to do:

- Edit standard XML files with all the tools of Word and Excel (like formulas and the spell checker).

- Take existing Word or Excel documents and output all or some of the content into any type of XML. This allows you to "plug" your documents into business processes and workflows. For example, your purchase order can be fed into any inventory management system, just by mapping the spreadsheet cells to the appropriate parts of a custom XML document.

- Take your XML and format it in a variety of ways. For example, you can create a Word document that contains a newspaper article, and convert it into rich HTML for a web site without disrupting the original format or using a line of code.

- Create "hybrid" XML documents that contain your data and the rich formatting information required for Office applications. This allows you to convert your data to XML and back to its native Office format, without causing the slightest change or loss of information.

- Mine the data in an XML Office document, using custom macros or applications—on any platform. For example, you could create a Visual Basic application that can read information about resume candidates from a series of Word resume documents.

- Create rich Word or Excel documents using any programming language, without even needing to have Office installed. All you need to do is generate the right XML.

You'll learn about all of these techniques in this book.

> **NOTE** *It's estimated that there is more data in Microsoft Excel spreadsheets than all the relational databases in the world combined, and Microsoft Word contains even more information. Opening up that data to other applications, platforms, and processes will take some time, but it could completely change the face of enterprise computing.*

Who Should Read This Book

This book is aimed at experienced Office users who want to use XML to unlock the data in Office spreadsheets and documents. You don't need to have any experience with XML in order to use this book, as it explains XML in detail. You also won't need to understand any type of programming, although basic knowledge of Visual Basic, VBScript, or Visual Basic .NET will help you use some of the more advanced tips and tricks shown in this book. Most of these examples are left to the end of each chapter. While impressive, they are entirely optional!

The one exception to this rule is Chapter 8, which shows how you can manage documents in an enterprise environment using Web services. I'll develop this approach using the freely downloadable .NET Framework and the free ASP.NET Web Matrix development tool. In order to reap the full benefits of this example, you'll need to get your hands dirty with a little Visual Basic .NET code.

What This Book Teaches You

This book provides the following:

- A detailed description of XML, and related standards like XML Namespaces, XML Schema, and XML Transformations. I'll also explain the philosophy behind XML, and when and why you should use it.

- A thorough explanation of the new XML mapping features in Word and Excel, and the XML importing and exporting features in Access.

- A close look at the WordML and SpreadsheetML formats, which allow you to store rich Word and Excel documents entirely in XML.

- An introduction to InfoPath, Microsoft's newest addition to the Office family, which allows you to create rich forms quickly for entering XML data.

- Code examples that mine XML data, generate Office documents dynamically, and use Web services to transmit data in large organizations.

What This Book Doesn't Teach You

Of course, it's just as important to point out what this book *doesn't* contain:

- An explanation of the basics of .NET, or any programming language. Office 2003 has a rich extensibility model that can be used with various languages and platforms, but this book won't explain them. (Apress provides many other fine books to fill this role.)

- A description of other new Office 2003 features (ones that don't involve XML). Also, this book won't use the more advanced Smart Document technology, which allows you to create XML expansion packs using full-fledged programming languages like Visual Basic 6 or Visual Basic .NET.

- A description of every possible related XML standard. Although I'll dissect the essentials, there are far too many related standards to cover in a single book!

Companion Content

In order to learn XML and its related standards, you need to see sample documents that show different formats, approaches, and content. In keeping with this philosophy, this book is packed full of a variety of realistic XML examples. Many of the chapters in this book present examples with sample XML files. You can download these files with the companion content for this book. Look for the files for a particular chapter in a directory named after the chapter. For example, *Chapter 03* will contain the initial Office and XML files you need to walk through the examples in Chapter 3. In addition, the companion content includes all the code examples presented in this book. To download these files, surf to http://www.prosetech.com or the Apress site at http://www.apress.com.

System Requirements

In order to use this book, you need the full Professional Edition or Enterprise Edition of Office 2003. The other Office versions (including Standard, Small Business, and Student and Teacher) don't provide the full XML features that this book explores. Also, you'll find that InfoPath is only included with the Enterprise Edition. Thus, if you're using the Professional Edition, you can safely skip Chapter 9. For more information about different Office versions and what they include, refer to http://www.microsoft.com/office/editions/howtobuy/compare.mspx.

All of the normal Office 2003 system requirements apply (as listed on http://www.microsoft.com/office). In addition, you'll see small code examples throughout this book that have been created using Visual Basic 6 or Visual Basic .NET. To run the .NET examples, you need to have the .NET runtime, which is about 23MB. If you don't already have it, you can install it using Windows Update by following these steps:

1. Go to the Windows Update web site. You can select Windows Update from the Start menu, or just go directly to http://windowsupdate.microsoft.com using your browser.

2. Scan for updates.

3. Select .NET Framework Version 1.1.

4. Choose to install it.

Additionally, if you have the Visual Basic 6 or Visual Basic .NET development tools installed, you'll be able to open the projects and look at the source code for these examples.

The case study in Chapter 8 has the following additional requirements:

- *Internet Information Services (IIS):* IIS is an optional component included with the Windows XP Professional and Windows 2000 Professional operating systems. It can be installed using the Add/Remove Windows Components section of the Add or Remove Programs dialog box.

- *Web Matrix:* This is the development tool you use to create .NET web applications. It's freely downloadable from http://www.asp.net.

- *The SOAP Toolkit:* This component allows applications to communicate with Web services. It's freely downloadable from http://msdn.microsoft.com/downloads/list/websrv.asp.

All of these components are free, and the installation and setup process for them is described in more detail in Chapter 8.

In addition, you might want to use some of the Office 2003 web downloads that are provided by Microsoft. These include Software Development Kits (SDKs) and Content Development Kits (CDKs) that show additional examples with Word and Excel XML, as well as full-blown sample applications written in various programming languages. For more information, refer to the list of downloads on Microsoft's MSDN site, at http://msdn.microsoft.com/downloads/list/office2k3.asp.

Feedback

You can send complaints, adulation, and everything in between directly to apress@prosetech.com. I can't solve your Office problems or critique your custom macro code, but I will benefit from information about what this book did right and wrong (and what it may have done in an utterly confusing way). Changes will be incorporated into future editions of this book.

Chapter Overview

This book is designed to give you the essentials you need to start using XML in Office 2003 as quickly as possible. I recommend that you read the chapters in order, because later chapters often rely on the background presented in the earlier chapters. If you are new to XML, you'll need to start with Chapter 1 and Chapter 2, which explain XML and its philosophy, before you get a chance to dig into any Office applications.

The next few sections give you a chapter-by-chapter preview of what's ahead.

Chapter 1: Understanding XML

This chapter presents XML from the ground up. You'll learn how XML works, and why it's so important to have a standard way to create structured documents. You'll also learn about the different types of XML documents that are possible, and see examples of data-oriented and narrative-style documents. The chapter also describes XML Namespaces, which allows you to distinguish and identify different XML-based formats, and introduces the promise of XML in Office 2003.

Chapter 2: XML Schema

XML is a flexible tool for structuring documents. Unfortunately, that very flexibility can lead to problems. Or to put it another way: with developers around the world creating their own XML languages, how do you allow them to communicate with one another? The answer is to define your document structure with an XML schema. In this chapter, you'll learn the basics of schema language, including ways to define structure, set data types, and apply more advanced rules.

Chapter 3: Mapping XML in Excel

Now that you've learned the basics of XML and XML Schema, it's time to put your knowledge to work with Office 2003. In this chapter, you'll learn how you can map an XML structure to a spreadsheet. This opens up two important opportunities. First of all, you can use Excel to graph and analyze XML data—even if this XML data is retrieved dynamically from a business application or the Internet. Secondly, you can use mapping to export the data in existing spreadsheets to XML. This allows other applications to process that data, rather than leaving it trapped inside Excel's proprietary format.

Chapter 4: Mapping XML in Word

Word also provides features that allow you to map XML structures to Word documents. These features revolve around one new innovation: Word's schema library. Once a schema is imported into the library, you can use it to open existing XML files or map new Word documents. In this chapter, you'll learn how to master the schema library, and use it to export XML. You'll also learn how to build a template that looks like an ordinary Word document, but contains hard-wired XML mapping information.

Chapter 5: Exporting and Importing XML in Access

The XML features in Access stop far short of Word and Excel's mapping features, but they still provide a few interesting tricks. Notably, you can export database records into XML documents, complete with schemas that describe the structure of these documents. You can also perform the same task in reverse, and load a database with information extracted from an XML file.

Chapter 6: WordML and SpreadsheetML

WordML and SpreadsheetML are two specialized XML languages that preserve all the information in Word documents and Excel spreadsheets. If you save your documents using these standards—and it only requires a few extra mouse clicks—you'll get pure XML content without losing information like rich formatting, styles, or graphics. This opens up some interesting possibilities for interacting with custom applications that can use the WordML and SpreadsheetML standards to extract data from your Office files, or generate new documents on the fly. This chapter dissects both languages.

Chapter 7: Transforming XML

In the business world, different applications use different types of XML, and it's often important to be able to transform one type of XML into another. The standard that makes this type of transformation possible is the Extensible Stylesheet Language (XSL), and you'll get a solid introduction to it in this chapter.

Chapter 8: Managing Workflow with XML Web Services

Now that you've learned about the various core XML standards and the Office XML features, how do you put it all together? In this chapter, you'll see one possible answer, with a custom solution that automates part of an expense report workflow. It uses Excel mapping, Web services, a little custom macro code, and an XSLT stylesheet to create a web page.

Chapter 9: InfoPath

InfoPath is Microsoft's newest Office application, and it's designed to solve XML data-entry challenges that are awkward or tedious with applications like Word and Excel. Using InfoPath, you can create interactive forms based on any XML schema. Other users can then fill out these forms and submit their data directly to a Web service. All in all, InfoPath just might help you automate the process of collecting data in an organization.

CHAPTER 1

Understanding XML

XML IS, AT ITS SIMPLEST, a remarkably flexible and elegant approach for storing and transmitting data. Contrary to popular assumption, XML isn't really a data format—instead, it's a language that allows you to define *your own* data format. The reason XML has proved so successful is because it allows anyone to quickly create simple, customized documents, while retaining enough power to handle much more dense and complex information. Today, XML is at work in fields ranging from law, finance, and software design to physics, journalism, and music notation. It's no exaggeration to say XML can handle any kind of information, including binary or image data, long free-flowing text, tables and grids, and semistructured documents.

This chapter introduces both the syntax and philosophy of XML. You'll learn how to create your own XML documents (and why you should), and how to structure all types of data. You'll also learn about XML namespaces, which allow you to distinguish different XML documents.

A Brief History of XML

XML, the Extensible Markup Language, is a descendant of a much more complex standard known as the Standard Generalized Markup Language (SGML). SGML was invented in the 1970s as a standardized system for defining any type of data format. Understanding SGML is not for the faint of heart—not only does the specification span over 150 extremely technical pages, but it also considers many special cases that are rarely encountered. Many software programs only support a subset of SGML, and different subsets aren't necessarily 100 percent compatible with one another. That said, SGML is still in use in the world today. It's found in the publishing industry, in the world of aeronautics, and in the military. SGML was also used to create HTML, the language of the Web.

In the mid 1990s, several SGML gurus worked to create a lighter version of SGML, one that would preserve its power and flexibility but eliminate features that were too complex, confusing, or redundant. This scaled-down version of SGML was XML, and it became an instant success when the World Wide Web Consortium (W3C) released it in 1998.

In the years that followed, the XML standard remained unchanged. At the time of this writing, there is only one official version of XML (version 1.0), although there is a proposed version (1.1) that introduces minor refinements for dealing with non-English character encodings.[1] The real enhancements to XML have taken the form of dozens of separate XML-related standards that have sprung up in the meantime. These standards deal with issues like validating, searching, transforming, and linking XML documents. Understanding this tangled thicket of core XML standards is what distinguishes the casual user from the XML guru.

Much as SGML was used to create HTML, XML has been applied in countless industries to define standard formats for everything from resumes and legal pleadings to voice mail systems. XML has also been incorporated into a number of new technologies, including Web services (where it's the format for messages exchanged between applications and over the Internet), and now Microsoft Office. You might use XML to define your own data formats, or maybe you'll just apply an industry standard. In either case, it's keenly important to understand the basics of XML syntax.

The XML Philosophy

XML was designed as a universal way to represent data. Having a universal standard allows businesses, developers, and knowledge workers to stop worrying about how to exchange data between different platforms, and get back to work thinking about what they want to do with that data.

Of course, no single format, no matter how rich it is, can concisely and easily represent everyone's data. E-commerce applications need to be able to track order details and product lists, news agencies need to create articles, and scientists need to model complex equations. It's impossible for any single markup language to define all these ingredients. For that reason, XML isn't really a language, but a *metalanguage*—in other words, it's a language used to create other languages. In the same way that SGML was used to create the HTML standard, XML can be used to create your own markup languages.

For example, you might create the following XML document to store a list of product names:

```
<ProductList>
    <Product>Rare China Teapot</Product>
    <Product>Exercise Video</Product>
    <Product>Blank CD Media</Product>
</ProductList>
```

---

1. For the somewhat intimidating technical lowdown on XML, see http://www.w3.org/TR/REC-xml (for XML 1.0) and http://www.w3.org/TR/xml11 (for XML 1.1).

This XML document stores three pieces of information: the product names Rare China Teapot, Exercise Video, and Blank CD Media. In addition, the document conveys the meaning of this information using *tags*, which are delineated using angle brackets (< and >). The tags aren't part of the data—instead, they provide the contextual information that explains what the data *is*. Compare it with this non-XML document, which contains the same data, but is more difficult to interpret:

```
Rare China Teapot,
Exercise Video,
Blank CD Media
```

Using the XML version, an application could search for all the <Product> tags to find out what products are available in your product list. The same task is possible with the non-XML version, but the application would need to make more assumptions about how the data is organized.

The most important characteristic of XML is its flexibility. The previous example uses exactly two tags: <ProductList> and <Product>. However, these tags aren't defined in the XML language. The author of this XML document created them because they provide a useful way to describe this data. Or, to look at in another way, you could say that the product list shown previously is created in a markup language I'll call ProductListML. ProductListML is a custom XML-based language that defines two tags, <ProductList> and <Product>, and is used to store product list information. There is no limit to how many languages XML can create. A conservative estimate would put the number of current XML-based markups in the thousands.

In fact, another user who wants to store similar information might very well create a similar but incompatible XML markup, like this one:

```
<products>
    <product>
        <name>Rare China Teapot</name>
    </product>
    <product>
        <name>Exercise Video</name>
    </product>
    <product>
        <name>Blank CD Media</name>
    </product>
</products>
```

The success of the XML standard is largely due to this simplicity, which makes it easy for XML parsers to be implemented on a wide range of platforms and used in applications that run in almost any language on any operating system. Another important factor is the flexibility of XML. The XML standard is a little like a common alphabet. Any application can use this common alphabet to define its own language, which is best suited to the kind of data it works with.

XML vs. HTML

If you've authored HTML web pages before, you might notice that XML has a superficial resemblance to HTML. Like an XML document, an HTML document is made up of tags. However, the similarities end there. To better understand the difference, consider the following example, which shows a web page that displays the product catalog data shown earlier:

```
<html>
    <head>
        <title>Our products</title>
    </head>
    <body>
        <p>Rare China Teapot</p>
        <p>Exercise Video</p>
        <p>Blank CD Media</p>
    </body>
</html>
```

You'll notice that the tags no longer convey any information about the data. Instead they provide information to the web browser about how the real content should be displayed. In this example, <html> is a start tag, and </html> is an end tag. Everything in between is part of the HTML content for the page. The <head> tag identifies the start of header-related information like the web page title, and the <body> tag indicates where the web page itself starts. Currently, this web page contains rather modest contents: a series of three <p> tags representing three paragraphs, each with a single line of text. When opened in a browser, this HTML document renders as a simple page that contains a list of products, as shown in Figure 1-1.

In an HTML document, the tags represent formatting. An experienced web designer adds tags to represent paragraphs, lists, images, and tables, as well as to specify fonts, justification, and positioning. Unlike HTML, most XML documents are primarily concerned with the *content* of the data, not its appearance. In other words, an XML document might supply tags that identify types of information, like names, addresses, products, and so on. It won't describe how to display this information.

Another difference is that HTML is limited to a set of about 100 known tags. You can't define your own tags and use them in an HTML document, because web browsers won't be able to interpret them. XML, on the other hand, has no predefined tags. Instead, it defines rules for creating and naming your own elements, based on your own data.

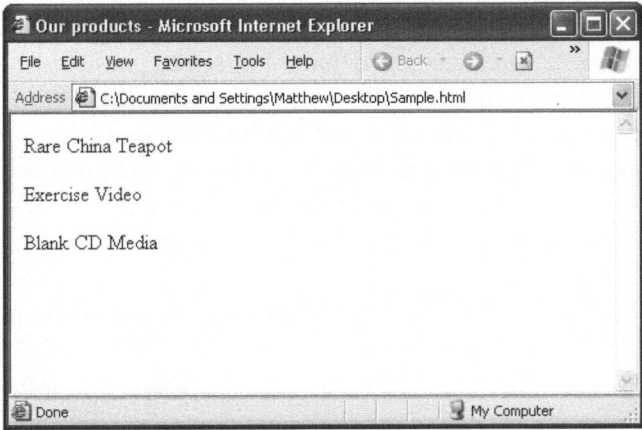

Figure 1-1. A simple HTML document

What XML Is Not

In all the excitement over XML, it's sometimes wedged into areas where it doesn't belong. This section debunks some of these myths.

- *XML is not a programming language.* XML documents aren't programs—and you can't "run" an XML document. An XML document is simply a container for data.

- *XML is not a relational database.* A database may contain some information stored in XML, or it might allow you to perform queries that return XML-formatted information (as does SQL Server 2000). These options use XML, but they aren't a part of the XML standard.

- *XML is not a network transport protocol.* If you want to send an XML document over the Internet, you have to use another standard.

- *XML is not a display language.* A web browser is not built to display XML documents, and XML documents rarely include any formatting information. XML is not a replacement for HTML.

- *An XML document is not necessarily a file.* It's convenient to think of an XML document as a physical file, and this is often the case. However, an XML document can just as easily reside in a database or in some application's memory.

Some of these myths are more widely believed than others. Even experienced developers are occasionally guilty of thinking they can replace their full-blown database systems (like Oracle or SQL Server) with a handful of XML files. If you understand the philosophy of XML, you'll recognize that this just isn't possible. Database systems are full-scale server products with a slew of advanced features. They allow multiple users to access and edit data at once without causing a conflict, and they cache information and precompile logic for optimum performance. These industrial-strength features are always required in a large business environment. In other words, XML determines what data looks like, but not how you interact with it.

XML documents often correspond to physical files on a computer's hard drive. For example, you might save the product list example to a file called Products.xml. XML documents can also exist solely in memory. For example, some types of XML documents are used to exchange information between Web services. In this case, the XML document is never stored anywhere; it's just sent over the network from one application to another.

Incidentally, it's possible to open an XML file in many web browsers, but all you'll see is the complete XML text. The latest versions of Internet Explorer are a little more sophisticated—they allow you to collapse and expand portions of an XML document, and they color-code text and tags, as shown in Figure 1-2.

If you want to test Internet Explorer's XML viewing features, start by creating an XML document. All XML files are stored in plain text, so you can't use a word processing application to create them.[2] Instead, use a simple text editor like Notepad. Save the file with the extension .xml, and then double-click it to launch Internet Explorer. Alternatively, you can drag and drop your XML file onto an open Internet Explorer window. Make sure you give the file the .xml extension, however, or IE will try to interpret it as HTML. Notepad, for example, will save all files with a .txt extension unless you explicitly select the All File option in the Save As Type field of the Save As dialog box. If you don't make this change, you'll end up with a file named something like Products.xml.txt, which won't display correctly in Internet Explorer.

---

2. Technically you could create a document in Word, and export it to plain text, but you would run into several problems, including replacing ordinary attribute quotes with curly quotes, and inadvertently splitting XML elements over line breaks. Both of these problems can cause errors reading the XML document. These are some of the issues that the XML integration in Office 2003 addresses.

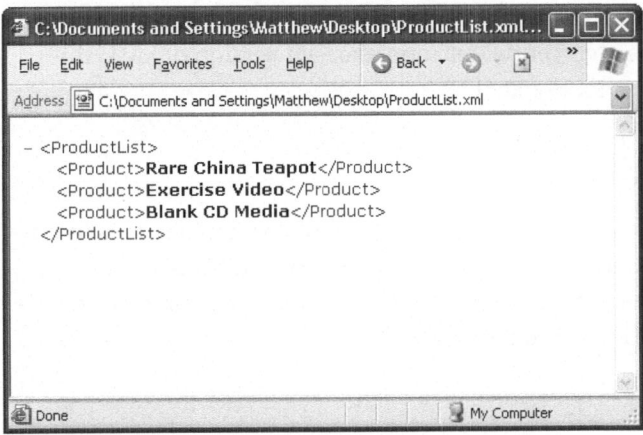

Figure 1-2. Looking at XML through a web browser

> **NOTE** *Being able to display XML in Internet Explorer is only a convenience. XML is meant for data storage, not data presentation. However, the XML standard does define a related standard for converting XML documents into presentation documents like web pages. This standard is XSLT, and we'll explore it in Chapter 7.*

The Rules of XML

So far, you've seen that an XML document is a simple text document made up of a combination of tags. In this section, you'll look at XML a little more closely, and learn the rules you need to follow when building your own XML documents.

The Document Prolog

The first line of an XML document is usually taken up with an XML declaration, or *document prolog*. This line indicates that the contents of the document are marked up using XML, and while it isn't required by all XML parsers, it's always recommended, as it removes the possibility of error. If you include the document prolog, it must be placed on the first line of the document, before any actual XML content. The examples listed in this book always include the document prolog, unless they are only showing part of an XML document.

At its simplest, the document prolog simply indicates the version of XML that is being used. Because there is currently only one released version of XML, this means the declaration always looks like this:

```
<?xml version="1.0" ?>
```

In addition, the prolog can indicate the text encoding, which becomes important if you are using a nonstandard character set. This is typically the case if you are creating an XML document in another language. Here's an example of a document prolog that indicates Unicode encoding:

```
<?xml version="1.0" encoding="Unicode" ?>
```

If you don't indicate the encoding, the XML parser may try to make a logical guess. The default depends on the platform and application. In a computer that runs the Windows 2000 or Windows XP operating system, you'll usually be dealing with UTF-8, which is a variable-length encoding that supports ordinary ASCII-encoded characters and special Unicode characters.

> **NOTE** *The basic idea behind UTF-8 is that ordinary characters are encoded the same way as they are in ASCII, using a single byte. This saves on disk and memory space. However, if you insert special characters—those that don't correspond to a number, letter, or standard symbol in the Western alphabet—they are encoded using up to 4 bytes. The bottom line is that UTF-8 is as efficient as ASCII for English documents, but it doesn't surrender the ability to use extended non-English alphabet characters if required.*

Encoding-related problems are rare, unless you are creating a non-English document. If you are creating a simple XML document using Notepad, you can choose the type of encoding for the file when you save the file, as indicated in Figure 1-3. Some early versions of Windows, such as Windows 95 and Windows 98, don't provide this feature. These operating systems are standardized on ASCII encoding. The end result is that you won't be able to correctly add non-English characters to an XML document with Notepad on these operating systems. You can find more information about Unicode and UTF-8 encodings at http://www.utf-8.com.

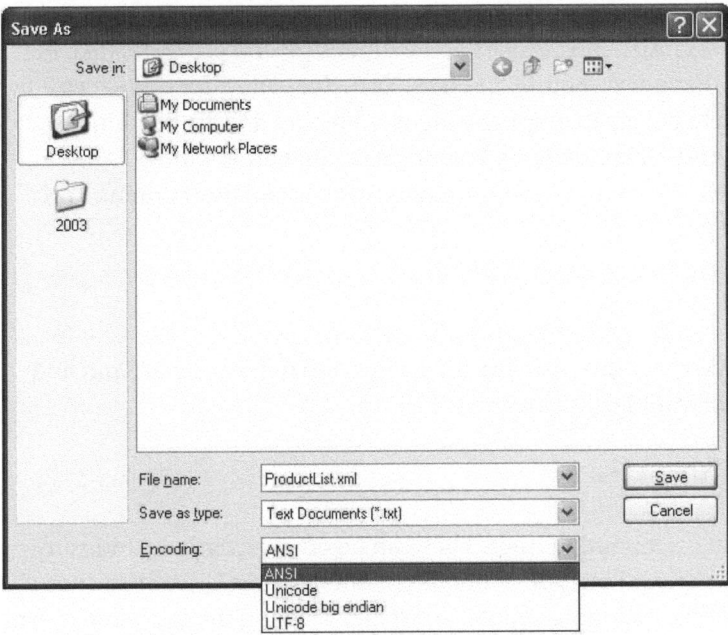

Figure 1-3. Setting the encoding for an XML text file

The document prolog is a type of processing instruction, and you can add additional instructions to convey some information to the XML parser about how it should process the document. However, most XML documents don't include any special processing instructions. You'll see one notable exception in Chapter 6, which looks at the native Office XML formats.

Elements and Tags

The basic building block for any XML document is the *element*. An element is composed of a start tag and an end tag. These tags are identical, except the end tag begins with the characters </ instead of just <.

Here's an example element named <MyTag>:

```
<MyTag>[Content goes here]</MyTag>
```

In XML, every start tag needs to have an end tag. This is much different than HTML, which tolerates much looser rules and includes several elements (like the line break tag <br>) that never require end tags. XML does allow for one exception, however. If you wish to create an empty element—one that doesn't contain any other content—you can indicate this by creating a tag that ends with />.

Here's an example of an empty element that can't contain any content, and doesn't need an end tag:

```
<MyTag />
```

Unlike HTML, XML tags are case sensitive. Thus, the following start and end tags don't match, and would cause an error:

```
<MyMismatchedTag></mymismatchedtag>
```

Tags follow fairly strict naming rules. They can be of any length, include any alphanumeric character, and include hyphens (-), underscores (_), and periods (.). Other special characters, including spaces, aren't allowed, and the tag name must start with an underscore or letter. XML documents also support characters from non-English alphabets.

These are all examples of valid tags:

```
<Month-Day-Year>...</Month-Day-Year>
<date_of_birth>...</date_of_birth>
<_BirthDate>...</_BirthDate>
<Année>...</Année>
```

These tags won't pass the test, and will be rejected by an XML parser:

```
<Month/Day/Year>...<Month/Day/Year>
<date of birth>...</date of birth>
<Customer's_BirthDate>...</Customer's_BirthDate>
<1Date>...</1Date>
```

> **TIP** *Of course, matters of style are quite separate from issues of syntactical correctness. Most XML standards avoid any special characters, including underscores, and separate values using capitalization, as in <birthDate> or <BirthDate>. The first example, where the element begins with a lowercase letter, is called* camel case, *and is a common approach.*

Element Contents

Elements can contain character data or other elements. For example, consider the following element, named <firstName>, which contains a single piece of information: the text "Joe."

```
<firstName>Joe</firstName>
```

Elements always contain text information, because XML is text-based. You can't directly store binary data, like images. However, applications can use different ways to "translate" binary data into text data if they need to insert it in an XML file. One common example is Base64 encoding, which changes binary data into a string of legal XML characters.

Following is an example of how a small picture stored in XML might look with Base64 encoding. The resulting XML isn't human-readable, but an application could convert it back to a stream of bytes and work with it as an image.

```
<myPicture>LZPVtzlndhYFJQIDAQABMAOGCSqGSIb3DQEBAgUAA1kACKrOPqphJYw1j+YPtcIqiWlFP
uN5jJ79Khfg7ASFxskYkEMjRNZV/HZDZQEhtVaU7Jxfzs2wfX5byMp2X3U/5XUXGx7qusDgHQGs7Jk9W
8CW1fuSWUgN4w==</myPicture>
```

Elements can also contain other elements. In fact, this is a basic principle for organizing information XML. For example, a <person> tag might represent information about a client. This information could be split into separate subelements, like <firstName> and <lastName>, both of which will be placed inside the <person> element. For good measure, the whole <person> element could be inserted into a <customers> element, which would represent a list of people. The final, completely valid XML document with the information from two customers is shown here:

```
<?xml version="1.0" ?>
<customers>

    <person>
        <firstName>Anne</firstName>
        <lastName>Marly</lastName>
    </person>

    <person>
        <firstName>Joe</firstName>
        <lastName>Mihevc</lastName>
    </person>

</customers>
```

You could enhance this document by adding more <person> elements (one for each customer), or adding more elements to represent person information, like <birthDate> and <countryOfResidence>.

This example adds some *whitespace* (empty lines and spaces) between the elements so that you can better see how they are organized. In this case, the more deeply an element is nested, the more it's indented. However, it's important to realize that this whitespace is completely ignored by any XML parser, and is just used to make it easier for human reading. In fact, the preceding example is completely equivalent to this much less legible version:

```
<?xml version="1.0" ?>
<customers><person><firstName>Anne</firstName><lastName>Marly</lastName></person>
<person><firstName>Joe</firstName><lastName>Mihevc</lastName></person>
</customers>
```

In this example the XML document takes three lines after the prolog, but that is also completely arbitrary. There's no reason that all the elements and their content couldn't be placed into a single awkwardly long line.

Element Relations

When an element is contained by another element, it's described as the *child* of that element. In the previous example, <firstName> and <lastName> are both child elements of the <person> element. In turn, <person> is the child element of <customers>. You can also look at it the other way round, and say that <customers> is the *parent* element of <person>.

Each element in an XML document has exactly one parent, except for the first element. This element is called the document or *root element*, and it contains all the other elements and data. In the sample document, <customers> is the root element.

An XML document can only contain a single root element. Once you close the root element, you can't add any more tags or information. That means that the following XML markup is not a valid XML document, because there are two root <person> elements.

```
<?xml version="1.0" ?>
<person>
    <firstName>Anne</firstName>
    <lastName>Marly</lastName>
</person>

<person>
    <firstName>Joe</firstName>
    <lastName>Mihevc</lastName>
</person>
```

Figure 1-4 and 1-5 show two different ways to conceptualize the sample customer list document shown earlier. Figure 1-4 shows how the elements are nested. It clearly shows that the <customers> element contains the rest of the document, the <person> element contains the first and last name information, and so on. However, it's often more convenient to think of an XML document as a tree, with the root node at its very base. Figure 1-5 shows a tree view of the XML document, which allows you to quickly identify how nodes are related.

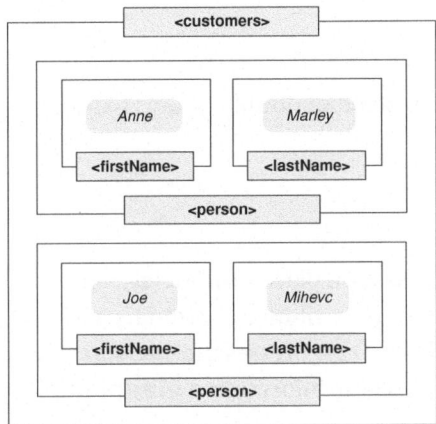

Figure 1-4. Nested elements in XML

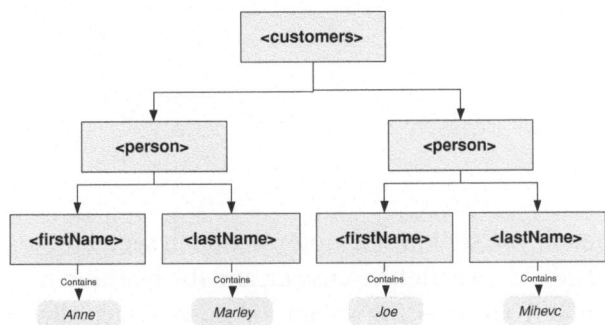

Figure 1-5. An XML tree

Note that only the deepest level of elements contains text content. This isn't a requirement (XML is very flexible), but it's a convention of data-centric XML documents. We'll consider it in more detail later in this chapter.

Attributes

So far, I've shown how you can add character data to an XML document inside a set of tags. But there is one other way to add data: by using *attributes*.

Attributes embed a piece of information into a start tag. Every attribute is made up of an attribute name and an attribute value. Following is an example that shows an attribute named id placed inside a <person> tag. The value for the id attribute is 400.

```
<person id="400" >...</person>
```

You can also use single apostrophe marks instead of double quotes to mark the attribute value:

```
<person id='400' >...</person>
```

There's no limit to the number of attributes you can place inside a tag, you simply need to separate them by spaces. You can add attributes to ordinary start elements, or to empty elements. Here's an example that compresses the <person> tag and its subelements into a single empty tag, with all the information in attributes:

```
<person firstName="Anne" lastName="Marly" />
```

This conveys the same amount of information as the following set of three nested elements:

```
<person>
    <firstName>Anne</firstName>
    <lastName>Marly</lastName>
</person>
```

The obvious question is whether you should store information in separate child elements or in attributes. There is no definitive answer, and the question is often a hot debate topic between XML gurus. Using separate elements is usually more flexible, as it allows you to easily include lengthy data fields, and add elements that contain other elements.

A basic rule of thumb is to use attributes when the information modifies the element in a subtle way, but use elements when you need to identify distinct pieces of related information. For example, imagine an XML document with order information. The <order> element contains all the details of the physical order record, including the order date, purchase amount, client, and product name, as shown here:

```
<order>
    <orderDate>2003-12-20</orderDate>
    <purchaseAmount>943.22</purchaseAmount>
    <clientName>Amax Systems</clientName>
    <productName>Rare China</productName>
</order>
```

However, this information on its own might not be entirely clear. A large multinational company might also need to track the type of currency that the order uses, as well as the time zone that should be used to interpret the date information. In addition, each order may be assigned a priority level by a sales manager after the fact. All of this contextual information is required by the applications that process the order XML document, but these details aren't a part of the original order record. For that reason, the company decides to store it using attributes as follows:

```
<order priority="10">
    <orderDate timeZone="GMT">2003-12-20</orderDate>
    <purchaseAmount currency="US">943.22</purchaseAmount>
    <clientName>Amax Systems</clientName>
    <productName>Rare China</productName>
</order>
```

Remember, whether or not you use attributes is a design decision. Other types of information that you might want to store outside the main XML document data in attributes includes anything that isn't directly related to the element content, like versioning information. Here's one example with an XML element that represents a news article:

```
<newsArticle versionState="Modified" version="1.2" lastUpdate="2003-10-10">
    <headline>All Is Quiet in Local City</headline>
    <story>Nothing much happened today.</story>
</newsArticle>
```

TIP *Order is not important when dealing with attributes. XML parsers treat attributes as a collection of unordered information relating to an element. On the other hand, the order of elements often is important. Thus, if you need a way of arranging information and preserving its order, use elements, not attributes.*

Entity References

There are a number of special characters that can't be used for XML content, because they have a special meaning in XML documents. For example, the angle brackets are used exclusively to denote tag names. That means the following XML is illegal:

```
<text>My favorite HTML element is the <p> paragraph.</text>
```

In this case, an XML parser will attempt to process the <p> text as though it were a tag name that starts a new element. An error will occur because there is no corresponding </p> tag to end the element.

In order to avoid this problem, you need to use an XML *entity reference.* Entity references allow you to insert special characters in an XML document using a special syntax that will always be correctly recognized. For example, the entity reference for the < angle bracket is < and > is the entity reference for the > angle bracket. Using these entity references, you can rewrite the preceding XML snippet like this:

```
<text>My favorite HTML element is the &lt;p&gt; paragraph.</text>
```

When you read the raw XML directly using an editor like Notepad, the entity reference looks quite different from the expected characters. However, when you load this XML into an XML parser like a web browser, the entity reference will be converted to the intended character. The same is true of the Office 2003 XML support. It will perform entity replacements automatically as needed, which means you won't need to worry about this issue.

XML includes the following predefined *character elements*:

Ampersand (&)	&amp;
Greater-than sign (>)	&gt;
Less-than sign (<)	&lt;
Apostrophe (')	&apos;
double quotation (")	&quot;

The last two aren't required, because you can use apostrophes and quotation marks inside XML text. However, they are sometimes useful when you set attribute values. For example, here's an attribute that contains a double quotation mark:

```
<text content="This is &quot;interesting&quot;"
```

You can also define your own entities and use them in XML documents, but this feature won't be covered in any detail in this book.

XML writers have one other option for dealing with illegal symbols like the angle brackets: They can define a special *CDATA section*, which will allow all special characters. A CDATA section begins with the instruction `<![CDATA[` and ends when the instruction `]]>` is encountered. Special characters are permitted in the content in between.

Here's an example that solves the earlier problem with a CDATA section:

```
<text><![CDATA[My favorite HTML element is the <p> paragraph.]]></text>
```

CDATA is usually used if you have a block of text with numerous special characters. Keep in mind that CDATA is a convenience for XML writers, and it doesn't affect the way your XML is treated once it's read and loaded into memory by an XML parser. In other words, both using a CDATA section and using entity replacement are equivalent approaches. If you were to create a custom order processing application that reads XML order documents, it would have no way to know whether the original XML files used entity replacement or CDATA sections, because the XML parser that's built into the programming language would perform this conversion automatically. The custom application would simply be able to access the converted data.

Finally, XML also supports numbered character entities. For example, the character entity `&#174;` represents the 174st character in the current character set, which by default is the ® symbol. Character entities are intended as a convenience for entering symbols that are otherwise difficult to type. You can also specify the character position using a hexadecimal number by prefixing the value with an x. Thus you can replace the character `&#174` with the hexadecimal value `&#xAE`.

Comments

The final XML ingredient discussed in this chapter is XML comments. Comments can be placed anywhere in a document, except before the XML declaration or inside a tag name. Comments are variable-length text that you insert between an initial `<!--` marker and a closing `-->` marker. Comments, like all XML content, can span multiple lines.

Here's an example that adds two comments to a document:

```
<?xml version="1.0" ?>
<customers>

    <!-- This is a person record. -->
```

```
<person>
    <firstName>Anne</firstName>
    <!-- Is the last name correct? -->
    <lastName>Marly</lastName>
</person>
</customers>
```

XML comments are completely ignored by XML parsers. That means that you won't see XML comments when you map XML data to an Office 2003 document (as you'll see in Chapters 3 and 4). It's also worth noting that XML comments have nothing to do with comments in Word or Excel.

Comments can be used to identify the purpose of a document, describe a tangled element hierarchy, or leave a message for another user who is editing the same document. Comments can also be used to "hide" parts of an XML document from an XML parser. For example, the following XML document appears to contain two <person> elements, but one is commented out. That means that the XML parser will only retrieve and process the first <person> element.

```
<?xml version="1.0" ?>
<customers>
    <person>
        <firstName>Anne</firstName>
        <lastName>Marly</lastName>
    </person>

    <!-- The next element is hidden in a comment
        <firstName>Joe</firstName>
        <lastName>Mihevc</lastName>
    </person> -->
</customers>
```

This technique can be useful if you are testing a modification to an XML document or trying to solve a problem.

NOTE *Comments are only used when you are directly editing a raw XML file. For that reason, this book won't use them often. Instead, you'll concentrate on how to import and export XML documents through the XML parsers built into the Office 2003 applications.*

Well-Formed XML

XML is a fairly strict standard. This strictness is designed to preserve broad compatibility. When it comes to storing business data, small variations in syntax and structure can't be ignored. If different applications interpret the same document in different ways it could cause catastrophic problems. (This isn't a concern for HTML, which is much more lenient, because it simply needs to display data in a browser. As a result, it's quite possible to create an HTML web page with errors that will be successfully rendered in one browser but will be interpreted differently in another. This isn't acceptable in XML.)

To prevent this sort of problem, all XML parsers perform a few basic quality checks. If an XML document doesn't meet these standards, it's rejected outright. If the XML document does follow these rules, it's deemed to be *well formed*. Well-formed XML isn't necessarily correct XML—for example, it could still contain incorrect data—but it can be parsed by an XML processor.

To be considered well formed, an XML document must meet these criteria:

- Every start tag must have an end tag.

- An empty element must end with />.

- Elements can never overlap. In other words,
  <person><firstName></firstName></person> is valid, but
  <person><firstName></person></firstName> is not.

- An element can't have two elements with the same name (because there will be no way to distinguish them from each other). However, you can have elements with the same name in different places. For example, you can place a <name> element inside multiple <product> elements and a separate <customer> element.

- A document can only have one root element.

- All attributes must have quotes around the value.

- The document must not contain illegal characters.

- Comments and processing instructions can't be placed inside tags.

To quickly test whether an XML document is well formed, try opening it in Internet Explorer. Figure 1-6 shows an error reported by Internet Explorer when it discovers improperly nested tags.

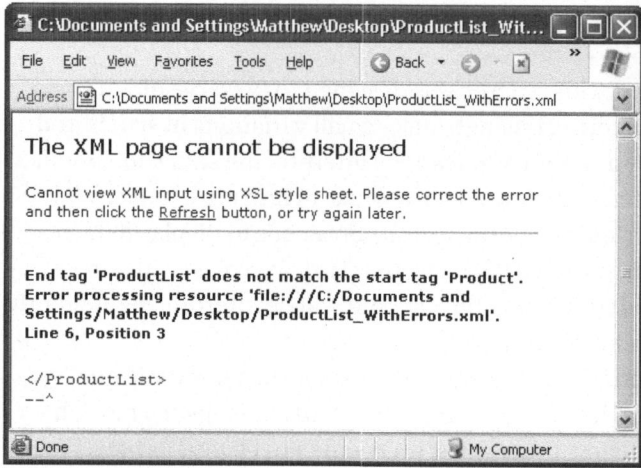

Figure 1-6. Diagnosing an XML document that is not well formed

Types of XML Documents

The previous sections have dissected the basic building blocks of XML in detail. To create your own XML document, you simply decide how you want to organize your data, what tag names you want to use, and how your elements should be arranged. You can then insert the actual data into the appropriate elements.

XML allows a wide variety of different document structures. However, most of these document structures fall into one of two categories:

- *Data-centric:* They hold lists of information, like tables of customers, items, orders, and so on.

- *Document-centric:* They follow a looser, free-flowing structure and are used for traditional document types like news articles, resumes, essays, short stories, and so on.

The next two sections present a few examples of both types of documents.

Data-Centric XML

Data-centric documents follow a rigid tree model. They are most often used to store information used in a business process (like a shipment confirmation) or retrieved from a database (like a product catalog). In a data-centric document, an element can contain other elements *or* text data—not both. The actual text content is only contained in the deepest layer of elements.

The following example shows a classic data-centric document that represents a product catalog. It starts with some generic product catalog information, followed by a product list with itemized information about two products.

```
<?xml version="1.0" ?>
<productCatalog>
    <catalogName>Acme Fall 2003 Catalog</catalogName>
    <expiryDate>2004-01-01</expiryDate>

    <products>
        <product id="1001">
            <productName>Magic Ring</productName>
            <productPrice>342.10</productPrice>
        </product>
        <product id="1002">
            <productName>Flying Carpet</productName>
            <productPrice>982.99</productPrice>
        </product>
    </products>
</productCatalog>
```

Data-centric documents can easily store more than one list. For example, a product catalog might realistically store a list of product categories and a list of products. An application parsing this catalog can map products to categories using the categoryID information, although this step won't take place automatically.

```
<?xml version="1.0" ?>
<productCatalog>
    <categories>
        <category id="1">
            <categoryName>One-of-a-Kind Items</categoryName>
        </category>
        <category id="2">
            <categoryName>Housewares</categoryName>
        </category>
        <category id="3">
            <categoryName>Fresh Food</categoryName>
        </category>
    </categories>

    <products>
```

```
        <product id="1001">
            <productName>Magic Ring</productName>
            <productPrice>342.10</productPrice>
            <categoryID>1</categoryID>
        </product>
        <product id="1002">
            <productName>Flying Carpet</productName>
            <productPrice>982.99</productPrice>
            <categoryID>1</categoryID>
        </product>
    </products>
</productCatalog>
```

There's another way to organize this data: using a parent-child list. In this case, products would be nested under the category elements they belong to. This structure is typically more complex, but it's also easier to analyze, because the relationship of different items is obvious.

```
<?xml version="1.0" ?>
<productCatalog>
    <categories>
        <category id="1">
            <categoryName>One-of-a-Kind Items</categoryName>

            <products>
                <product id="1001">
                    <productName>Magic Ring</productName>
                    <productPrice>342.10</productPrice>
                </product>
                <product id="1002">
                    <productName>Flying Carpet</productName>
                    <productPrice>982.99</productPrice>
                </product>
            </products>
        </category>

        <category id="2">
            <categoryName>Housewares</categoryName>
            <!-- Other products go here. -->
        </category>
        <category id="3">
            <categoryName>Fresh Food</categoryName>
            <!-- Other products go here. -->
```

```
        </category>
    </categories>

</productCatalog>
```

Which model you use depends on a number of factors, including the applications you use to process the XML (including Office 2003), and the ways you want to manipulate that data. Chapters 3 and 4 will delve into this issue in more detail.

Document-Centric XML

Document-centric data (also known as narrative or free-form data) usually adopts a mixed structure that mingles elements and text. As in a data-centric document, the outer layer of document-centric XML is primarily made up of elements that contain other elements. These elements establish the role of various text blocks. Here's a partial example:

```
<?xml version="1.0" ?>
<resume>
    <firstName>Sally</firstName>
    <lastName>Markov</lastName>
    <body>
        <objective></objective>
        <education></education>
        <workHistory></workHistory>
    </body>
</resume>
```

The difference between document-centric and data-centric XML data is found in the text content. In document-centric XML, the text data might include a combination of additional tags that indicates additional information, embedded objects like pictures, formatting, and so on. This is called *mixed content*, because XML elements and text data can be mixed in various ways, and aren't locked in a fixed hierarchical structure. In the resume document, the <objective>, <education>, and <workHistory> elements are likely to contain mixed content.

```
<?xml version="1.0" ?>
<resume>
    <firstName>Sally</firstName>
    <lastName>Markov</lastName>
    <body>
```

```
        <objective>To become an XML guru.</objective>
        <education>Study at numerous education instutions, including the
          <school>Julliard Academy</school> and <school>M.I.T.</school>.
        </education>
        <workHistory>Worked at a number of companies. At
          <company>Microsoft</company> I learned that XML is an important
          technology in the web-enabled world. At <company>IBM</company> I
          developed my own XML documents to store computer inventory information.
          This allowed us to automate production.
        </workHistory>
    </body>
</resume>
```

The benefits of this approach should be obvious. Automated programs that parse XML can easily filter out specific XML elements, even without any ability to understand the English language. By using elements like <company> and <school> in mixed mode, you make it possible for an application to mine important information and use it in reports, searches, and other tasks.

Similarly, formats for complex documents like news articles or books will also use mixed mode, possibly to indicate where pictures should be inserted, where technical terms are used, where cross-references should be created, and so on. One commonly used XML markup language is DocBook (see http://www.docbook.org for more information), which was designed by a consortium of companies and organizations for writing technical documentation. DocBook consists of several hundred defined tags that allow authors to create everything from short reference sheets to multiple-volume book sets. The following example shows how a portion of this book might be marked up using DocBook XML.

```
<?xml version="1.0"?>
<book>
    <title>XML for Office 2003 Power Users</title>
    <author>Matthew MacDonald</author>

    <chapter id="XMLIntro">
        <title>Understanding XML</title>

        <para><FirstTerm>XML</FirstTerm> is, at its simplest, a remarkably flexible
and elegant approach for storing and transmitting data. Contrary to popular
assumption, XML isn't really a data format. Instead, it's a language that allows
you to define <emphasis>your own data</emphasis> format ...</para>
        <para>This chapter introduces both the syntax and philosophy of XML.
  You'll learn ...</para>
```

```
<sect1>
    <title>A Brief History of XML</title>
    <para> XML, the Extensible Markup Language, is a descendant of a more
complex standard known as the Standard Generalized Markup Language ...</para>
        <figure id="simple-HTML-document">
    </sect1>


</chapter>
</book>
```

Note that the DocBook standard follows the XML philosophy by not explicitly specifying format information. Instead, it indicates information about the type of data. For example, you might use inline elements in a <para> element that identify technical terms, cross-references, footnotes, emphasized words, acronyms, footnotes, quotations, computer syntax, and so on. However, you don't specify how these items should be formatted. Another document is used to map the XML data to the appropriate type of output, allowing you to ensure that the XML data file remains clean and easy to edit.

> **TIP** *Crafting your own XML markup is an art. The best approach is to study as many examples as possible, particularly ones from your own industry. If possible, you may want to adopt an industry-standard XML markup that's already defined for your data. On the other hand, if you are using applications that require XML in a specific format, you might have no choice but to adopt that fixed format.*

XML Namespaces

As the XML standard gained ground, dozens of XML markup languages (often called XML *grammars*) were created, many of them specific to certain industries, processes, and types of information. Organizations began to adopt these fledgling standards rather than invent their own markup, so as to standardize their applications and support easier integration. In many cases, it became important to extend one type of markup with additional company-specific elements, or even create XML documents that combine several different XML grammars.

This development posed a new problem. First of all, what happens if you need to combine two XML grammars that use elements with the same names? How do you tell them apart? A related, but more typical problem occurs when an application needs to distinguish between XML grammars in a document. For example, consider an XML document that has order-specific information using a standard named OrderML, and client-specific information using a standard named ClientML. This document is sent to an order-fulfillment application that's only interested in the OrderML details. How can this application quickly filter out the information that it needs, and ignore the unrelated details? A similar problem might be created in document-oriented XML data if you need to insert an equation object using one XML standard, and vector graphics using another standard.

The solution is found in a standard that was released shortly after the XML 1.0 standard became official: XML Namespaces. The core idea behind this standard is that every XML markup language has its own namespace, which is used to uniquely identify all related elements. Technically, namespaces *disambiguate* elements, by making it clear what markup language they belong to.

All XML namespaces use Universal Resource Identifiers (URIs). Typically, these URIs look like a web page URL. For example, http://www.mycompany.com/mystandard is a typical name for a namespace. Though the namespace looks like it points to a valid location on the web, this isn't required (and shouldn't be assumed).

The reason that URIs are used for XML namespaces is because they are more likely to be unique. Typically, if you create a new XML markup, you'll use a URI that points to a domain or web site you control. That way, you can be sure that no one else is likely to use that URI. For example, the XML Schema standard (described in the next chapter), uses the namespace http://www.w3.org/2001/XMLSchema, because it was developed by the W3C, which controls the www.w3.org namespace. In this case, the URL does actually point to a web document—one that describes the standard. This is often a useful convention, but it's by no means required, and many namespaces don't point to anything at all.

> **TIP** *Namespace names must match exactly. If you change the capitalization in part of a namespace, add a trailing / character, or modify any other detail, it will be interpreted as a different namespace by the XML parser.*

To specify that an element belongs to a specific namespace, you simply need to add the xmlns attribute to the start tag, and indicate the namespace. For example, the following element is part of the http://mycompany/OrderML namespace:

```
<order xmlns="http://mycompany/OrderML"></order>
```

If you don't explicitly assign a namespace, the element will not be a part of any namespace.

It would be cumbersome if you needed to type in the full namespace URI every time you wrote an element in an XML document. Fortunately, when you assign a namespace using the xmlns attribute, it becomes the default namespace for all child elements. For example, in the following XML document, the <order> and <orderItem> elements are both placed in the http://mycompany/OrderML namespace:

```
<?xml version="1.0"?>
<order xmlns="http://mycompany/OrderML">
    <orderItem>...</orderItem>
    <orderItem>...</orderItem>
</order>
```

You can declare a new namespace for separate portions of the document. For example, here's an XML document where the <order> and <orderItem> elements are in the http://mycompany/OrderML namespace, and the <client>, <firstName>, and <lastName> elements are in the http://mycompany/ClientML namespace.

```
<?xml version="1.0"?>
<order xmlns="http://mycompany/OrderML">
    <client xmlns="http://mycompany/ClientML">
        <firstName>...</firstName>
        <lastName>...</lastName>
    </client>

    <order>
        <orderItem>...</orderItem>
        <orderItem>...</orderItem>
    </order>
</order>
```

When you use this approach, it's not always obvious which namespace an element belongs to. For that reason, it's far more common to use *namespace prefixes*. Namespace prefixes are short character sequences that you can insert in front of a tag name to indicate its namespace. You define the prefix in the xmlns attribute by inserting a colon (:) followed by the characters you want to use for the prefix.

Here's the order document rewritten with prefixes:

```
<?xml version="1.0"?>
<ord:order xmlns:ord="http://mycompany/OrderML"
 xmlns:cli="http://mycompany/ClientML">
    <cli:client>
        <cli:firstName>...</cli:firstName>
```

```
        <cli:lastName>...</cli:lastName>
    </cli:client>

    <ord:orderItem>...</ord:orderItem>
    <ord:orderItem>...</ord:orderItem>
</ord:order>
```

Namespace prefixes are simply used to map an element to a namespace. The actual prefix you use isn't important as long as it remains consistent. For example, the following document uses different prefixes, but is identical:

```
<?xml version="1.0"?>
<o:order xmlns:o="http://mycompany/OrderML"
 xmlns:c="http://mycompany/ClientML">
    <c:client>
        <c:firstName>...</c:firstName>
        <c:lastName>...</c:lastName>
    </c:client>

    <o:orderItem>...</o:orderItem>
    <o:orderItem>...</o:orderItem>
</o:order>
```

If you define a namespace without using a namespace prefix, it becomes the default namespace for that portion of the document. However, if you define a namespace prefix, that namespace *won't* be applied by default. In other words, if you define a namespace prefix, make sure you use it! In the next XML snippet, a namespace is defined, but it's not applied. Thus, the <order> element is not a part of any namespace.

```
<order xmlns:o="http://mycompany/OrderML">
```

Here's how you would correct the mistake:

```
<o:order xmlns:o="http://mycompany/OrderML">
```

Namespaces allow you to build complete modular XML documents that combine multiple XML grammars. They are used extensively in this book.

> **NOTE** *Namespaces aren't just an add-on to XML—they represent a key way to cat-alog different XML-based standards. All the Office applications use namespaces, and some—like Word—force you to use them in your XML documents.*

Namespaces and Attributes

Attributes act a little differently than elements when it comes to namespaces. You can use namespace prefixes with both elements and attributes. However, attributes don't use the default namespace of a document. That means if you don't add a namespace prefix to an attribute, the attribute will *not* be placed in the default namespace. Instead, it will have no namespace.

The following document demonstrates this point with a custom id attribute. The id attribute in the <client> tag is explicitly placed in the http://mycompany/ClientML namespace. On the other hand, the id attributes on the <orderItem> tags have no namespace at all.

```
<?xml version="1.0"?>
<ord:order xmlns:ord="http://mycompany/OrderML"
 xmlns:cli="http://mycompany/ClientML">
    <cli:client cli:id="1001">
        <cli:firstName>...</cli:firstName>
        <cli:lastName>...</cli:lastName>
    </cli:client>

    <ord:orderItem id="1">...</ord:orderItem>
    <ord:orderItem id="2">...</ord:orderItem>
</ord:order>
```

This probably isn't the behavior you expect, but it was a necessary tradeoff when the XML Namespaces standard was first created to ensure backward com-patibility in some applications. It won't be a real problem as long as you remember to always use namespace prefixes.

Testing Namespaces

If you'd like to practice with namespaces, you can use the simple test program included with the companion content for this chapter. This application requires the .NET Framework, and can be launched using the GetXMLNamespaces.exe file. To use the GetXMLNamespaces utility, you select an XML file (using the Browse button) and then click the Get Namespaces button. The display will show a list of all the elements in the XML document, and the namespace of each node. Figure 1-7 shows the output you will receive if you use the simple order XML file.

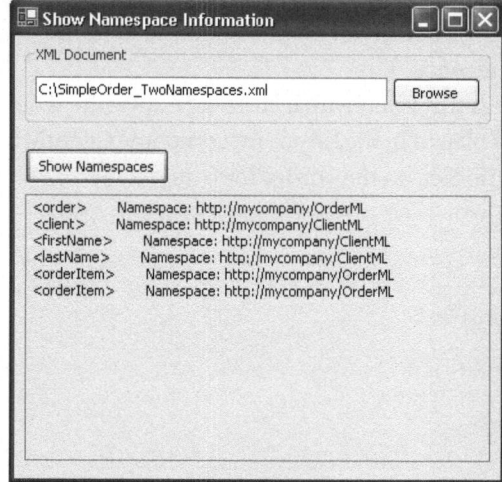

Figure 1-7. Testing namespaces with the GetXMLNamespaces utility

The Visual Basic .NET source code for this application is also provided in case you want to start exploring basic techniques for programming with XML.

The Promise of XML in Office 2003

Now that you've had a thorough introduction to XML, you're ready to consider the roles it can play in an enterprise system that uses Office 2003. XML is often described as an *enabling* technology, because it allows organizations and companies to build various types of automated solutions, without requiring a specific approach or technology.

By using XML in Office 2003, Microsoft introduces several new possibilities:

- Office applications can integrate with other XML-enabled Microsoft applications and technologies. Examples include SQL Server 2000, which can return query results as a custom XML document, and ASP.NET Web services, which can send all types of information over the Internet using XML.

- Office applications can integrate with custom applications. These applications might only consist of a few individual utilities built in the Office VBScript language, or they might include complete end-to-end systems designed around Visual Basic 6, the .NET Framework, or any other programming language.

The Office 2003 applications don't all support XML in the same way, or to the same degree. Word and Excel include some of the most full-featured support for importing and exporting XML data, while Access and Visio lag a little farther behind, and Outlook and PowerPoint lack XML features altogether. The next few sections present a quick summary of the XML features of different Office 2003 applications.

Word

First of all, Word includes the capability to edit almost any XML file. If you need to create XML documents, this allows you to leverage Word features like macros, spell check, drag-and-drop, and so on when working with XML data.

A much more useful feature is the ability to map XML elements to Word documents (an ability explored in Chapter 4). Using this approach, you can create a Word document that can export some of its data to custom XML markup. You can even retrofit existing documents and templates, unlocking data and exposing it to other applications and processes. You can use the exported XML data to mine important pieces of information, or you can apply other XML standards, like XSLT (presented in Chapter 7) to convert it to other formats, like an HTML web page.

Figure 1-8 diagrams one possible way that Word can be used in an enterprise system. Here, resume documents are mapped to a specific XML markup. Then, this XML can be transformed into a rich web page and posted to a partner web site, or made available to a custom search application that scans batches of XML files to filter out candidates with specific credentials.

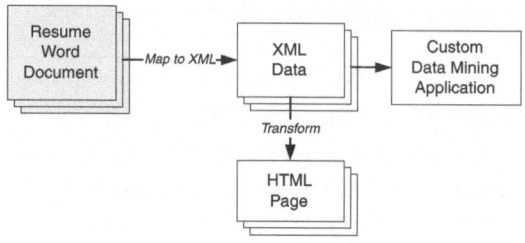

Figure 1-8. Mapping Word documents to XML

Finally, Word also includes a new option to export your documents to an XML format called *WordML*. This is a proprietary XML markup that preserves all Word-related information, including versioning, pictures, and formatting. WordML extends the reach of Word documents. Applications can create simple Word documents on the fly, just by writing an XML file in the WordML format. Applications can also extract any mapped XML data from inside the full-flown WordML document. Chapter 6 presents both of these techniques.

Excel

Excel has the capability to save spreadsheets in XML since Office XP. This format, called *SpreadsheetML,* doesn't include everything—charts and macro code won't be preserved, for example—but it does faithfully retain all the data and formatting.

Excel 2003 includes enhanced abilities to import XML data, and map XML data to spreadsheet cells (as you'll see in Chapter 3). This feature is similar to Word's mapping abilities, and it allows the same possibilities for mining data and reusing content. However, Excel also plays a unique role in data analysis. For example, you might create a spreadsheet that incorporates data from several XML sources (perhaps representing sales reports and profit forecasts), and then create charts and graphs to study the information. If the information changes, you can import the new results into your spreadsheet, and update the related charts, with a simple mouse click.

This ability becomes particularly useful when you consider where the XML data might be coming from. For example, you could read the XML document returned by a Web service. Assuming that this Web service returns the latest results from a server-side database, you can create a spreadsheet that never goes out of date. Figure 1-9 shows an example in which a spreadsheet imports the most up-to-date product catalog from a remote web server. The user then creates an order based on that data, and exports the order information to a different XML format. This XML format is fed to some sort of automated order processor (and can be submitted through e-mail, another Web service, a direct upload, or whatever technique suits best).

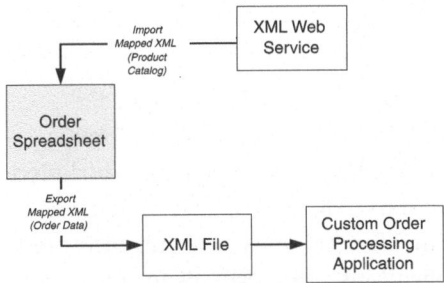

Figure 1-9. Analyzing XML data in Excel

Unfortunately, it still isn't possible to automate a workflow like this without writing some custom code (although it may become easier in future versions of Office as the XML foundation is solidified). Chapter 8 explores your options with an Office XML solution that integrates with a Web service.

Access

Access doesn't provide full integration with XML—in fact, full integration probably isn't possible or desirable. Relational database technology is fundamentally different from the structure of XML, although the two developments often complement one another. Access breaks data into related tables, stores it in a compact binary form, and is optimized for search and update operations with several users. XML doesn't replace these features, but it can play an important role when exchanging data with other applications.

The XML features in Access focus on allowing you to import data from XML into a database, and write database information to XML files. Chapter 5 explores these features.

Visio

Visio has provided the ability to save diagrams in XML since Visio XP. The latest release tweaks the file format to support Scalable Vector Graphics (SVG), a W3C standard XML markup for vector graphics. Custom XML data can be embedded in a Visio XML file, and extracted by another application or process. This book doesn't explore the Visio XML format.

PowerPoint, Outlook, and FrontPage

These three Office applications lack significant XML features. FrontPage does include a graphical tool for creating XSLT stylesheets that you can use to format XML, but it requires another Microsoft tool (SharePoint Services, which is included with Windows 2003 Server). Sadly, there are no stand-alone XML features. Power-Point and Outlook don't include any XML-related functionality, and currently there is no way to export data in either of these applications to an XML file format, although this may change in future releases.

InfoPath

InfoPath is an entirely new addition to the Office family, and it's designed with XML and Web services in mind. InfoPath allows you to design data entry forms that are based on XML documents. Once these forms are created, any user can create the appropriate type of XML documents using the graphical form. The features of InfoPath stretch beyond the XML mapping in Word or Excel to handle a variety of different types of information. Best of all, creating the forms is largely a drag-and-drop exercise.

Finally, InfoPath simplifies the stage that takes place after data entry—workflow. You can use InfoPath to submit data to a Web service or forward it via e-mail. InfoPath also allows you to present the same document in a variety of different views. This allows it to support different stages of a workflow, where different types of users need to enter or edit different parts of the document. Of course, InfoPath isn't required at every stage—as you would expect, everything you save in InfoPath is pure XML. Chapter 9 introduces InfoPath.

The Last Word

Now that this lightning tour of XML basics is drawing to a close, you should have a basic understanding of what XML is, how it looks, and why the world needs a structured document format. XML represents a new tool for breaking down the barriers between different businesses and platforms—it's nothing less than a universal toolkit for storing and communicating all types of information.

The key benefits of XML include the following:

- *XML is an open standard.* It's not tied to any company, and thus it isn't at risk of bankruptcy now that the dot-com boom has ended. It isn't tied to any software or technology, so it doesn't limit you to Windows computers, Apple computers, Unix, Java, C++, Visual Basic, or the Internet. XML isn't even tied to a specific writing system. You can create XML documents using Chinese symbols, the Russian alphabet, or any other language that has its own character encoding.

- *XML is flexible.* You can tailor XML so that you store your data in the format that makes most sense to you.

- *XML is simple.* It's easy for both applications and humans to read and understand average XML content. XML add-ons are handled by separate standards, all of which are entirely optional.

- *XML is established.* You can find XML markups for almost any industry, including the world of finance, retail, real estate, travel and hospitality, and much more.

XML on its own is a remarkable innovation. However, to get the most out of XML you need to embrace other standards that allow you to validate XML, transform XML from one markup to another, convert XML data output you can display (like web pages), and search XML for specific information. As you'll see, the core XML standard is only one piece of a large and elaborate structure of complementary standards. We'll dive into all these standards in this book, starting with the next chapter where you'll learn how you can use XML schemas to define your custom flavors of XML.

CHAPTER 2

XML Schema

IN THE PREVIOUS CHAPTER, you learned that XML is a standard that allows you to create your own custom markup languages. This allows for great flexibility when you're using XML within the bounds of a single small business, but it raises a few problems when you need to exchange information with the rest of the world. Essentially, how can you ensure that other businesses and organizations can understand your custom XML?

For example, consider a personal finance application like Microsoft Money or Quicken. As one of its tasks, this application needs to download the user's transaction records from online sources like banks and credit card companies. These transaction records will probably be transmitted in an XML format, which ensures that they can be read by applications running in virtually any programming language and on any operating system. However, the application developer needs to know precisely what tags are used, and what structure they follow, in order to extract the required information. *Reading* the XML isn't a problem, but *interpreting* it is.

Trial and error doesn't seem like a realistic option. What's more, even if the developer can discover the element names and document structure by looking at some examples, there's still no easy way to quickly determine if an XML document conforms to the required standard. For example, you might create an XML document using an XML grammar developed by another organization with all the correct element names, but use the wrong data types! Or the data and structure might be correct, but the data might not fit into an allowable range. XML simply doesn't provide any ability to define these types of rules.

Fortunately, another standard fills in the gaps: XML Schema. *Schemas* are formal definitions that describe additional rules an XML document must follow. In a perfect world, every flavor of XML markup would have a corresponding schema that defines it. Anyone who wants to be able to create or process XML documents that use that markup could then use the schema to verify that it's correct. Best of all, this process of validation takes place automatically as long as you use an XML parser that supports schema validation.

In this chapter, we'll explore schemas in detail, and look at numerous examples of how you can create schema documents for your own XML grammars. We'll look at how you define document structure, the best way to organize a schema, and the types of rules you can enforce (including data types, allowed value ranges, maximum and minimum lengths, and more). Schemas play a key role in many Office 2003 XML features. Without them, you won't be able to map Excel and Word documents to XML.

The Role of XML Schema

A good part of the success of the XML standard is due to its remarkable flexibility. Using XML, you can create exactly the markup language you need. This flexibility also raises a few problems. With developers around the world creating their own XML grammars, how do you allow them to communicate with one another?

The solution is to create a formal document that states the rules of your custom markup language. These "rules" won't include syntactical details (like the requirement to use angle brackets or properly nest tags) because these requirements are already a part of the basic XML standard. Instead, the schema document will list the logical rules that pertain to your type of data. They include

- *Document vocabulary:* This determines what element and attribute names are used in your XML documents.

- *Document structure:* This determines where tags can be placed, and can include rules specifying that certain tags must be placed before, after, or inside others. You can also specify how many times an element can occur.

- *Supported data types:* This allows you to specify whether data is ordinary text, or must be interpretable as numeric data, date information, and so on.

- *Allowed data ranges:* This allows you to set constraints restricting numbers to certain ranges, or only allows specific values.

When an XML document meets the rules of a particular schema, it's said to *conform* to that schema. The process of checking whether an XML document is well formed, and testing whether it conforms to the appropriate schemas, is called *validation*.

Schemas work with all types of XML documents, but they are particularly well suited to data-centric XML, because of the support for strict validation with all kinds of data. Depending on your needs, you may create your own XML language and an XML schema for it, or you may simply adopt an existing XML standard, and use the corresponding schema to validate the documents you create. This is a scenario that Office 2003 makes particularly convenient, as you'll see in the next two chapters. To look at a registry that includes a variety of schema documents, organized by industry, visit http://www.xml.org/xml/registry.jsp.

XML Schema and Other Standards

XML Schema is not the first schema standard. Several other schema standards exist and are in use today, including Schematron, XDR, and Relax NG. Other XML developers rely on the Document Type Definition (DTD) standard, which predates XML, and can be used to formalize any type of SGML document. Each of these standards has its own strengths and weaknesses, but XML Schema provides three compelling benefits:

- XML Schema documents are written using XML markup. That means you'll see the same familiar angle brackets and nested structure. Of course, you'll still need to learn about the specific elements that are used in XML schemas.

- XML Schema supports data typing, which means you can specify that certain values can only contain numeric information, while others require dates, and so on. This key requirement, which underlies many business applications, is not provided by DTDs.

- XML Schema supports the XML Namespaces standard, allowing you to easily validate documents that contain a combination of markup languages. DTDs predate the XML Namespaces standard, and don't provide this support.

XML Schema is also a W3C standard, and it's integrated into all the Office 2003 XML features. That means that not only will the XML Schema be the schema standard for most XML authors, but it's also the schema standard of Microsoft Office.

TIP *The XML Schema standard is also referred to as XML Schema Definition, and abbreviated as XSD.*

Testing a Schema

In the examples in this chapter, I'll show you how to develop a variety of schema documents. When working with a new schema, it's often helpful to have a test application that can validate XML documents and see whether they conform to the schema. One simple test application is included with the companion content for this book. It's shown in Figure 2-1.

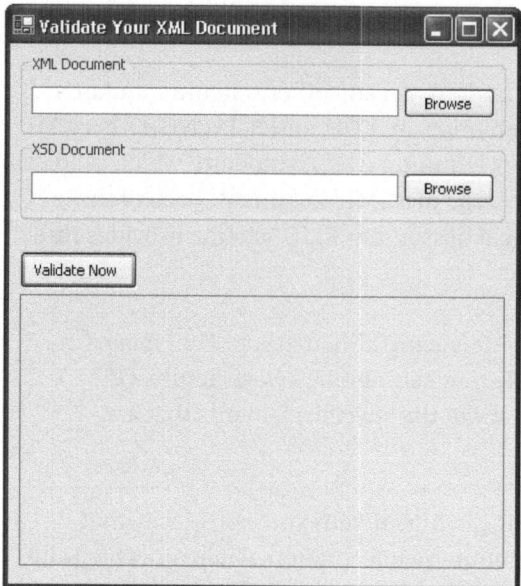

Figure 2-1. An XML schema test application

To start this application, run the file named ValidateXML.exe. To use this application, you simply need to select an XML file (which will usually have the extension .xml) and a schema file (which will usually have the extension .xsd), and click Validate Now. The application will then report any validation errors.

> **TIP** *All of the schemas that are discussed in this chapter are included in the companion content, along with sample XML documents. That allows you to test validation, and experiment with making changes.*

This simple application is written using Visual Basic .NET code, and the source code is provided if you'd like to learn how to validate XML in .NET, or adapt the application for your own purposes.

Every modern programming language provides its own XML parser, and most of these support schema-based validation. Office 2003 also includes a built-in XML parser. As you'll see in later chapters, you can map Excel and Word documents to a schema, and then use Office 2003 to validate whether the document follows or violates those schema rules.

Basic Schemas

Your exploration into XML schemas begins with the simplest possible XML document—a document that contains a single element with string information. Here's one example:

```
<?xml version="1.0"?>
<quotation>One thing is for certain: if you don't change the path you're on, you
will end up where you are headed.</quotation>
```

The schema document you would create to define the structure of this XML is as follows:

```
<?xml version="1.0"?>
<xsd:schema xmlns:xsd="http://www.w3.org/2001/XMLSchema">
    <xsd:element name="quotation" type="xsd:string"/>
</xsd:schema>
```

This schema document packs a lot of information into a small package. The first thing it does is import the namespace http://www.w3.org/2001/XMLSchema and map it to the xsd prefix.

```
<?xml version="1.0"?>
<xsd:schema xmlns:xsd="http://www.w3.org/2001/XMLSchema">
    <xsd:element name="quotation" type="xsd:string"/>
</xsd:schema>
```

As you'll remember, namespaces are used to distinguish different XML grammars. In this case, schema documents need to use their own specific set of elements, which serve one purpose: describing the structure and data for an XML document. In order to make sure that these tags don't conflict with any other XML language (including the one you're using to write your XML document), they are placed into a distinct namespace. This makes it easy for you to separate the two types of markup, and it even allows you to embed a schema right inside the document it validates with no chance of confusion.

> **NOTE** *By convention, the schema namespace is usually mapped to the prefix xsd. However, some schema documents map it to the prefix xs. Any sequence of characters is legitimate, provided it points to the same namespace and is consistently used in the rest of the document. Remember, the namespace prefix is just a convenience that you use to avoid writing the full namespace name.*

The schema document uses an element from the http://www.w3.org/2001/ XMLSchema namespace to start the document definition. This element is always named <schema>, and it's always the root element in an XML schema document.

```
<?xml version="1.0"?>
<xsd:schema xmlns:xsd="http://www.w3.org/2001/XMLSchema">
    <xsd:element name="quotation" type="xsd:string"/>
</xsd:schema>
```

Inside the <schema> element, you add the elements that define the structure of your target document. In this case, the target document consists of a single element, named <quotation>. In the schema document, this element is represented by the <element> tag. The <element> tag defines the name of the <quotation> tag, and defines it as an ordinary text string, which means that it can contain any sequence of valid XML characters.

```
<?xml version="1.0"?>
<xsd:schema xmlns:xsd="http://www.w3.org/2001/XMLSchema">
    <xsd:element name="quotation" type="xsd:string"/>
</xsd:schema>
```

Validating with the Simple Schema

You can now use this simple schema to validate quotation documents. Any document that contains a single <quotation> element will be successfully validated. You can freely change the following details without creating an invalid document:

- The text of the <quotation> element (you can even leave it completely empty)

- The spacing around the <quotation> element, which is ignored by the XML parser

- The document prolog on the first line, which indicates how the XML document is encoded

There are also a number of details that would break the schema rules. For example, the following document contains different capitalization for the <quotation> element, so the XML parser will interpret it as a completely different tag name.

```
<?xml version="1.0"?>
<QUOTATION>One thing is for certain: if you don't change the path you're on, you
will end up where you are headed.</QUOTATION>
```

The document shown that follows contains an element that isn't defined in the schema. It doesn't matter where you place this element; it isn't allowed.

```
<?xml version="1.0"?>
<quotation>One thing is for certain: if you don't change the path you're on,
you will end up where you are headed. <Source>Chinese Proverb</Source>
</quotation>
```

To test schema validation, you can use the utility provided with the companion content for this chapter. Figure 2-2 shows the result of trying to validate the quotation document just shown with the schema. As you can see, the error message clearly indicates the problem: an unrecognized element named <Source>.

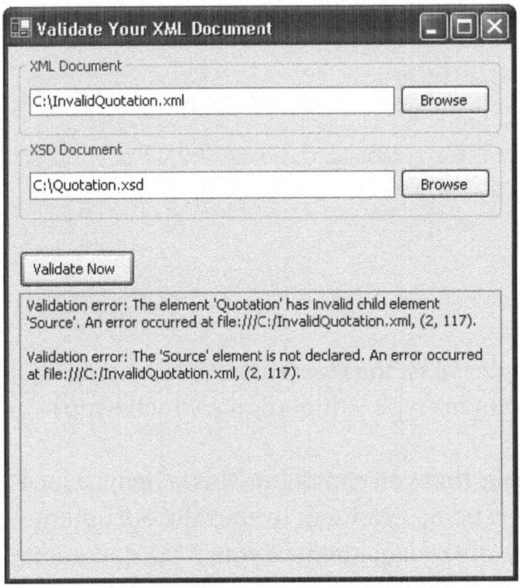

Figure 2-2. Validating the simple XML schema

This schema doesn't make use of any rules for element structure, data types, or data ranges. To address these issues, you'll need to create a more sophisticated document.

Simple and Complex Types

Schemas can contain two different element types:

- *Simple types* can only contain character data (which includes any combination of letters, numbers, and special characters). In the sample quotation schema, the <quotation> element is a simple type. Simple types cannot have attributes.

- *Complex types* can contain character data *and* other elements. In addition, complex types can have attributes.

Whenever you use a complex type in your schema, you'll specify exactly what other elements and attributes it can contain. However, if you use a simple type, you don't have these options. Simple types don't support attributes or nested elements.

For an example, consider the revamped quotation XML shown here, which incorporates several additional pieces of information in three nested elements:

```xml
<?xml version="1.0"?>
<quotation>
    <text>One thing is for certain: if you don't change the path you're on,
        you will end up where you are headed.</text>
    <source>Chinese Proverb</source>
    <category>Ancient Wisdom</category>
</quotation>
```

In this example, there are three simple types: the elements <text>, <source>, and <category>. There is also a single complex type, <quotation>, which wraps these three elements.

The following example shows one way that you can define this schema. Once again, this schema document uses the <schema> element to start the document, and it uses the <element> tag to indicate the root element of your XML document. The difference is what's found *inside* the <element> tag.

```xml
<?xml version="1.0"?>
<xsd:schema xmlns:xsd="http://www.w3.org/2001/XMLSchema">
    <xsd:element name="quotation">
        <xsd:complexType>
            <xsd:sequence>
                <xsd:element name="text" type="xsd:string"/>
                <xsd:element name="source" type="xsd:string"/>
```

```
            <xsd:element name="category" type="xsd:string"/>
        </xsd:sequence>
      </xsd:complexType>
    </xsd:element>
</xsd:schema>
```

In this example, the <element> tag contains a <complexType> that is made up of several subelements. These elements are wrapped into a <sequence> element, which indicates that they must all be present in the document in exactly this order. If you rearrange the <text>, <source>, and <category> elements in the XML document and attempt to validate this changed document, the validation will fail.

> **TIP** *Notice in this example that every piece of information is being described as the data type* string, *which means that any text is allowed. Later on in this chapter you'll see how you can restrict elements to specific types of data, like numbers.*

This should give you some insight into the way that schemas are constructed. Basically, schemas serve as a structural layout plan that maps out the structure and elements of allowed documents. Every <element> maps directly to an element in the source document. That means you can quickly isolate the basic structure of a schema just by picking out the various declared elements:

```
<?xml version="1.0"?>
<xsd:schema xmlns:xsd="http://www.w3.org/2001/XMLSchema">
    <xsd:element name="quotation">
      <xsd:complexType>
        <xsd:sequence>
            <xsd:element name="text" type="xsd:string"/>
            <xsd:element name="source" type="xsd:string"/>
            <xsd:element name="category" type="xsd:string"/>
        </xsd:sequence>
      </xsd:complexType>
    </xsd:element>
</xsd:schema>
```

If you use this approach with complex XML documents, you'll wind up with lengthy, deeply nested schema documents (which is completely acceptable). However, schema documents often use a more modular design, and break up their information several distinct pieces so certain complex types can be easily reused, either in multiple places in the same document, or in various different documents. To understand this type of schema design, you'll need to understand the difference between anonymous and named types—a distinction that's explained in the next section.

Anonymous and Named Types

The previous schema demonstrated an example of *anonymous types*. Anonymous types are complex types that are embedded directly into your document structure. The problem with anonymous types is that the information they contain isn't easy to reuse. For example, consider the following XML document, which might represent a typical high-school yearbook entry:

```xml
<?xml version="1.0"?>
<student>
    <firstName>Lucy</firstName>
    <lastName>Timpani</lastName>
    <favoriteQuotation>
        <text>Great people talk about ideas, average people talk about things,
            and small people talk about wine.</text>
        <source>Fran Lebowitz</source>
        <category>Contemporary</category>
    </favoriteQuotation>
    <favoriteFood>Donuts</favoriteFood>
    <lastWords>
        <text>Democracy is not something you believe in or a place to hang your
            hat, but it's something you do. You participate. If you stop doing
            it, democracy crumbles.</text>
        <source>Abbie Hoffman</source>
        <category>Politics</category>
    </lastWords>
</student>
```

This XML document actually contains two separate quotes. It's easy enough to create the XML schema for this document, but it's fairly repetitive, and it repeats the <text>, <source>, and <category> definitions for each quote element. Here's how it would look:

```xml
<?xml version="1.0"?>
<xsd:schema xmlns:xsd="http://www.w3.org/2001/XMLSchema">
```

```
<xsd:element name="student">
    <xsd:complexType>
        <xsd:sequence>
            <xsd:element name="firstName" type="xsd:string"/>
            <xsd:element name="lastName" type="xsd:string"/>

            <xsd:element name="favoriteQuotation">
                <xsd:complexType>
                    <xsd:sequence>
                        <xsd:element name="text" type="xsd:string"/>
                        <xsd:element name="source" type="xsd:string"/>
                        <xsd:element name="category" type="xsd:string"/>
                    </xsd:sequence>
                </xsd:complexType>
            </xsd:element>

            <xsd:element name="favoriteFood" type="xsd:string"/>

            <xsd:element name="lastWords">
                <xsd:complexType>
                    <xsd:sequence>
                        <xsd:element name="text" type="xsd:string"/>
                        <xsd:element name="source" type="xsd:string"/>
                        <xsd:element name="category" type="xsd:string"/>
                    </xsd:sequence>
                </xsd:complexType>
            </xsd:element>

        </xsd:sequence>
    </xsd:complexType>
</xsd:element>

</xsd:schema>
```

Essentially, this schema states that the <student> element is a complex type made up of a sequence of elements. Two of these elements are themselves complex types that are made up of a sequence of elements: <favoriteQuotation> and <lastWords>.

Another way to represent the same document is to define a *named type* for quotations. This named type would include the three elements that are always a part of any self-respecting quotation: <text>, <source>, and <category>. To define the named type, you simply move the <complexType> element up the hierarchy so that it's directly under the <schema> element. You must then give it a name, using the name attribute. Here's how it would look:

```
<xsd:complexType name="quotation">
   <xsd:sequence>
      <xsd:element name="text" type="xsd:string"/>
      <xsd:element name="source" type="xsd:string"/>
      <xsd:element name="category" type="xsd:string"/>
   </xsd:sequence>
</xsd:complexType>
```

Note that the name you give your complex type (in this case it's quotation) is only used in the schema. It identifies the structure so you can reuse it in more than one place. It doesn't need to have the same names as the element in the XML document you're validating.

Now you can use the quotation type to declare other elements. For example, you can use the following syntax to insert a <favoriteQuotation> element:

```
<xsd:element name="favoriteQuotation" type="quotation"/>
```

The complete, revised schema follows. Although this schema validates the same XML in the same way, its more modular structure makes it easier to understand. It's also shortened 29 lines of schema content down to a leaner 20 lines.

```
<?xml version="1.0"?>
<xsd:schema xmlns:xsd="http://www.w3.org/2001/XMLSchema">

   <!-- This is the definition of a custom complex type for quotations. -->
   <xsd:complexType name="quotation">
      <xsd:sequence>
         <xsd:element name="text" type="xsd:string"/>
         <xsd:element name="source" type="xsd:string"/>
         <xsd:element name="category" type="xsd:string"/>
      </xsd:sequence>
   </xsd:complexType>

   <!-- This is the structure of the document itself. -->
   <xsd:element name="student">
      <xsd:complexType>
         <xsd:sequence>
            <xsd:element name="firstName" type="xsd:string"/>
            <xsd:element name="lastName" type="xsd:string"/>
            <xsd:element name="favoriteQuotation" type="quotation"/>
```

```
            <xsd:element name="favoriteFood" type="xsd:string"/>
            <xsd:element name="lastWords" type="quotation"/>
        </xsd:sequence>
    </xsd:complexType>
</xsd:element>

</xsd:schema>
```

The differences become even more dramatic if you have a complex type that contains another complex type. For example, the quotation type might contain an <author> element with <firstName> and <lastName> information. In this case, there are two complex types: quotation and person. You can define the person type as an anonymous type embedded inside the quotation itself, or you can define the person and quotation separately, as shown here:

```
<?xml version="1.0"?>
<xsd:schema xmlns:xsd="http://www.w3.org/2001/XMLSchema">

    <xsd:complexType name="person">
        <xsd:sequence>
            <xsd:element name="firstName" type="xsd:string"/>
            <xsd:element name="lastName" type="xsd:string"/>
        </xsd:sequence>
    </xsd:complexType>

    <xsd:complexType name="quotation">
        <xsd:sequence>
            <xsd:element name="text" type="xsd:string"/>
            <xsd:element name="author" type="person"/>
            <xsd:element name="category" type="xsd:string"/>
        </xsd:sequence>
    </xsd:complexType>

    <!-- This is the structure of the document itself. -->
    <xsd:element name="student">
        <xsd:complexType>
            <xsd:sequence>
                <xsd:element name="firstName" type="xsd:string"/>
                <xsd:element name="lastName" type="xsd:string"/>
                <xsd:element name="favoriteQuotation" type="quotation"/>
                <xsd:element name="favoriteFood" type="xsd:string"/>
                <xsd:element name="lastWords" type="quotation"/>
            </xsd:sequence>
```

```
        </xsd:complexType>
    </xsd:element>

</xsd:schema>
```

Most published schemas follow this style. They begin by defining their own complex types, and then map out the document structure using these types. Sometimes type definitions are even reused across different schema documents. Keep in mind, however, that the global type definitions are just a convenience. To validate the document, the XML parser must match the document's root element to the root <element> tag in the schema document.

There is one other option. You can create a schema that defines multiple root elements. In this case, the XML parser will use the first match. Here's an example that defines the <quotation> complex type, and supplies two root elements: <quotation> and <student>, which are highlighted in bold.

```
<?xml version="1.0"?>
<xsd:schema xmlns:xsd="http://www.w3.org/2001/XMLSchema">

    <xsd:complexType name="quotation">
        <xsd:sequence>
            <xsd:element name="text" type="xsd:string"/>
            <xsd:element name="source" type="xsd:string"/>
            <xsd:element name="category" type="xsd:string"/>
        </xsd:sequence>
    </xsd:complexType>

    <xsd:element name="quotation" type="quotation"/>

    <xsd:element name="student">
        <xsd:complexType>
            <xsd:sequence>
                <xsd:element name="firstName" type="xsd:string"/>
                <xsd:element name="lastName" type="xsd:string"/>
                <xsd:element name="favoriteQuotation" type="quotation"/>
                <xsd:element name="favoriteFood" type="xsd:string"/>
                <xsd:element name="lastWords" type="quotation"/>
            </xsd:sequence>
        </xsd:complexType>
    </xsd:element>

</xsd:schema>
```

This schema can validate an XML document that contains a single <quotation> element (as presented earlier), or one that contains a single student element (with an embedded quotation). This flexibility occasionally comes in very useful, but it usually isn't the behavior you want. Usually, it's more important for you to isolate every single version of a file to prevent problems. (For example, you wouldn't want to accidentally end up with the XML quotation document used instead of the XML student document in a high school yearbook.)

Groups and Sequences

As you've seen, complex types are used to represent elements that contain a combination of subelements. In other words, complex types represent a *grouping* of different elements.

When defining a complex type in a schema, you specify the way that the subelements should be ordered. You have three choices:

- *Sequence:* In this case, the elements must appear in the XML document in the same order as you list them in the schema document. You create this construction with a <sequence> element.

- *Choice:* In this case, only one of the elements will appear in the complex type. You create this construction with a <choice> element.

- *All:* In this case, all of the elements must occur in the XML document, but the order is not important. You create this construction with an <all> element.

So far, the examples in this chapter have used sequences, by nesting all the subelements of a complex type inside a <sequence>. But the other types of grouping are just as easy to use. For example, here's a schema for quotations that allows the information to be provided in any order:

```
<?xml version="1.0"?>
<xsd:schema xmlns:xsd="http://www.w3.org/2001/XMLSchema">
    <xsd:element name="quotation">
      <xsd:complexType>
        <xsd:all>
            <xsd:element name="text" type="xsd:string"/>
            <xsd:element name="source" type="xsd:string"/>
            <xsd:element name="category" type="xsd:string"/>
        </xsd:all>
```

```
        </xsd:complexType>
    </xsd:element>
</xsd:schema>
```

Now the following rearranged XML document becomes valid:

```
<?xml version="1.0"?>
<quotation>
    <source>Chinese Proverb</source>
    <category>Ancient Wisdom</category>
    <text>One thing is for certain: if you don't change the path you're on,
            you will end up where you are headed.</text>
</quotation>
```

The assumption here is that the program processing this type of file will search specifically for the <text> element inside the <quotation> element, rather than just assuming it's the first contained element. Development platforms have lots of tools that make this sort of manipulation easy.

Choices, on the other hand, are most commonly used when a portion of an XML document supports several different types of content. For instance, in the yearbook example, you might allow two different types of quotations: the standard quotation format, and another entry representing a citation from a printed source. The schema would then define both of these complex types, as shown here:

```
<xsd:complexType name="quotation">
    <xsd:sequence>
      <xsd:element name="text" type="xsd:string"/>
      <xsd:element name="source" type="xsd:string"/>
      <xsd:element name="category" type="xsd:string"/>
    </xsd:sequence>
</xsd:complexType>

<xsd:complexType name="printCitation">
    <xsd:sequence>
      <xsd:element name="text" type="xsd:string"/>
      <xsd:element name="bookTitle" type="xsd:string"/>
      <xsd:element name="bookAuthor" type="xsd:string"/>
    </xsd:sequence>
</xsd:complexType>
```

Now when you define the structure of the XML document, you can use a <choice> element to indicate that the user can supply either a <favoriteQuotation>

or a <favoriteBookQuote>. The <lastWords> element, on the other hand, must always be a quotation.

```
<xsd:element name="student">
    <xsd:complexType>
        <xsd:sequence>
            <xsd:element name="firstName" type="xsd:string"/>
            <xsd:element name="lastName" type="xsd:string"/>

            <xsd:choice>
                <xsd:element name="favoriteBookQuote" type="printCitation"/>
                <xsd:element name="favoriteQuotation" type="quotation"/>
            </xsd:choice>

            <xsd:element name="favoriteFood" type="xsd:string"/>
            <xsd:element name="lastWords" type="quotation"/>
        </xsd:sequence>
    </xsd:complexType>
</xsd:element>
```

Note that when using a choice, you must supply elements with different names. For example, this choice would not be allowed:

```
<xsd:choice>
    <xsd:element name="favoriteQuotation" type="printCitation"/>
    <xsd:element name="favoriteQuotation" type="quotation"/>
</xsd:choice>
```

The problem here is that there's no way to determine which choice is used in the XML document, because both elements have the same name. That means that the XML parser won't be able to validate this portion of the document, because it won't be able to decide whether it should validate the content as a printCitation or a quotation.

> **TIP** *As a general rule, the more flexibility you allow in your schema, the more complexity you'll introduce to the applications and XML authors that use it. If you don't need constructs like <choice> and <all>, stick with the simpler <sequence> group.*

Minimums, Maximums, and Lists

In many schemas, certain elements can occur multiple times. This is particularly true in data-centric XML, which focuses on tables and lists. For example, a product list will contain an undetermined number of products, a customer list will contain multiple customers, and order will contain multiple order items, and so on. You can handle repeating data in a schema by adding the minOccurs and maxOccurs attributes to an <element> tag. The minOccurs attribute specifies the minimum number of times that an element must appear at that location, while the maxOccurs attribute specifies the maximum number of times it can be included. By default, if you omit this information (as in the previous examples), both minOccurs and maxOccurs will be one, which means the element must occur exactly one time.

As an example, the following schema document defines a list of quotations. This list must include at least one quotation, but it can allow up to ten.

```
<?xml version="1.0"?>
<xsd:schema xmlns:xsd="http://www.w3.org/2001/XMLSchema">

    <xsd:complexType name="quotation">
      <xsd:sequence>
        <xsd:element name="text" type="xsd:string"/>
        <xsd:element name="source" type="xsd:string"/>
        <xsd:element name="category" type="xsd:string"/>
      </xsd:sequence>
    </xsd:complexType>

    <xsd:element name="quotationList">
      <xsd:complexType>
        <xsd:sequence>
          <xsd:element name="quotation" type="quotation" minOccurs="1"
            maxOccurs="10"/>
        </xsd:sequence>
      </xsd:complexType>
    </xsd:element>

</xsd:schema>
```

Here's a sample document that you might validate with this schema:

```
<?xml version="1.0"?>
<quotationList>
```

```
<quotation>
    <text>One thing is for certain: if you don't change the path you're on,
        you will end up where you are headed.</text>
    <source>Chinese Proverb</source>
    <category>Ancient Wisdom</category>
</quotation>
<quotation>
    <text>Always forgive your enemies; nothing else annoys them so
        much.</text>
    <source>Oscar Wilde</source>
    <category>Literary</category>
</quotation>
<quotation>
    <text>Justice will only exist where those not effected by injustice are
        filled with the same amount of indignation as those offended.</text>
    <source>Plato</source>
    <category>Ancient Wisdom</category>
</quotation>
</quotationList>
```

In many cases, you'll want to allow an unlimited number of occurrences of a certain element. In this case, you use the special value "unbounded" for the maxOccurs attribute, as shown here:

```
<xsd:element name="quotation" type="quotation" minOccurs="1"
 maxOccurs="unbounded"/>
```

The minOccurs attribute is also useful for defining an optional element. For example, the quotation schema shown here defines the category as optional, which means it may or may not be present in valid documents.

```
<xsd:complexType name="quotation">
  <xsd:sequence>
    <xsd:element name="text" type="xsd:string"/>
    <xsd:element name="source" type="xsd:string"/>
    <xsd:element name="category" type="xsd:string" minOccurs="0"
      maxOccurs="1"/>
  </xsd:sequence>
</xsd:complexType>
```

It's not always obvious how minOccurs and maxOccurs work with the different types of groupings in a complex type. For example, the elements in an <all> group can only use values of 0 or 1 for maxOccurs and minOccurs. That means you can create an <all> grouping that includes optional elements, but you can't create one that allows element lists.

The <choice> element has its own subtleties when used with lists. You can use the minOccurs and maxOccurs attribute to specify a range for the <choice> element, but this range applies to *all* elements in the choice. For example, consider the following choice group:

```
<xsd:choice minOccurs="1" maxOccurs="6">
    <xsd:element name="favoriteBookQuotation" type="printCitation"/>
    <xsd:element name="favoriteQuotation" type="quotation"/>
</xsd:choice>
```

The matching XML can include six elements, and these elements can be <favoriteQuotation> tags, <favoriteBookQuotation> tags, or any combination of the two. There is no way for you to specify a more advanced choice that limits how often each contained element can be used.

Mixed Content Type

The quotation and yearbook documents are examples of data-centric XML. In data-centric XML, simple types contain character data and complex types contain other elements.

Another model exists for XML data: document-centric XML. Document-centric XML is a more free-flowing approach that's often used for narrative documents like articles, essays, and resumes. It freely mixes character data and subelements.

The last chapter presented document-centric XML with the resume example shown here:

```
<?xml version="1.0" ?>
<resume>
    <firstName>Sally</firstName>
    <lastName>Markov</lastName>
    <body>
        <objective>To become an XML guru.</objective>
        <education>Study at numerous education instutions, including the
            <school>Juilliard Academy</school> and <school>M.I.T.</school>.
        </education>
        <workHistory>Worked at a number of companies. At
            <company>Microsoft</company> I learned that XML is an important
            technology in the web-enabled world. At <company>IBM</company> I
```

```
        developed my own XML documents to store computer inventory information.
        This allowed us to automate production.
    </workHistory>
  </body>
</resume>
```

In this example, the <education> and <workHistory> elements contain mixed content that includes text *and* tags. You can specify this type of element by setting the mixed attribute, as shown here:

```
<xsd:complexType name="education" mixed="true">
. . .
</xsd:complexType>
```

You still need to declare what elements are allowed to appear. In the resume example, the embedded <school> and <company> tags can occur an unlimited number of times, and order is unimportant. The easiest way to model this requirement is to use an unbounded <choice> group.

```
<xsd:complexType name="education" mixed="true">
    <xsd:choice minOccurs="0" maxOccurs="unbounded">
        <xsd:element name="school" type="xsd:string"/>
    </xsd:choice>
</xsd:complexType>
```

The complete resume schema is shown here:

```
<?xml version="1.0"?>
<xsd:schema xmlns:xsd="http://www.w3.org/2001/XMLSchema">

  <xsd:complexType name="education" mixed="true">
    <xsd:choice minOccurs="0" maxOccurs="unbounded">
      <xsd:element name="school" type="xsd:string"/>
    </xsd:choice>
  </xsd:complexType>

  <xsd:complexType name="workHistory" mixed="true">
    <xsd:choice minOccurs="0" maxOccurs="unbounded">
      <xsd:element name="company" type="xsd:string"/>
    </xsd:choice>
  </xsd:complexType>

  <xsd:complexType name="resume">
```

```
    <xsd:sequence>
        <xsd:element name="firstName" type="xsd:string"/>
        <xsd:element name="lastName" type="xsd:string"/>
        <xsd:element name="body">
            <xsd:complexType>
                <xsd:sequence>
                    <xsd:element name="objective" type="xsd:string"/>
                    <xsd:element name="education" type="education"/>
                    <xsd:element name="workHistory" type="workHistory"/>
                </xsd:sequence>
            </xsd:complexType>
        </xsd:element>
    </xsd:sequence>
</xsd:complexType>

<xsd:element name="resume" type="resume"/>
</xsd:schema>
```

Schemas that use mixed content obviously allow a more flexible document structure. For that reason, they aren't as easy to use with the Office XML features, and won't be supported in many scenarios.

Attributes

Attributes, like elements, must be defined in a schema. You define an attribute by adding the <attribute> element to a complex type definition. For example, consider the following quotation document, which uses an ID attribute to record a unique numeric identifier (which might correspond to a record number in a database):

```
<?xml version="1.0"?>
<quotation id="1034">
    <text>One thing is for certain: if you don't change the path you're on,
        you will end up where you are headed.</text>
    <source>Chinese Proverb</source>
    <category>Ancient Wisdom</category>
</quotation>
```

The schema for this document defines a complex type with three elements and one attribute. Note that attribute declaration must come *after* the element declarations.

```
<?xml version="1.0"?>
<xsd:schema xmlns:xsd="http://www.w3.org/2001/XMLSchema">
   <xsd:complexType name="quotation">
      <xsd:sequence>
         <xsd:element name="text" type="xsd:string"/>
         <xsd:element name="source" type="xsd:string"/>
         <xsd:element name="category" type="xsd:string"/>
      </xsd:sequence>
      <xsd:attribute name="id" type="xsd:string"/>
   </xsd:complexType>

   <xsd:element name="quotation" type="quotation"/>
</xsd:schema>
```

Attributes have certain limitations when compared to elements. First of all, attributes can't themselves be complex types, because they can't contain other elements or attributes. Attributes also don't support the minOccurs and maxOccurs attributes, because you can't have more than one attribute with the same name. More importantly, order isn't important with attributes, so you can't use grouping constructs like <any> and <sequence>.

You can also create elements that only contain attributes, not elements. One example of an empty element that provides all its information through attributes is the <img> tag in HTML.

```
<img src="logo.gif" alt="ACME Logo">
```

To model this in an XML schema, you would declare a complex type like this:

```
<xsd:complexType name="img">
   <xsd:attribute name="src" type="xsd:string"/>
   <xsd:attribute name="alt" type="xsd:string"/>
</xsd:complexType>
```

NOTE *You don't need to declare attributes that are used to define namespaces or specify the schema that an XML document will use. XML validators ignore these attributes.*

Attributes must be defined inside a complex type. This raises a problem if you need to create an ordinary tag with simple character content that uses an attribute. Here's one possible example:

```
<quotation id="1034">We must learn to live together as brothers or perish
  together as fools.</quotation>
```

To define this element in a schema, you need to create a new complex type, and then add the <simpleContent> element. Inside the <simpleContent> element, you need to define an <extension> element that indicates the type of data that is contained inside the element. In this case, you'll use the basic string type, because I haven't yet discussed the different data types that are available. You can then add any <attribute> elements inside the <extension> element.

```
<xsd:complexType name="quotation">
   <xsd:simpleContent>
      <xsd:extension base="xsd:string">
         <xsd:attribute name="id" type="xsd:string"/>
      </xsd:extension>
   </xsd:simpleContent>
</xsd:complexType>
```

The Any Element

The <element> tag defines a specific element. The <attribute> tag defines a specific attribute. In addition, you can use two special tags, <any> and <anyAttribute>, to match any element or attribute from any namespace. No restrictions are placed on the content of the element, its namespaces, or even whether it contains other nested elements.

The <any> and <anyAttribute> elements allow you to create extremely flexible schemas. However, they can also cause problems, and even result in nondeterministic schemas—schemas that can't be validated because there is more than one way to interpret the same structure. This is commonly a problem if you use the <any> element in a <choice>, or if you create it in a list by setting minOccurs or maxOccurs to anything other than the default value 1. Generally, the Office applications restrict the use of the <any> and <anyAttribute> elements when mapping documents to XML. Excel won't allow them at all, and Word will allow them only if they don't lead to nondeterministic structures.

Data Types

So far, you've taken a close look at the rules for structuring a schema document. You've learned how to validate data-centric and document-centric XML, how to deal with ordering, repetition, and choices, and how to define nested structures with elements that contain other elements. But there is still a significant part of the XML Schema standard that hasn't been considered: data typing. Data types help you distinguish numbers from names, limit text length, and even validate simple fields.

The XML Schema standard defines 44 different built-in data types. So far, all the schema examples have used elements and attributes that are based on the string data type. Strings can contain any sequence of characters, numbers, and special characters. The other 44 types can be divided into the following categories:

- Numeric types

- String types

- Date and time types

- The Boolean type

- Binary types

- XML reserved types

You'll get a chance to explore all of these data types briefly, except for the specialized XML types, which are used to represent certain XML constructs that haven't been introduced. The very technical details of the XML Schema standard can be found online at http://www.w3.org/XML/Schema. Microsoft also provides a handy reference for schema data types with the online documentation for their MSXML component. You can find it at http://msdn.microsoft.com/library/en-us/xmlsdk/htm/xsd_ref_5bc5.asp.

Numeric Data Types

Some of the most obvious data types are numbers. As programmers will attest, not all numeric types are the same. Some don't support fractional values, while others can only contain positive values. Some reserve more space to accommodate a broader range of values. (For example, a 16-bit integer can hold whole numbers that range in value from –32768 to 32767, while a 32-bit integer can hold values from –2,147,483,648 through positive 2,147,483,647.)

Table 2-1 lists the numeric data types defined in the XML Schema standard. Many of these types overlap. Some specify a size (which determines the maximum and minimum allowed values), while others do not. Generally, schemas will use types that closely map to a specific application. As a basic rule of thumb, use an integer for whole numbers, decimal for currency values, and float or double for large fractional numbers in scientific applications. The other numeric data types are used in special cases, often because they map directly to data types used in a particular piece of application code.

Table 2-1. Numeric Data Types

Name	Description	Allowed Range
xsd:float	32-bit floating-point number	−3.402823e38 . . . 3.402823e38 and special values like −INF (negative infinity), INF (infinity), and NaN (not a number)
xsd:double	64-bit floating point number	−1.79769313486232e308 . . . 1.79769313486232e308 and special values like −INF (negative infinity), INF (infinity), and NaN (not a number)
xsd:decimal	Decimal number	Numbers of various precision
xsd:integer	An integer	−50000000000000000000000 . . . 4567349873249832649873624958
xsd:nonPositiveInteger	An integer less than or equal to zero	0, −1, −2 . . .
xsd:negativeInteger	An integer less than zero	−1, −2, −3 . . .
xsd:long	A large 64-bit integer	−922337203685477580 . . . 9223372036854775807
xsd:int	A standard 32-bit integer	−2147483648 . . . 2147483647
xsd:short	A small 16-bit integer	−32768 . . . 32767
xsd:byte	An 8-bit integer	−128 . . . 127
xsd:nonNegativeInteger	An integer greater than or equal to zero	0, 1, 2, . . .
xsd:unsignedLong	A 64-bit integer with no positive/negative sign	0, 1, 2 . . . 18446744073709551615
xsd:unsignedInt	A 32-bit integer with no positive/negative sign	0, 1, 2 . . . 4294967295
xsd:unsignedShort	A 16-bit integer with no positive/negative sign	0, 1, 2 . . . 65535
xsd:unsignedByte	A 8-bit integer with no positive/negative sign	0, 1, 2 . . . 255
xsd:positiveInteger	An integer greater than zero	1, 2, 3 . . .

String Types

The XML Schema standard defines three types of strings that can be used to represent different types of text. These include the basic string type, which has no restrictions at all, the normalized string, which rejects line breaks and tabs, and the token, which doesn't allow line breaks, tabs, or trailing or leading spaces. These three types are outlined in Table 2-2. The most common is the standard string, which all the examples have relied on so far.

Table 2-2. String Data Types

Name	Description
xsd:string	A sequence of zero or more Unicode characters. Can include any characters that are allowed in an XML document.
xsd:normalizedString	A string that doesn't contain any tabs, carriage returns, or line feeds.
xsd:token	A string with no leading or trailing whitespace, no tabs, no line feeds, and not more than one consecutive space.

Date and Time Types

Agreeing on the proper way to represent dates, years, and time intervals is an often sticky issue. The XML Schema standard defines nine data types for date and time information, all of which require you to use a fixed international representation (in other words, no more month-day-year patterns). Out of these, the most commonly used for isolating a specific date is the date type, or the dateTime type (which includes time of day information). In addition, you can indicate some of the components of a date using the types that start with the letter "g," such as gDay, gMonth, and gYear. If you need to record a duration of time, you must use the duration data type with its somewhat obscure period-year-month-day-hour-minute-second format. Table 2-3 lists the date and time types.

Table 2-3. Date Data Types

Name	Type	Example
xsd:dateTime	A particular moment in Coordinated Universal Time, up to a fraction of a second	1999-05-31T13:20:00.000
xsd:date	A specific date in the year	2003-10-31
xsd:time	A specific time of day	14:30:00.000

(Continued)

Table 2-3. Date Data Types (Continued)

Name	Type	Example
xsd:gDay	A day	--31
xsd:gMonth	A month	--10--
xsd:gYear	A year	2003
xsd:gYearMonth	A specific month in a specific year	2003-10
xsd:gMonthDay	A date without the year component	--10-31
xsd:duration	A length of time, to a fraction of a second	P2000Y10M31DT09H32M7

The Boolean Type

The Boolean data type can take one of two values: true or false. You can also substitute true with 1, or false with 0, which are equivalent.

Binary Types

Some types of data can't be easily accommodated in XML. This includes binary information (like image data). When represented as text, this information can include special characters that aren't allowed in XML documents. If you need to include this type of information in an XML document, you'll need to encode it using Base64 encoding or hexadecimal encoding. *Hexadecimal encoding* works by writing out the number value of each byte in sequence (these values range from 00 to FF). It looks like this:

```
EA6C807F41F332127323432147A4E345EC54CC8D52198000FF
```

To designate a field as containing hexadecimal content, you set the element type to hexBinary.

Base64 encoding works by translating every set of three bytes into a combination of two XML-legal characters. Base64 encoding is generally preferred over hexadecimal encoding, because it's more compact (it increases the size of encoded data by a third, while hexadecimal encoding doubles it). Base64 encoding typically looks something like this:

```
BjWiJo2ir3HJuY7elYB7y5ROsTr1/fFwmjkHwpbpzed1LE=
```

To designate a field as containing Base64-encoded data, you set the element type to base64Binary.

> **NOTE** *This book won't focus on binary data types in much detail, because they aren't easily usable in Office 2003. The problem is that Office 2003 won't know how it should treat your binary data and what it represents. Without that knowledge, applications like Word and Excel won't be able to display or use embedded binary data.*

A Typed Schema

You can use all of these data types natively in your schema. The XML parser that validates the document will check that the data matches the required data types.

For an example, consider the product catalog introduced in the last chapter. It took the following form:

```xml
<?xml version="1.0" ?>
<productCatalog>
    <catalogName>Acme Fall 2003 Catalog</catalogName>
    <expiryDate>2004-01-01</expiryDate>

    <products>
        <product id="1001">
            <productName>Magic Ring</productName>
            <productPrice>342.10</productPrice>
            <inStock>true</inStock>
        </product>
        <product id="1002">
            <productName>Flying Carpet</productName>
            <productPrice>982.99</productPrice>
            <inStock>true</inStock>
        </product>
    </products>
</productCatalog>
```

You can create a schema for this document that recognizes the numeric, date, and Boolean data types that it contains.

```xml
<?xml version="1.0"?>
<xsd:schema xmlns:xsd="http://www.w3.org/2001/XMLSchema">

    <xsd:complexType name="product">
        <xsd:sequence>
            <xsd:element name="productName" type="xsd:string"/>
```

```
            <xsd:element name="productPrice" type="xsd:decimal"/>
            <xsd:element name="inStock" type="xsd:boolean"/>
        </xsd:sequence>
        <xsd:attribute name="id" type="xsd:integer"/>
    </xsd:complexType>

    <xsd:element name="productCatalog">
        <xsd:complexType>
            <xsd:sequence>
                <xsd:element name="catalogName" type="xsd:string"/>
                <xsd:element name="expiryDate" type="xsd:date"/>

                <xsd:element name="products">
                    <xsd:complexType>
                        <xsd:sequence>
                            <xsd:element name="product" type="product"
                              maxOccurs="unbounded"/>
                        </xsd:sequence>
                    </xsd:complexType>
                </xsd:element>
            </xsd:sequence>
        </xsd:complexType>
    </xsd:element>

</xsd:schema>
```

You can use the validation test utility to try out what happens if you break these data type rules. For example, even though the following document has the correct structure, it has several data type errors, which are highlighted in bold:

```
<?xml version="1.0" ?>
<productCatalog>
    <catalogName>Acme Fall 2003 Catalog</catalogName>
    <expiryDate>Jan 1, 2004</expiryDate>

    <products>
        <product id="1001">
            <productName>Magic Ring</productName>
            <productPrice>$342.10</productPrice>
            <inStock>true</inStock>
        </product>
        <product id="1002">
            <productName>Flying Carpet</productName>
```

```
        <productPrice>982.99</productPrice>
        <inStock>Yes</inStock>
      </product>
    </products>
</productCatalog>
```

Figure 2-3 shows the results of attempting to validate this document with the typed schema using the ValidateXML.exe test application.

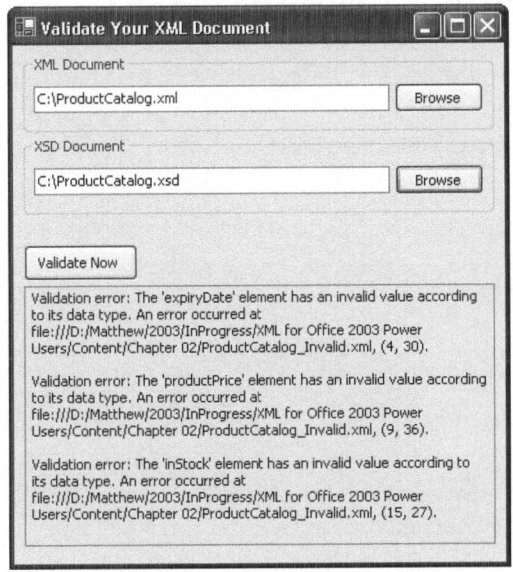

Figure 2-3. Failed validation with data type errors

Deriving Custom Data Types

Restricting elements to specific data types gives you a basic level of protection. It can stop users from typing letters into numeric fields, for example. However, it can't catch a host of more subtle problems, like strings that are too long, numbers that are too large, or special values that don't match the proper format (like e-mail addresses, phone numbers, and postal codes).

Fortunately, the XML Schema standard defines an extensible system you can use to force XML data to play by your own rules. You use this system by declaring *facets*, additional rules that restrict the values allowed for an element. To create a facet for an element, you must first declare the element as a new <simpleType>. Then, you can add a child <restriction> element, which specifies the basic data type you want to use. Inside the <restriction> element, you add another element that defines the exact type of restriction that applies. This last ingredient is the actual facet, and you can add as many as you need.

The next few sections explain the different ways you can use facets.

Restricting String Length

To restrict the length of the string data types, you can use the <minLength> and <maxLength> facets. For example, consider the following schema document, which includes a definition for a <Quotation> element that must contain between 1 and 1,000 characters:

```xml
<?xml version="1.0"?>
<xsd:schema xmlns:xsd="http://www.w3.org/2001/XMLSchema">

    <!-- Define the restricted type. -->
    <xsd:simpleType name="quotation">
      <xsd:restriction base="xsd:string">
          <xsd:minLength value="1"/>
          <xsd:maxLength value="1000"/>
      </xsd:restriction>
    </xsd:simleType>

    <!-- Define the structure of the document. -->
    <xsd:element name="Quotation" type="quotation">

</xsd:schema>
```

Now if you attempt to validate a document with a longer quotation, an error will occur.

> **TIP** *You can also use a <whitespace> facet to tell the XML parser how to treat whitespace in an element (either ignoring it, or including it in the value, which is the default). This feature isn't used in this book.*

Restricting Number Ranges

The approach for restricting ranges of numbers is very similar to the technique you use to restrict string length. The difference is that you must base the simple type on a numeric data type, and you must use the following four facets:

- <maxInclusive> sets an upper bound. The document value must be less than or equal to this number.

- <maxExclusive> sets an upper bound. The document value must equal this number.

- <minInclusive> sets a lower bound. The document value must be greater than or equal to this number.

- <maxExclusive> sets a lower bound. The document value must be greater than this number.

In addition, you can control the number of digits and decimal places that are allowed with these two attributes:

- <totalDigits> sets the maximum number of digits allowed. (For example, 1234.56 has six digits.)

- <fractionDigits> sets the maximum number of digits allowed in the fractional part of the element. (For example, 1234.56 has two fractional digits.)

Here's how you might define restrictions for a simple type that represents a price in a product catalog, so that it can't be more precise than a single cent, and must be positive:

```
<xsd:simpleType name="price">
  <xsd:restriction base="xsd:decimal">
      <xsd:minExclusive value="0"/>
      <xsd:factionDigits value="2"/>
  </xsd:restriction>
</xsd:simleType>
```

Restricting Values with Enumerations

Ranges work well for numeric data types, but they aren't much help if you need to constrain an element to preset values. This is where enumerations become very useful. Enumerations allow you to define a list of allowed values. The element must use one of these values in order to be valid.

All enumerations are derived from the basic string data type. The following example restricts a color field to one of five values. This might make sense if the element corresponds to a product that's only offered in five colors.

```
<xsd:simpleType name="color">
    <xsd:restriction base="xsd:string">
        <xsd:enumeration value="Gray"/>
        <xsd:enumeration value="White"/>
        <xsd:enumeration value="Black"/>
        <xsd:enumeration value="Beige"/>
        <xsd:enumeration value="Silver"/>
    </xsd:restriction>
  </xsd:simpleType>
```

Restricting Values with Patterns

One of the most generic and powerful facets is the <pattern>, which defines a regular expression pattern that the element must match. *Regular expressions* are a platform-independent syntax for describing patterns in text. What makes regular expressions particularly useful are their rich set of wildcards. Using the basic facets, you can limit string text and numeric ranges. But using a regular expression, you can impose the following much richer types of rules:

- The element must be a certain number of words long.

- The element must contain specific characters (position is not important).

- The element must be made up of a string using only these allowed characters.

- The element must match a well-known format, like a postal code, telephone number, e-mail address, URL, and so on.

A full discussion of regular expressions is far beyond the scope of this chapter. In fact, regular expressions really represent a whole language of their own, and entire books have been written on the subject. However, even if you don't master

the finer points of regular expression syntax, that doesn't mean you can't use the
<pattern> facet. Using a research tool like the Web, you might even look up a regu-
lar expression that matches your type of data, instead of creating it on your own.

All regular expressions are made up of two kinds of characters: literals and
metacharacters. *Literals* represent a specific defined character, like the letter "w."
Metacharacters are wildcards that can represent a range of values. You're probably
familiar with the concept of wildcards if you've ever used a command like del *.* in
the console window. In this case, * is a wildcard that represents everything, and so
this command translates into "delete files with all names and all extensions."

Regular expressions don't use the asterisk—they define a much richer and
larger set of wildcards. For example, \s represents any whitespace character (like a
space or tab). \w represents any "word" (alphanumeric) character. \d represents
any digit. Thus, the regular expression that follows represents four groups of digits,
separated by dashes (as in 412-333-9026):

```
\d\d\d-\d\d\d-\d\d\d\d
```

And it can even be written in the following more compact format:

```
\d{3}-\d{3}-\d{4}
```

Another staple of regular expressions is the character range. For example, you
can define a range of allowed characters using square brackets. [a-c] would match
any single character from "a" to "c" (lowercase only). The following expression will
match any word that starts with a letter from "a" to "c," continues with a variable
number of characters from "a" to "z," and ends with "ing". Possible matches
include acting and counting.

```
[a-c][a-z]+ing
```

Table 2-4 lists a few regular expression examples. Using that table, the following schema fragment shows how you can apply a regular expression with a pattern
facet to make sure an element contains a valid e-mail address. As with the enumeration facet, patterns can only be applied to the basic string data type.

```
<xsd:simpleType name="email">
  <xsd:restriction base="xsd:string">
    <xsd:pattern value="([\w\-]+\.)*[\w\-]+@([\w\-]+\.)+([\w\-]{2,3})"/>
  </xsd:restriction>
</xsd:simpleType>
```

Table 2-4. A Few Regular Expression Examples

Type of Data	Expression	Rules Imposed
E-mail address	([\w\-]+\.)*[\w\-]+ @([\w\-]+\.)+ ([\w\-]{2,3})	Must consist only of word characters, must include an @, and must end with a period and an extension of two or three characters (e.g., someone@somewhere.com).
Phone number	\d{3}-\d{3}-\d{4}	Digits must be separated by hyphens (e.g., 416-777-9344). You can use a similar approach for social security numbers.
Specific-length text	\w{4,10}	A password that must be at least four characters long, but no longer than ten characters (e.g., "hello").

Schemas and Namespaces

Different types of markup have different rules and, as a result, XML schemas can't afford to ignore namespaces. Instead, schema validators carefully check the namespaces used in an XML document when performing validation. For example, a <name> element in an order namespace and a <name> element in a client namespace are treated as completely separate elements—as they should be. Similarly, if you have two documents that have the same elements but are in different namespaces, you'll need to create a separate schema for each one.

For example, consider the simple quotation document shown at the beginning of this chapter. You can easily modify this document to place it inside a specific namespace. The following example uses the namespace http://www.prosetech.com/Schemas/Quotation.

```
<?xml version="1.0"?>
<quotation xmlns="http://www.prosetech.com/Schemas/Quotation">One thing is for
certain: if you don't change the path you're on, you will end up where you are
headed.</quotation>
```

If you try to validate this document with the existing schema, you'll receive an error message informing you that the <quotation> element is not defined. (Technically, the problem really results because the <quotation> element is not defined in the correct namespace.)

To resolve this problem, you simply add the targetNamespace attribute to the <schema> element in your schema document.

```
<?xml version="1.0"?>
<xsd:schema xmlns:xsd="http://www.w3.org/2001/XMLSchema"
 targetNamespace="http://www.prosetech.com/Schemas/Quotation">
  <xsd:element name="quotation" type="xsd:string"/>
</xsd:schema>
```

With more complex documents, you need to take a little more care. For a good example, consider the quotation list, which defines a custom complex type named quotation. In order to create a namespace-aware schema for this document, you must start by adding the elementFormDefault attribute to the <schema> element, and set it to qualified. This ensures that the nested elements you define in the schema will be placed in the same namespace as their parents.

```
<xsd:schema xmlns:xsd="http://www.w3.org/2001/XMLSchema"
 targetNamespace="http://www.prosetech.com/Schemas/QuotationList"
 elementFormDefault="qualified" >
```

Next, you need to make sure that every time you use a new complex type, you explicitly indicate the target namespace. To do this, you'll need to create a prefix for the namespace.

```
<xsd:schema xmlns:xsd="http://www.w3.org/2001/XMLSchema"
 targetNamespace="http://www.prosetech.com/Schemas/QuotationList"
 elementFormDefault="qualified"
 xmlns:ql="http://www.prosetech.com/Schemas/QuotationList" >
```

And you'll need to use this namespace every time you use a type attribute that isn't referring to one of the built-in schema data types.

```
<xsd:element name="quotation" type="ql:quotation" />
```

Here's the completed schema document for the quotation list:

```
<?xml version="1.0"?>
<xsd:schema xmlns:xsd="http://www.w3.org/2001/XMLSchema"
 targetNamespace="http://www.prosetech.com/Schemas/QuotationList"
 elementFormDefault="qualified"
 xmlns:ql="http://www.prosetech.com/Schemas/QuotationList" >

  <xsd:complexType name="quotation">
    <xsd:sequence>
      <xsd:element name="text" type="xsd:string"/>
      <xsd:element name="source" type="xsd:string"/>
```

```
        <xsd:element name="category" type="xsd:string"/>
      </xsd:sequence>
    </xsd:complexType>

    <xsd:element name="quotationList">
      <xsd:complexType>
        <xsd:sequence>
          <xsd:element name="quotation" type="ql:quotation"
            minOccurs="1" maxOccurs="10" />
        </xsd:sequence>
      </xsd:complexType>
    </xsd:element>

</xsd:schema>
```

> **TIP** *For examples of schemas that use namespaces, look in the Namespaces sub-directory of the companion content for this chapter. You'll see the familiar quotation, detailed quotation, quotation list, and yearbook examples, all enhanced with namespaces.*

Locating Schemas

In this chapter, you've seen several examples of XML documents and the schemas you need to validate them. You've even used a simple schema test program (shown in Figure 2-1) that allows you to validate a document using the corresponding schema. In this application, you are in charge of selecting the XML document and the schema you want to use. Clearly, if you tried to use the yearbook schema to validate a quotation list document, the validation would fail. In this case, the problem isn't that the schema is wrong, just that it's the wrong schema for that type of data.

Unfortunately, life becomes a little murkier when you're dealing with automated applications. For example, although you know that a certain document should be validated by a certain schema (probably by looking at the filenames used in the samples), the application has no way to make the same sort of decision. That means developers are left with a few undesirable options:

- Don't perform validation.

- Create applications that only process one type of XML. The application can then assume that every XML document it deals with uses the same schema.

- Try to match the schema using the name of the file. Unfortunately, different documents will have different filenames, and they can't all match the schema. And many applications will receive XML data that's sent directly, and never stored in a file.

- Use XML namespaces. The application can then use different schema files for different documents, depending on their namespace.

The last option is clearly the best choice, and it's often used. Because namespaces uniquely identify different XML languages, they can also be used to organize the related schema documents. However, even if you use this approach, the application still needs to keep some sort of list that links different namespaces to different schemas. In fact, there's another, more convenient option: The XML file itself can store information about the linked schema.

In order to make this connection, you need to add one of the following attributes to your XML document:

- *noNamespaceSchemaLocation* indicates the schema that should be used to validate elements that don't have a namespace.

- *schemaLocation* indicates the schema that should be used to validate elements in a specific namespace. If your document contains multiple namespaces, you can use multiple schemaLocation attributes to indicate the schema for each namespace.

The location itself can be anURL that points to a web site (like http://www.mycompany.com/MySchema.xsd) or absolute path (like file:///C:\MySchema.xsd), but usually it's just a filename. Most schema validators will automatically look for the schema validation file in the same directory as the schema document. If the schema document can't be found, you'll receive an error. In the simple test utility included with the download for this chapter, you'll receive the "Cannot load schema" error.

Both the noNamespaceSchemaLocation and schemaLocation attributes are defined in the XML Schema standard. In order to use these attributes, you need to use the http://www.w3.org/2001/XMLSchema-instance namespace in your document. Usually, the first element in the document maps this namespace to a prefix, and then defines all linked schemas (although you can put this information in another element).

The next example shows the quotation document with no namespace. It uses the noNamespaceSchemaLOcation attribute to point to the Quotation.xsd schema file.

```
<?xml version="1.0"?>
<Quotation xmlns:xsi="http://www.w3.org/2001/XMLSchema-instance"
 xsi:noNamespaceSchemaLocation="Quotation.xsd">One thing is for certain: if
 you don't change the path you're on, you will end up where you are
 headed.</Quotation>
```

If you load this document into the validating utility, you don't need to specify the schema separately. That's because the XML validator will automatically retrieve the specified schema and use it for validation.

It's almost as easy to validate a document that uses a namespace. In this case, you need to use the schemaLocation attribute, which maps a namespace to a location. For example, the following schemaLocation attribute maps the namespace http://www.prosetech.com/Schemas/Quotation to the file Quotation_Namespace.xsd.

```
xsi:schemaLocation =
 "http://www.prosetech.com/Schemas/Quotation Quotation_Namespace.xsd"
```

The following example shows the full quotation document that uses a namespace:

```
<?xml version="1.0"?>
<Quotation xmlns="http://www.prosetech.com/Schemas/Quotation"
 xmlns:xsi="http://www.w3.org/2001/XMLSchema-instance"
 xsi:schemaLocation =
  "http://www.prosetech.com/Schemas/Quotation Quotation_Namespace.xsd">One thing
 is for certain: if you don't change the path you're on, you will end up where
 you are headed.</Quotation>
```

The <Quotation> element actually takes three steps. First, it defines the default namespace for the document. Then, it defines the namespace used for the schemaLocation attribute. Finally, it uses the schemaLocation attribute to specify the linked schema document.

If a document contains multiple namespaces, you must include a schemaLocation tag for each one in order for the validation to complete successfully. You can test validation with linked schemas using the sample XML documents and schemas included with this chapter.

> **TIP** *For examples of linked schemas, look in the LinkedSchemas subdirectory of the companion content for this chapter.*

Are There Tools for Creating Schemas?

Unfortunately, there is no single standard tool for creating XML schemas. Many products include this functionality, however—two examples are Microsoft's BizTalk Server and Visual Studio .NET.

One excellent product that targets XML and XML Schema is Altova's XML Spy, which is free to try and costs a nominal feel to keep (download from http://www.xmlspy.com). XML Spy allows you to write XML, build schemas graphically, validate your data, and much more. If you plan to get some more hands-on experience with XML before you tackle Office 2003, I recommend it heartily.

The Last Word

This chapter has presented a thorough look at schemas, and how they define structure, data typing, and custom rules. Even though you've covered a good deal of ground, there's actually much more depth to the XML Schema standard. For example, there are issues that arise if you want to share complex type definitions across multiple schemas, and declare schemas that work with multiple namespaces. If your enthusiasm for XML schema has been awakened, you might want to consult a dedicated book on the subject. And even if you're still digesting the avalanche of new concepts, you're still ready to apply XML and XML schemas to the Office world. The following three chapters apply these XML concepts, and use them to develop some interesting examples with Excel, Word, and Access. In the process, you'll see why XML will be at the heart of the next generation of business solutions.

CHAPTER 3

Mapping XML in Excel

THE LAST TWO CHAPTERS gave a quick but comprehensive introduction to XML and its overall philosophy. Armed with this knowledge, you're ready to explore the new XML features in Office 2003. This chapter begins the exploration with Excel 2003, Microsoft's premiere spreadsheet and data analysis tool.

Every Office 2003 application uses XML in a slightly different way. Both Excel and Word support features for mapping ordinary XML data to rich Office documents. Excel is most at home working with data-oriented XML, which typically includes repeating elements such as lists of products, customers, expenses, order items, and so on. On the other hand, Word is ideal for less structured narrative-style XML, like news articles and print documents.

In Excel, you'll find three levels of XML support:

- Limited support for opening, viewing, and editing XML files directly in Excel.

- Strong support for importing XML data into part of an Excel spreadsheet. This feature gives you a broad range of possibilities for analyzing XML data in Excel.

- Strong support for exporting part of the data in an Excel spreadsheet to an XML document. This feature is ideal when you want to feed your Excel spreadsheet data into some sort of automated business application.

You can combine the last two approaches to create a spreadsheet that both consumes *and* creates XML. One possible example is a spreadsheet that allows you to view and modify an XML price list. A more exciting example is a spreadsheet that reads an XML price list, lets you use it to create an order, and then exports the finalized order to XML using a completely different XML markup. This scenario transforms Excel from a "closed box" tool for end users into an active part of an XML workflow. But before you get to that stage, you need to learn the basics of XML lists and XML mapping in Excel.

NOTE *This chapter uses a variety of sample XML documents and Excel spread-sheets to demonstrate different features. As always, if you want to try out these steps on your own computer, you can download the files with the companion content online.*

XML Lists

XML lists are the key building block in Excel's support for XML. Essentially, an XML list is a series of one or more rows in an Excel spreadsheet that corresponds to a group of repeating elements in an XML document. These lists have a few interesting features:

- They expand or shrink to accommodate the data. In other words, you can define a single row in a spreadsheet, and it will grow into an entire table when you import an XML document.

- They automatically convert deeply nested XML structures into rectangular tables that Excel can display. This process, known as *denormalization,* is explored in more detail later in this chapter.

- They support built-in filtering and sorting to help you navigate the data.

- They also allow you to insert extra columns with calculated values.

- They allow you to combine data that has an identical structure from multiple different XML files.

XML lists are really at the heart of how Excel sees XML data. To get a better understanding of how they work, it helps to perform a simple test.

Importing and Exporting a Basic XML List

First of all, consider the ProductList.xml file shown here (and included with the sample content for this chapter in the Lists subdirectory). This document lists a series of items from Microsoft's fictional IBuySpy e-commerce shop.

```xml
<?xml version="1.0" ?>
<Products>
  <Product>
    <ProductID>356</ProductID>
    <ModelName>Edible Tape</ModelName>
    <ModelNumber>STKY1</ModelNumber>
    <UnitCost>3.99</UnitCost>
    <CategoryName>General</CategoryName>
  </Product>
  <Product>
    <ProductID>357</ProductID>
    <ModelName>Escape Vehicle (Air)</ModelName>
    <ModelNumber>P38</ModelNumber>
    <UnitCost>2.99</UnitCost>
    <CategoryName>Travel</CategoryName>
  </Product>

  <!-- Other products omitted. -->

</Products>
```

You can open this XML document directly in XML (either by dragging and dropping it, or by using the time-honored File ➤ Open command). When you do, Excel will present the dialog box shown in Figure 3-1, asking how you want to import the XML. Choose the first option, "As an XML list."

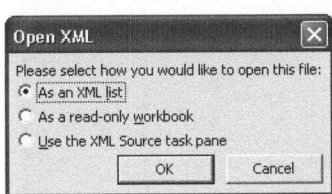

Figure 3-1. Opening an XML file in Excel

The next step Excel will take is to search for any information in the document that identifies the corresponding schema. If Excel can find the schema, it will use the data types and structure defined there. Otherwise, you'll see the dialog box shown in Figure 3-2, alerting you that Excel will need to infer the schema from the document. Usually, this process of making an educated guess will work fine. However, you won't gain the ability to validate data types.

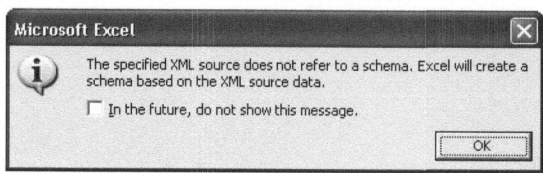

Figure 3-2. Importing XML without a schema

Once you click OK, Excel generates a new XML list based on the data in the document, and adds it to a new spreadsheet. The XML list looks more or less like an ordinary range of cells, except for the blue border that's marked around it. You'll also notice that every element name is turned into a column heading with a drop-down button next to it. Attributes are treated identically, and also converted into columns. This default view is shown in Figure 3-3.

	ProductID	ModelName	ModelNumber	UnitCost	CategoryName
1	ProductID	ModelName	ModelNumber	UnitCost	CategoryName
2	356	Edible Tape	STKY1	3.99	General
3	357	Escape Vehicle (Air)	P38	2.99	Travel
4	358	Extracting Tool	NOZ119	199	Tools
5	359	Escape Vehicle (Water)	PT109	1299.99	Travel
6	360	Communications Device	RED1	49.99	Communications
7	362	Persuasive Pencil	LK4TLNT	1.99	Communications
8	363	Multi-Purpose Rubber Band	NTMBS1	1.99	Munitions
9	364	Universal Repair System	NE1RPR	4.99	Tools
10	365	Effective Flashlight	BRTLGT1	9.99	Tools
11	367	The Incredible Versatile Paperclip	INCPPRCLP	1.49	Munitions
12	368	Toaster Boat	DNTRPR	19999.98	Travel
13	370	Multi-Purpose Towelette	TGFDA	12.99	Protection
14	371	Mighty Mighty Pen	WOWPEN	129.99	Munitions
15	372	Perfect-Vision Glasses	ICNCU	129.99	General
16	373	Pocket Protector Rocket Pack	LKARCKT	1.99	Protection
17	374	Counterfeit Creation Wallet	DNTGCGHT	999.99	Deception
18	375	Global Navigational System	WRLD00	29.99	Travel
19	376	Cloaking Device	CITSME9	9999.99	Deception
20	377	Indentity Confusion Device	BME007	6.99	Deception

Figure 3-3. An XML list in Excel

TIP *You aren't limited to files on the local hard drive when entering an XML source. You can freely use network paths, UNC paths (like //TheServer/TheShare/ TheFile.xml), and even URLs (like http://www.mysite.com/document.xml). Of course, downloading data from a web server is a one-way affair—you won't be able to export your changes back to the web site.*

Editing, Refreshing, and Exporting the List

You can perform three basic editing tasks with an XML list:

- *Editing rows:* This is easy—you simply need to modify the cell values.

- *Deleting rows:* Right-click the row number (at the far left) to select the entire row, and choose Delete from the pop-up menu.

- *Inserting rows:* Right-click the row number where you want to insert the row, and choose Insert. Or, to add a row to the end of the list, go to the last empty row (which has an asterisk [*] next to it) and start typing.

As you make these changes, you aren't actually modifying the original XML. Instead, you're modifying the copy of the XML that's been imported into the spreadsheet. When you save your work, you'll be prompted to save the document as a new .xls Excel spreadsheet. This document will contain the XML data, but it won't be in an XML format any longer.

This might seem like a limitation in Excel, but it's actually a design decision that makes a fair bit of sense. Excel isn't designed to be an all-purpose XML editing tool—many other utilities fill this gap more naturally. Instead, Excel is an application for *viewing and analyzing* XML data. Microsoft's vision is that you will import XML data into Excel to calculate formulas, chart results, plot trends, and so on. In this respect, importing XML data into your Excel spreadsheet is conceptually the same as importing data from a back-end database. Because you use the full Excel spreadsheet format when you save the document, you can add graphics, formatting, graphs, and any other kind of embedded content.

> **TIP** *In order to understand the philosophy of XML in Office 2003, you need to understand that the Office applications aren't intended to be fancy XML editors. Instead, each application can integrate with XML data in the way that makes most sense for that application. In Excel, this means you treat XML as just another data source with information you need to analyze, chart, and manipulate.*

When you import XML data as an XML list, Excel stores information about the data source in your spreadsheet. However, it doesn't actually use that file again unless you explicitly instruct it to. That means you can modify or even delete the source file without affecting the spreadsheet with the XML list.

You have three options for managing the jump from XML to Excel and back.

- *Refresh:* If the XML source changes, it's easy to refresh the list with the new contents. Just click inside the list, and select Data ➤ XML ➤ Refresh XML Data from the menu.

- *Import:* You can import XML data from another file with the same structure. In this case, click inside the list, select Data ➤ XML ➤ Import, and then choose a new XML file. The new XML data will flow into the existing XML list, replacing the original data, and the list will be resized accordingly.

- *Export:* You can export the data in the list into a new XML document. Click inside the list, select Data ➤ XML ➤ Export, and then choose a new XML file. Optionally, you can choose to replace the original XML source with the new XML file.

In the product list example, this means you could import the product list; change, delete, and add new product entries; and then export the finished product list back to XML with the same structure. However, not all XML documents can be successfully exported. This is particularly a problem with XML documents that have complex, deeply nested structures, and it's a topic covered later in this chapter.

All of these options—refreshing, importing, and exporting—can be accessed more quickly from the List toolbar, which appears by default at the far right of the Excel window. Figure 3-4 shows the toolbar with the individual buttons labeled. The toolbar includes a few additional options that are covered later in this chapter.

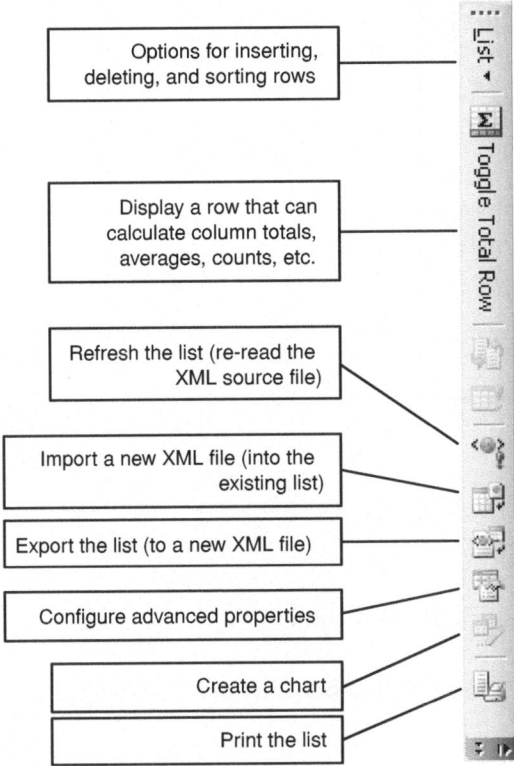

Options for inserting, deleting, and sorting rows

Display a row that can calculate column totals, averages, counts, etc.

Refresh the list (re-read the XML source file)

Import a new XML file (into the existing list)

Export the list (to a new XML file)

Configure advanced properties

Create a chart

Print the list

Figure 3-4. The List toolbar

For even more fun with lists, select Data ➤ Form from the menu. This displays an unusual window where you can edit each row using neatly organized text boxes in a dialog box (see Figure 3-5). A scrollbar allows you to move from record to record, and records can be inserted and removed with a single button click. This one-record-at-a-time browser probably isn't as convenient as working directly with the spreadsheet, but it is useful if you have so many columns of data that you can't edit a whole record at once in the normal spreadsheet view.

NOTE *There is one choice that this chapter doesn't consider—using Excel's custom XML format to export the full spreadsheet information to an XML document. This issue is more complex and usually won't be your first approach. It's dealt with in more detail in Chapter 6.*

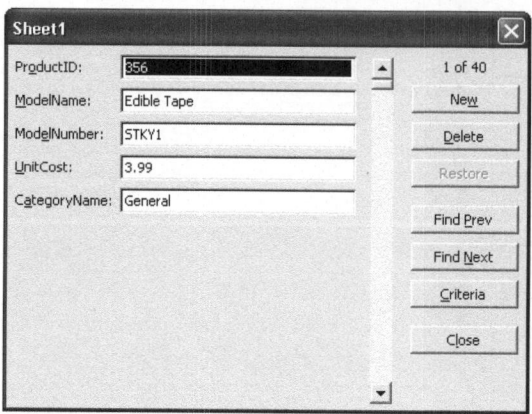

Figure 3-5. The form view of an XML list

Sorting and Filtering Lists

XML lists provide a few basic conveniences. These include

- *Sorting:* This allows you to order the data alphabetically or numerically by column.

- *Filtering:* This allows you to limit the list of information based on specific criteria.

You can quickly apply sorting and filtering using the drop-down column headers. To apply a new sort order, choose a column, click the drop-down box, and then choose one of the first two options (Sort Ascending or Sort Descending). The type of sort is determined by the data type of the column. Usually, Excel can successfully recognize numeric-only columns when it imports data. For example, in the product list example, the price column is correctly treated as numeric data, and sorting by that column performs a numeric sort, rather than an alphabetical sort. If you want to apply a sort using a combination of multiple column values, select Data ➤ Sort from the menu.

TIP *A numeric sort compares the whole number value, while an alphabetic sort compares text strings one character at a time. Thus, 92 is less than 102 in a numeric sort, but the text "92" is greater than "102" in an alphabetic sort, because 9 occurs after 1 in the alphabet.*

In some cases, XML might not be able to identify numeric data automatically. This is the case if your XML mixes other characters with the number (for example, the $ currency symbol). In this situation, you might want to write a VBA macro that fixes up the formatting of values. In many cases, XML will recognize currency values as "numbers stored as text." You can simply highlight the offending cells, click the exclamation icon that appears next to them, and choose Convert to Number from the pop-up menu.

Excel also allows you to change how you look at imported data with filtering. Using filtering, you can cut down a mass of data to the select rows that actually interest you. Filtering, like sorting, is performed through the drop-down column headings. You can choose to restrict rows in several ways:

- By a specific column value. For example, if you select Communications from the CategoryName field in the product list example, the list will only show the products that are in the Communications category (about five records).

- By limiting columns to the top ten values. This option is only supported for numeric columns. For example, if you choose (Top 10) under the UnitCost field in the product list example, you'll see the ten most expensive products.

- By limiting the columns with a custom condition. Just select (Custom) from the column header and enter your filter expression.

Figure 3-6 shows the sort and filter options available in a column.

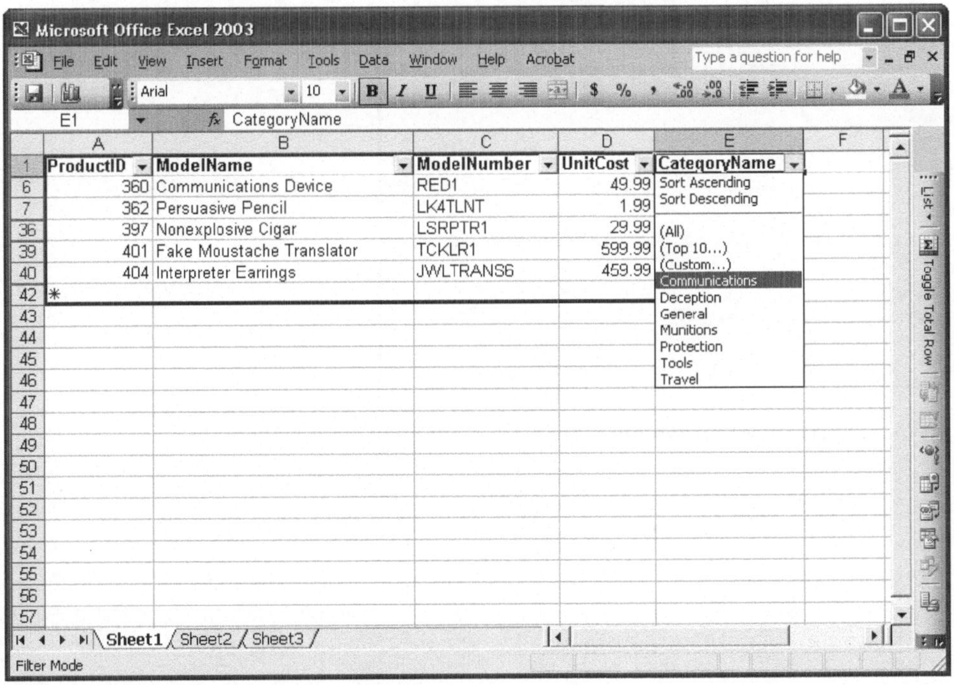

Figure 3-6. Filtering and sorting XML lists

The (Top 10) option actually pops up a dialog box where you can choose a number of items to display. This number is 10 by default. You can also choose to display only the bottom items (those with the smallest values). Figure 3-7 shows your options.

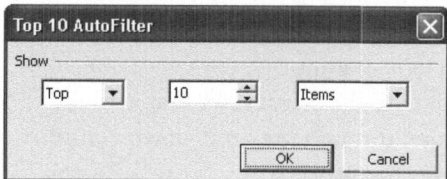

Figure 3-7. The (Top 10) option

If you want more control with your filtering, you can create a custom filter condition, which matches rows based on the criteria you specify. You can choose to match rows that are exactly equal to, greater than, or less than a specific value. You can also find values in a range by combining two conditions. For example, if you want to find all the products that range in cost from 50 to 100 dollars in the product list example, you could combine a greater than 50 condition with a less than 100 condition on the UnitCost field. Similarly, you could find all the products that start with the letter "E" using the alphabetical comparison shown in Figure 3-8.

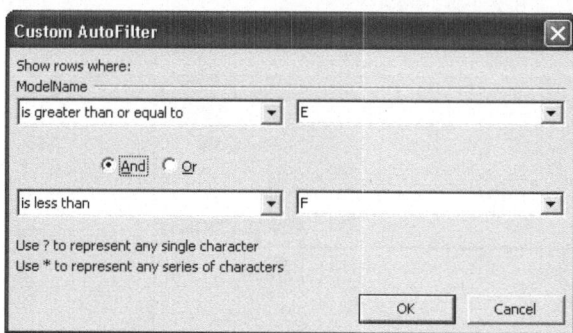

Figure 3-8. A custom filter condition

For even more advanced filtering, you can use two wildcards. The asterisk (*) is used to match any series of characters, while the question mark (?) matches a single character. That means the filter expression ModelName equals *Tool* matches any model names that contain the word "Tool." The filter expression ModelNumber equals P??X matches any four-character model number that starts with P and ends with X.

There are a few issues to keep in mind when using column filtering. First of all, filters are cumulative. That means that if you add a filter condition to two columns, you will only see the rows that match both conditions. To remove a condition, select (All) from the drop-down column header.

It's also important to understand how Excel handles filtered data when you save the document. Even though the full list isn't visible, all the data will be stored with the spreadsheet. However, if you export the XML list, the exported file will *only* contain the filtered rows. Finally, refreshing the display and importing new data won't remove the filter conditions. That means you should remove filtering before you import new data. Otherwise, you might not see all the data you import, because rows that don't match the filter conditions will be hidden.

Mapping Cells to XML

Up until this point, the examples have relied on Excel's default behavior for translating XML data into an XML list. This works well for simple documents, but it doesn't work out as well when Excel is confronted with more challenging data. In these situations, you need a few more tricks and a little more flexibility—both of which are provided through Excel's XML mapping features.

With XML mapping, you explicitly define how spreadsheet cells and XML elements are related. Excel gives you two basic ingredients to create a workbook mapping: single-cell mappings, and the infamous XML list.

To start creating a mapped spreadsheet, open an XML document, and choose the last option, "Use the XML Source task pane," from the dialog box shown in Figure 3-1. Excel won't import the data immediately. Instead, it will open a blank spreadsheet with the XML Source pane on the right of the window. The XML Source pane shows the structure of the XML document you want to import. You can then map some or all of these elements to the new spreadsheet. Figure 3-9 shows the XML Source pane inferred based on the ProductList.xml file.

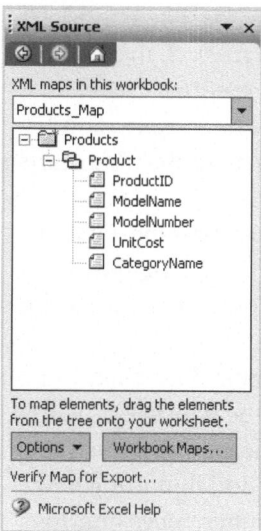

Figure 3-9. The XML Source pane

To map these elements to your spreadsheet, you simply need to follow these steps:

1. Select the element in the XML Source pane.

2. Drag the element from the XML Source pane to the appropriate place on the spreadsheet. If it's a repeating element, a column header will be created. If it's a single element, a single cell will be created and outlined in blue on the screen (as shown in Figure 3-10).

3. Return to step 1 and repeat the process until you've mapped all the elements. No data will be inserted into the document until you complete the mapping process and click the refresh button (the exclamation mark on the List toolbar) or select Data ➤ XML ➤ Refresh from the menu.

When multiple columns belong to the same XML list, it's often easiest to drag these elements onto your spreadsheet in one operation. You can select multiple elements by holding down the Ctrl key while you select items in the XML Source pane, or by selecting a parent element. In the product list example, selecting the Product node in the XML Source pane would select all the elements that are part of the product. You can then drag them all at once. It's entirely up to you whether you create your XML list as a series of contiguous columns, or as separate columns spread out over your spreadsheet. Either way, the data is equivalent.

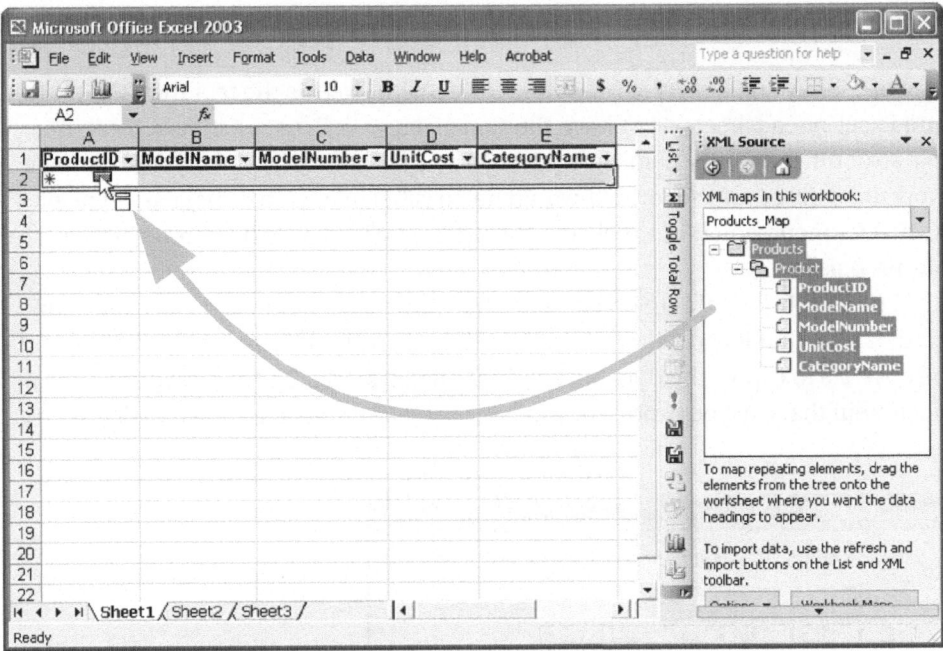

Figure 3-10. Mapping XML elements

You don't need to map the whole document before refreshing the data. It's quite possible that you might only want to map some elements and work with a part of the data. However, if you don't map a cell, it won't be stored with the spreadsheet. As a result, if you export the XML data, only the cells in the document will be exported. If you are using a schema that requires certain elements, and your Excel spreadsheet omits one of these elements, you'll receive a validation error when you attempt to export the data.

Before continuing with the rest of this chapter, you might want to open the same ProductList.xml document and perform the mapping on your own. Every element can be mapped only once. If you change your mind while creating a mapping, you can remove it by right-clicking the corresponding element in the XML Source pane, and choosing Remove.

XML mapping isn't just a means to fine-tune the way columns are organized on a spreadsheet. It also gives you the opportunity to handle XML documents that can't be represented in a single XML list because their structure is too complex. The next section presents several examples of these problem documents, and how you can safely map their structure by hand.

Importing Complex Structures

One of the key challenges to integrating XML with Excel is the fact that XML data and Excel spreadsheets don't have the same shape. XML uses a hierarchical, tree-like structure, while Excel fits everything into a tabular structure on a rectangular worksheet. In a perfect world, it would be possible to import almost any type of XML document, edit it in Excel, and then export it back to XML. However, this isn't always possible.

Excel's prime goal is to consume XML. That means it attempts to import any kind of XML that it can. However, depending on the type of document, it may not be possible to export the data back to XML. If you select the Export option with a document that can't be exported, you'll see the error message shown in Figure 3-11.

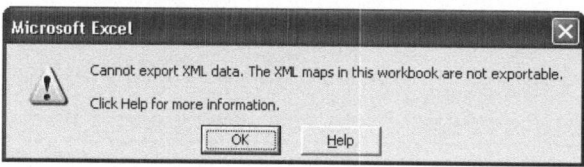

Figure 3-11. Trying to export unexportable XML

Typically, this problem occurs when Excel is forced to change the structure of the XML document to fit the list format. Depending on the structure of the original XML, this process of translation isn't always reversible. In some cases, you can solve the problem by fine-tuning the XML mapping, as discussed later in this chapter. In other cases, the problem is an unavoidable fact of life, and the only way out is to accept read-only XML.

To understand this problem, why it occurs, and how you can avoid it, you need to know a little more about the steps Excel takes to translate XML data into an XML list. In the next three sections, you'll see three types of XML structure that can cause a problem.

Tables and Headers

The product list example uses an XML file that contains a single series of repeating elements. It's common in XML to combine this simple repeating structure with a few elements that appear only once. For example, an alternate product list XML format might use additional elements to declare some information about the company, when the catalog was generated, and so on. Here's an example:

```
<?xml version="1.0" ?>
<Products>
  <Company>IBuySpy Store</Company>
  <Created>2004-01-01</Created>
  <Product>
    <ProductID>356</ProductID>
    <ModelName>Edible Tape</ModelName>
    <ModelNumber>STKY1</ModelNumber>
    <UnitCost>3.99</UnitCost>
    <CategoryName>General</CategoryName>
  </Product>
  <Product>
    <ProductID>357</ProductID>
    <ModelName>Escape Vehicle (Air)</ModelName>
    <ModelNumber>P38</ModelNumber>
    <UnitCost>2.99</UnitCost>
    <CategoryName>Travel</CategoryName>
  </Product>

  <!-- Other products omitted. -->

</Products>
```

When Excel loads this XML, it converts the entire document into a single rectangular list. To succeed, it needs to add the basic catalog data (the <Company> and <Created> elements) to each row. Figure 3-12 shows how this XML document appears if you open it directly as an XML list, without performing any custom mapping. The two denormalized columns are highlighted for emphasis. (You can test this example using the ProductList_Header.xml file included with the companion content for this book.)

This approach introduces some problems. For example, consider what would happen if you change the Company field in one row, but not in the other rows. In this case, Excel would have no way to represent the new data using the original document structure. Because of this ambiguity, this conversion is a one-way only affair. Excel won't let you export the product list.

This process of mapping a single value to multiple elements is called *denormalization*. It can occur with both elements and attributes. Fortunately, you can resolve this problem by manually mapping the additional elements to another part of the same document.

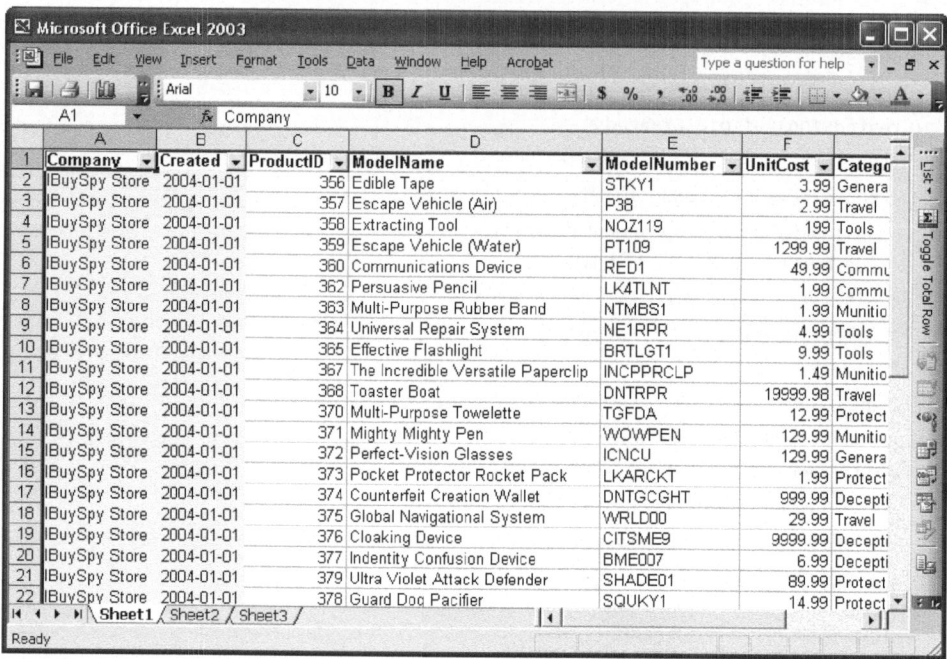

Figure 3-12. An XML list based on a document with header data

Here's how you can safely map the ProductList_Header.xml file to a spreadsheet:

1. Open the ProductList_Header.xml file and choose "Use the XML Source task pane."

2. Map the Company information to a single cell (use B1) by dragging and dropping the heading from the XML Source pane. When you drop the element on your cell, an eight ball icon will appear. Click it to choose where you want the element heading to appear (see Figure 3-13). Choose the left, which is cell A1. The heading becomes a static part of your spreadsheet, and it's not part of the XML map.

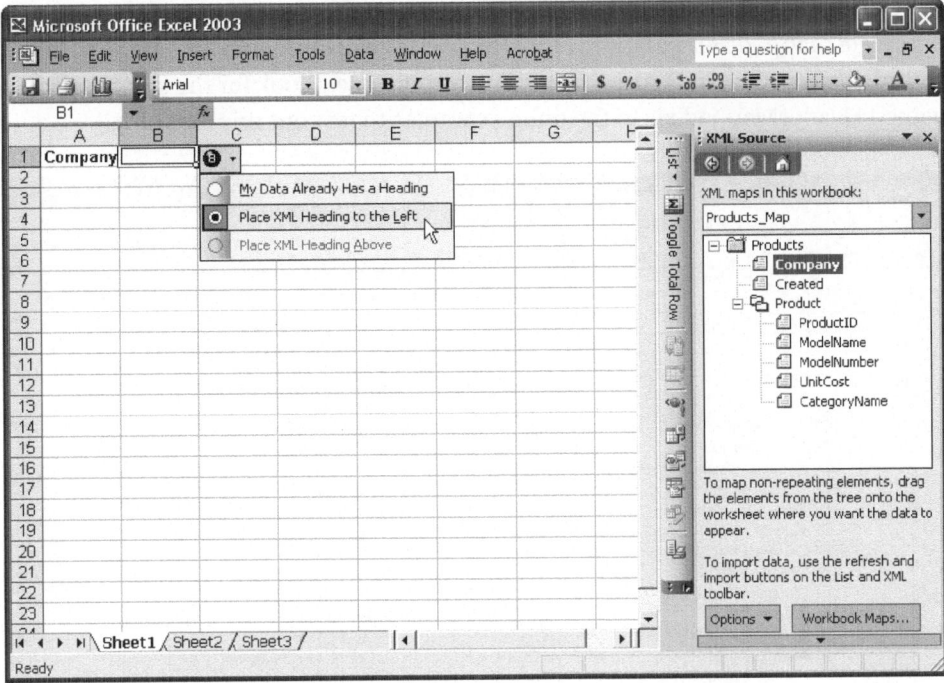

Figure 3-13. Choosing a heading for a cell mapped to a single value

3. Map the Created information to a single cell (use B2). Choose to display the heading on the left.

4. Now click the Product element in the XML Source pane to select the remaining elements, and drag them to a list under the heading. You can drop the elements on cell A4.

5. Click the refresh button (the exclamation mark on the List toolbar) or select Data ➤ XML ➤ Refresh from the menu.

Once you've completed this mapping, the header values will be displayed in the single mapped cells, and the repeating values will appear in an XML list. This spreadsheet (shown in Figure 3-14) is fully exportable. (Look for the spreadsheet named HeaderMapped.xls in the online samples to test out this mapping.)

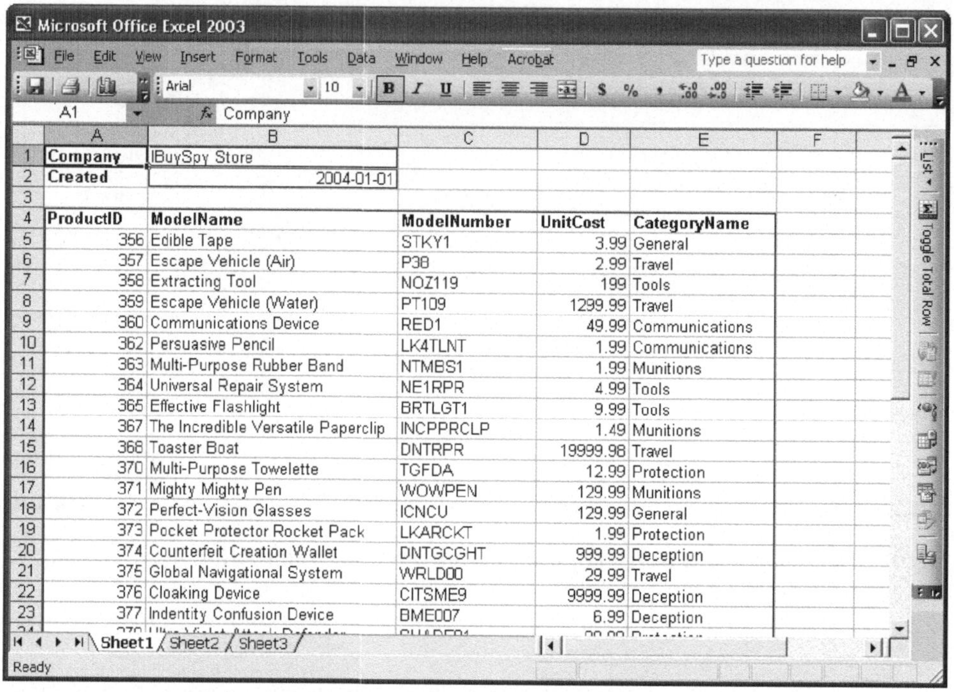

Figure 3-14. A properly mapped XML document with header information

Multitabular Data

Sometimes you might have an XML document that contains more than one series of repeating elements. For example, consider the following XML document, which includes both a list of products and a list of categories:

```
<?xml version="1.0" ?>
<Data>

  <Categories>
    <Category>
      <CategoryID>14</CategoryID>
      <CategoryName>Communications</CategoryName>
    </Category>
```

```
    <!-- Other categories omitted. -->
  </Categories>

  <Products>
    <Product>
      <ProductID>356</ProductID>
      <ModelName>Edible Tape</ModelName>
      <ModelNumber>STKY1</ModelNumber>
      <UnitCost>3.99</UnitCost>
      <CategoryName>General</CategoryName>
    </Product>

    <!-- Other products omitted. -->
  </Products>

</Data>
```

Excel's default conversion fails miserably with this type of information. It still treats the XML document as a single table, and attempts to fuse the <Category> and <Product> elements into a single row. This leads to the somewhat counterintuitive list shown in Figure 3-15. (You can test this example using the XML file ProductList_MultiTable.xml.)

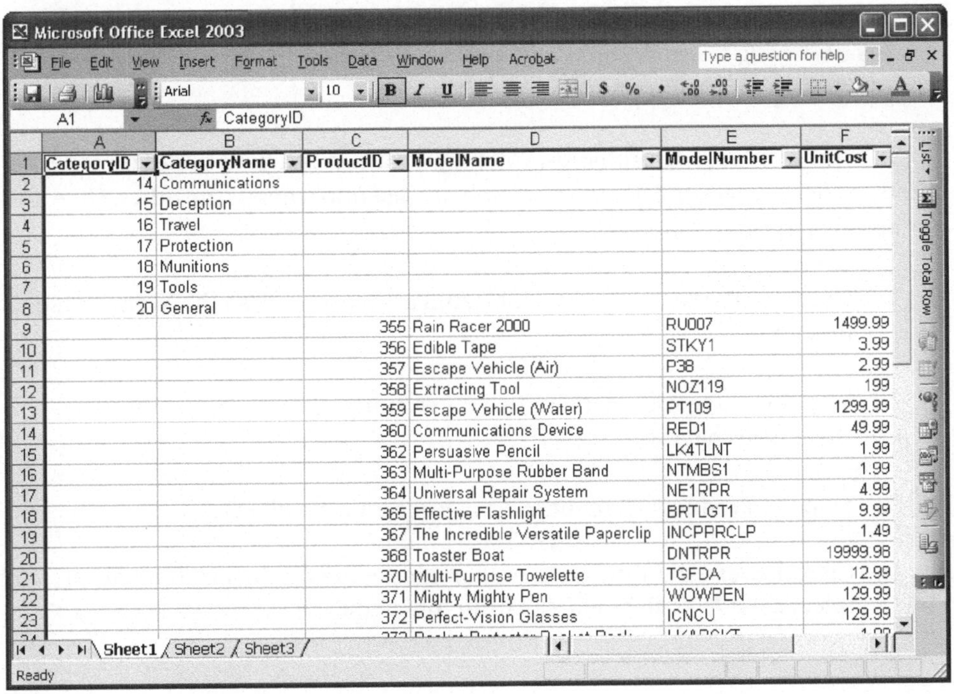

	A	B	C	D	E	F
1	CategoryID	CategoryName	ProductID	ModelName	ModelNumber	UnitCost
2	14	Communications				
3	15	Deception				
4	16	Travel				
5	17	Protection				
6	18	Munitions				
7	19	Tools				
8	20	General				
9			355	Rain Racer 2000	RU007	1499.99
10			356	Edible Tape	STKY1	3.99
11			357	Escape Vehicle (Air)	P38	2.99
12			358	Extracting Tool	NOZ119	199
13			359	Escape Vehicle (Water)	PT109	1299.99
14			360	Communications Device	RED1	49.99
15			362	Persuasive Pencil	LK4TLNT	1.99
16			363	Multi-Purpose Rubber Band	NTMBS1	1.99
17			364	Universal Repair System	NE1RPR	4.99
18			365	Effective Flashlight	BRTLGT1	9.99
19			367	The Incredible Versatile Paperclip	INCPPRCLP	1.49
20			368	Toaster Boat	DNTRPR	19999.98
21			370	Multi-Purpose Towelette	TGFDA	12.99
22			371	Mighty Mighty Pen	WOWPEN	129.99
23			372	Perfect-Vision Glasses	ICNCU	129.99

Figure 3-15. An XML list based on two tables

Once again, manual mapping is the answer. This time, you need to map the two tables separately (into two XML lists). You need to take some care when creating these two lists to avoid overlapping problems. If you create the product list starting at A1, and the category list starting at A10, there won't be a problem, because the category list will be automatically shifted down when the product list grows. If you use the reverse arrangement, however, a problem will occur. That's because the category list is smaller than the product list, and so it overlaps only some of the product list columns. As the category list grows, the first few product columns will be dislocated from the rest of the product list columns, causing an error. If you attempt to refresh the spreadsheet with this mapping, you'll see the error shown in Figure 3-16 and the information won't be imported.

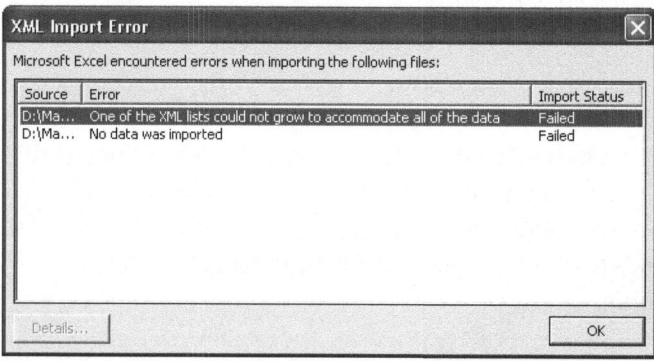

Figure 3-16. Trying to import data with overlapping lists

To avoid overlapping problems, you might want to put your tables on separate sheets, or side-by-side, rather than placing one list underneath the other. Here are the steps you need to follow:

1. Open the ProductList_MultiTable.xml and choose "Use the XML Source task pane."

2. Map the Categories element to a range starting on the left of the worksheet (use cell A3).

3. Map the Products element to a range starting at cell D3.

4. Click the refresh button (the exclamation mark on the List toolbar) or select Data ➤ XML ➤ Refresh from the menu.

The properly mapped spreadsheet, with imported data, is shown in Figure 3-17 (and provided online as the file MultiTableMapped.xls).

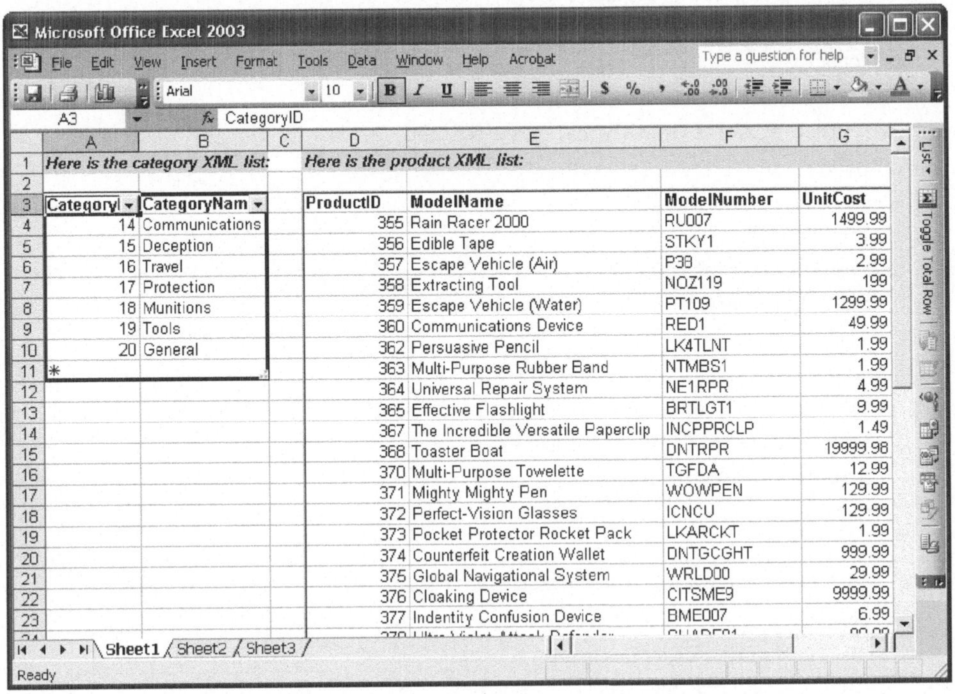

	A	B	C	D	E	F	G
1	*Here is the category XML list:*			*Here is the product XML list:*			
2							
3	CategoryI	CategoryNam		ProductID	ModelName	ModelNumber	UnitCost
4	14	Communications		355	Rain Racer 2000	RU007	1499.99
5	15	Deception		356	Edible Tape	STKY1	3.99
6	16	Travel		357	Escape Vehicle (Air)	P38	2.99
7	17	Protection		358	Extracting Tool	NOZ119	199
8	18	Munitions		359	Escape Vehicle (Water)	PT109	1299.99
9	19	Tools		360	Communications Device	RED1	49.99
10	20	General		362	Persuasive Pencil	LK4TLNT	1.99
11	*			363	Multi-Purpose Rubber Band	NTMBS1	1.99
12				364	Universal Repair System	NE1RPR	4.99
13				365	Effective Flashlight	BRTLGT1	9.99
14				367	The Incredible Versatile Paperclip	INCPPRCLP	1.49
15				368	Toaster Boat	DNTRPR	19999.98
16				370	Multi-Purpose Towelette	TGFDA	12.99
17				371	Mighty Mighty Pen	WOWPEN	129.99
18				372	Perfect-Vision Glasses	ICNCU	129.99
19				373	Pocket Protector Rocket Pack	LKARCKT	1.99
20				374	Counterfeit Creation Wallet	DNTGCGHT	999.99
21				375	Global Navigational System	WRLD00	29.99
22				376	Cloaking Device	CITSME9	9999.99
23				377	Indentity Confusion Device	BME007	6.99

Figure 3-17. A properly mapped XML document with multiple lists

Relational (or Nested) Data

Another problem occurs if you have nested tables (or lists of lists). For example, in the product list example, each <Product> element includes information about the corresponding category in a nested <CategoryName> field. The multitable example shows a scenario where you might want to store more information about the category. Another possibility is that you might want to alter the document to arrange the products in groups based on their category. Here's one example of how you might use this sort of nested structure in XML:

```
<?xml version="1.0" ?>
<Data>
  <Category>
    <CategoryID>14</CategoryID>
    <CategoryName>Communications</CategoryName>
```

```
    <Product>
      <ProductID>360</ProductID>
      <ModelName>Communications Device</ModelName>
      <ModelNumber>RED1</ModelNumber>
      <UnitCost>49.99</UnitCost>
    </Product>

    <!-- Other products in this category omitted. -->
  </Category>

  <Category>
    <CategoryID>15</CategoryID>
    <CategoryName>Deception</CategoryName>
    <Product>
      <ProductID>374</ProductID>
      <ModelName>Counterfeit Creation Wallet</ModelName>
      <ModelNumber>DNTGCGHT</ModelNumber>
      <UnitCost>999.99</UnitCost>
    </Product>

    <!-- Other products in this category omitted. -->
  </Category>

  <!-- Other categories and products omitted. -->
</Data>
```

In this example, the nested structure represents a relationship between categories and products. Each parent <Category> element contains one or more child <Product> elements. Unfortunately, Excel has no concept of related sets of data. It can't understand that the nested XML structure shown previously represents a relationship between categories and products. When you import this document into an XML list, Excel will fill all the category information into every related row. This creates the type of table shown in Figure 3-18. Note how each product has a column value for CategoryID and CategoryName, even though this information isn't actually defined in the <Product> element, but in the parent <Category> element.

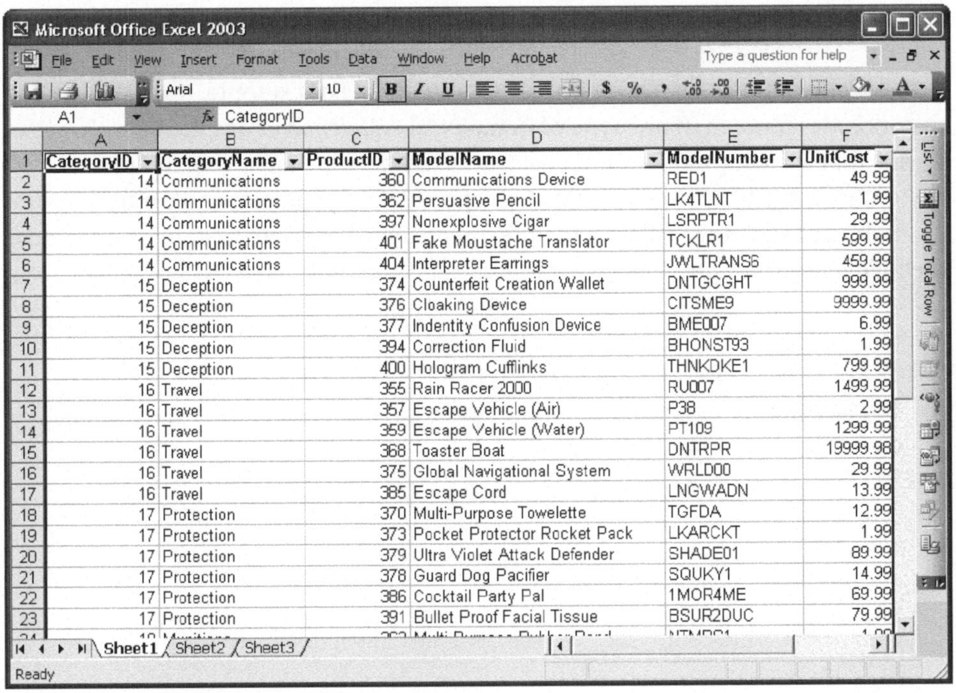

CategoryID	CategoryName	ProductID	ModelName	ModelNumber	UnitCost
14	Communications	360	Communications Device	RED1	49.99
14	Communications	362	Persuasive Pencil	LK4TLNT	1.99
14	Communications	397	Nonexplosive Cigar	LSRPTR1	29.99
14	Communications	401	Fake Moustache Translator	TCKLR1	599.99
14	Communications	404	Interpreter Earrings	JWLTRANS6	459.99
15	Deception	374	Counterfeit Creation Wallet	DNTGCGHT	999.99
15	Deception	376	Cloaking Device	CITSME9	9999.99
15	Deception	377	Indentity Confusion Device	BME007	6.99
15	Deception	394	Correction Fluid	BHONST93	1.99
15	Deception	400	Hologram Cufflinks	THNKDKE1	799.99
16	Travel	355	Rain Racer 2000	RU007	1499.99
16	Travel	357	Escape Vehicle (Air)	P38	2.99
16	Travel	359	Escape Vehicle (Water)	PT109	1299.99
16	Travel	368	Toaster Boat	DNTRPR	19999.98
16	Travel	375	Global Navigational System	WRLD00	29.99
16	Travel	385	Escape Cord	LNGWADN	13.99
17	Protection	370	Multi-Purpose Towelette	TGFDA	12.99
17	Protection	373	Pocket Protector Rocket Pack	LKARCKT	1.99
17	Protection	379	Ultra Violet Attack Defender	SHADE01	89.99
17	Protection	378	Guard Dog Pacifier	SQUKY1	14.99
17	Protection	386	Cocktail Party Pal	1MOR4ME	69.99
17	Protection	391	Bullet Proof Facial Tissue	BSUR2DUC	79.99

Figure 3-18. An XML list based on nested lists

This translation might be perfectly reasonable. However, it will prevent you from exporting the data, because Excel can't convert this structure back into the original hierarchical structure. You can use custom mapping to change the way Excel imports nested XML data—for example, you can map the category information and product information to different portions of the spreadsheet, so you can examine this information separately. In this case, the spreadsheet will look the same as the one in Figure 3-17. However, no matter how you import this document, you'll be prevented from exporting it.

To sidestep this issue, you might want to convert the XML data into a normalized format before you import it. In the product list example, you would have to add the <CategoryID> and <CategoryName> elements directly into each <Product> element, and change the structure of the document so it is only one level deep. This requires more work, but it allows you to import and export the data. Chapter 7 discusses XSLT, an XML-based standard you can use to convert one type of XML into another.

Irregular Rows

Other problems can occur with less structured data. For example, if you have a list that includes more than one type of item, Excel will *denormalize* the data. That means that a list of products and customers will become an aggregate "product customer" list. The list will include all the product and customer columns in a single table, and each row will only include the values that relate to it. In other words, the following structure:

```
<Items>
  <ItemA>
    <ID>1001</ID>
    <ColumnA>Sample Value A</ColumnA>
  </ItemA>
  <ItemB>
    <ID>1002</ID>
    <ColumnB>Sample Value B</ColumnB>
  </ItemB>
</Items>
```

becomes this XML list:

ID	ColumnA	ColumnB
1001	Sample Value A	
1002		Sample Value B

Once again, there's no way around this problem. You can use Excel to analyze the XML data, but it can't be round-tripped. The problem is that once data is denormalized, possible ambiguities are introduced. For example, in the previous XML document, what happens if there is a value placed in <ColumnA> for <ItemB>? Even a data transformation language like XSLT can't solve this problem. The bottom line is that Excel is tailored for XML data that has a tablelike structure. Other types of XML documents can be analyzed, but not modified or exported.

Importing XML Documents with Schemas

So far, the examples presented in this chapter have relied on Excel's ability to infer the structure of your XML document by examining your data. A more cautious approach is to use an XML schema that explicitly defines the XML markup you want to work with.

You have two options for using an XML schema in Excel:

- Use a schema location attribute in the XML source file. In this case Excel will automatically use the linked schema file.

- Manually attach a schema file before opening the XML document.

In the first case, Excel will automatically try to find the linked schema file. If it can find it, Excel will use the structure it defines to create the XML Source pane. If it can't find the schema file, Excel will display an error message and prompt you to continue (in which case it will infer the schema). One benefit with this approach is that the linked schema is always used. One potential downfall is that the schema must be available in the same directory or in the location you specify, which makes this approach less flexible in organizations that are constantly reorganizing their XML documents and schemas.

Another option is to manually attach the schema before you import the XML data. To take this approach, you'll need to follow several steps. You can practice these steps using some of the schemas examples from the previous chapter, such as the quotation list document and schema.

1. Open the spreadsheet in which you'd like to add the XML schema.

2. Select XML ➤ Data ➤ XML Source from the menu to open the XML Source pane.

3. Click the Workbook Maps button on the XML Source pane.

4. In the XML Maps dialog box, click the Add button.

5. Browse to your XML schema file, and click OK.

6. Click OK to close the XML Maps dialog box. You'll now see the schema-defined elements in the XML Source pane.

7. You can drag the elements from the XML Source pane to the spreadsheet as normal. When you're finished, import an XML document that has this structure by selecting Data ➤ XML ➤ Import.

> **TIP** *An Excel document can contain multiple maps. The only requirement is that each element in a map is only linked to one list or cell, and the maps don't overlap. Each map is given a unique name when you add the schema, and usually there's no need to change this name.*

When using an XML schema, Excel can perform validation with the schema data types to prevent invalid input. If you want to use this feature, you have to manually enable it for the document. Select Data ➤ XML ➤ XML Map Properties from the menu. In the list of options (shown in Figure 3-19), click the first checkbox, "Validate data against schema for import and export."

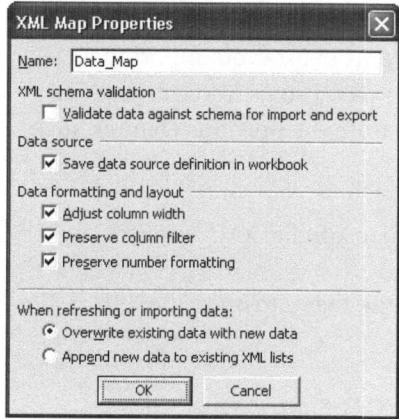

Figure 3-19. Additional options for configuring an XML map

Even when you enable validation, it won't be performed while you edit the document. In fact, it's completely acceptable to create an Excel spreadsheet that contains mapped XML data that doesn't conform to its schema rules! The validation only springs into effect whenever you import or export data. If you try to import an invalid document you'll receive an error message. Similarly, if you've broken the schema rules, you won't be able to export invalid data to a new XML document.

As a simple example, consider the schema for the simple product list used in the first few examples in this chapter (and provided in the online samples as ProductList.xsd):

```
<?xml version="1.0"?>
<xsd:schema id="Products" xmlns:xsd="http://www.w3.org/2001/XMLSchema">
```

```
<xsd:element name="Products">
  <xsd:complexType>
    <xsd:choice maxOccurs="unbounded">
      <xsd:element name="Product">
        <xsd:complexType>
          <xsd:sequence>
            <xsd:element name="ProductID" type="xsd:int" />
            <xsd:element name="ModelName" type="xsd:string" />
            <xsd:element name="ModelNumber" type="xsd:string" />
            <xsd:element name="UnitCost" type="xsd:decimal" />
            <xsd:element name="CategoryName" type="xsd:string" />
          </xsd:sequence>
        </xsd:complexType>
      </xsd:element>
    </xsd:choice>
  </xsd:complexType>
</xsd:element>
</xsd:schema>
```

To perform a simple test, attach this schema to a workbook, import the product list data, and enable schema checking. Then, try to make an illegal change and export the data. Excel will display a dialog box that lists all the errors it encountered. Figure 3-20 shows an example of what you might see if you try to insert text into the numeric product ID field.

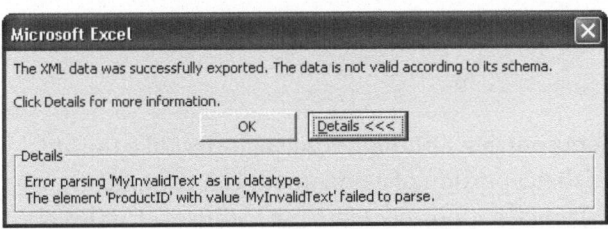

Figure 3-20. Validating with a schema

Here are a few more tricks to working with schemas in Excel:

- Excel only distinguishes between a limited set of data types, including dates, numbers, strings, and Boolean (true or false) values. Excel doesn't natively recognize all the data types that can be used in XML schemas. However, Excel will faithfully preserve the formatting of all fields, including dates, binary values, and so on.

- Excel doesn't completely support <choice> groups. Instead, Excel will just add all the possible elements to the XML Source window. For example, if you use the YearbookEntry_Choice.xsd schema from Chapter 2, you'll be able to map the <quotation> and <printCitation> elements. However, you'll need to map these elements to separate cells. You'll also run into problems exporting the data, in which case you'll end up with extra blank elements.

- Some schemas have more than one root <element> tag, and can be used to validate different types of documents. In this case, Excel will prompt you to choose which root you want to use when you import the schema. For example, Figure 3-21 shows what happens if you use the YearbookOrQuotation.xsd schema file from the Chapter 2 samples, which validates documents that contain a <student> or <quotation> root element.

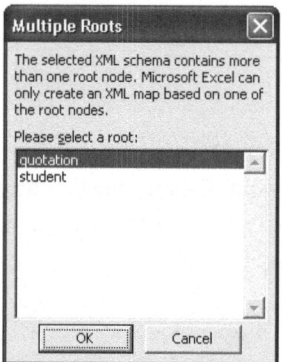

Figure 3-21. Using a schema with two roots

- Excel supports most schema entries, although some features (like the any data type, which declares that a portion of a document can contain any combination of elements) aren't supported. For a full listing of all of Excel's XML idiosyncrasies, you can refer to the detailed documentation included with the Excel Content Development Kit (CDK). Download this kit from http://msdn.microsoft.com/downloads/list/office2k3.asp.

Clearly, Excel's schema validation could be enhanced. It's not hard to imagine a version that underlines suspect values at runtime with a red mark, or prompts the user with valid values from a schema-defined enumeration using IntelliSense. (You'll see some of these features in Word, as discussed in the next chapter.) Unfortunately, Excel's XML integration doesn't provide that level of friendliness yet.

Aggregating and Analyzing XML

Importing XML into Excel is a bit of a compromise. Clearly, the rigid table-based structure Excel uses means that it isn't always the easiest tool for editing and viewing XML. So why use Excel at all? The most common reason for importing XML data into Excel is to use Excel's real strengths: crunching numbers and analyzing data. This section takes a closer look at how Excel formulas and graphs work with XML lists.

To understand the sequence of importing and exporting XML, it helps to consider a typical scenario. Sally, an experienced salesperson, receives an XML document with information about company sales. Sally decides to use Excel to analyze the data, and so she imports it into a spreadsheet as an XML list. She then adds other information to the spreadsheet, including calculated columns and a graph.

Next quarter, Sally receives a new XML document with updated sales figures. Rather than create a new Excel spreadsheet to analyze it, she returns to her existing spreadsheet. She then imports the new XML into the existing document. Because the new document has the same structure, the import operation works seamlessly. The only part of the spreadsheet that changes is the XML list—the charts and formulas remain, and are updated automatically with the new data.

Interestingly enough, you can even import data from multiple XML sources into the same XML list. In this case, you just need to tweak the XML settings slightly. Choose Data ➤ XML ➤ XML Map Properties from the menu, which displays the window shown in Figure 3-19. Then, choose the "Append new data to existing data" option at the bottom of the window. Now, every time you import or refresh XML data, it will be added to your list. This allows you to consolidate the information from multiple files, but you need to be careful that you don't accidentally end up with duplicates, as Excel won't try to catch these. In other words, clicking the refresh button multiple times will add multiple copies of the same data to your XML list, which probably isn't what you want.

The Total Row

XML lists make it easy to calculate totals, averages, standard deviations, and other common formulas for a column. First, enable the total row by clicking in the list, and selecting Data ➤ List ➤ Total Row. (You can also use the List toolbar.) Next, scroll down to the bottom of the list to the total row, and find the numeric column that you want to work with. If you click in the cell, a drop-down list will appear with preset options. Choose the type of calculation that you want, as shown in Figure 3-22.

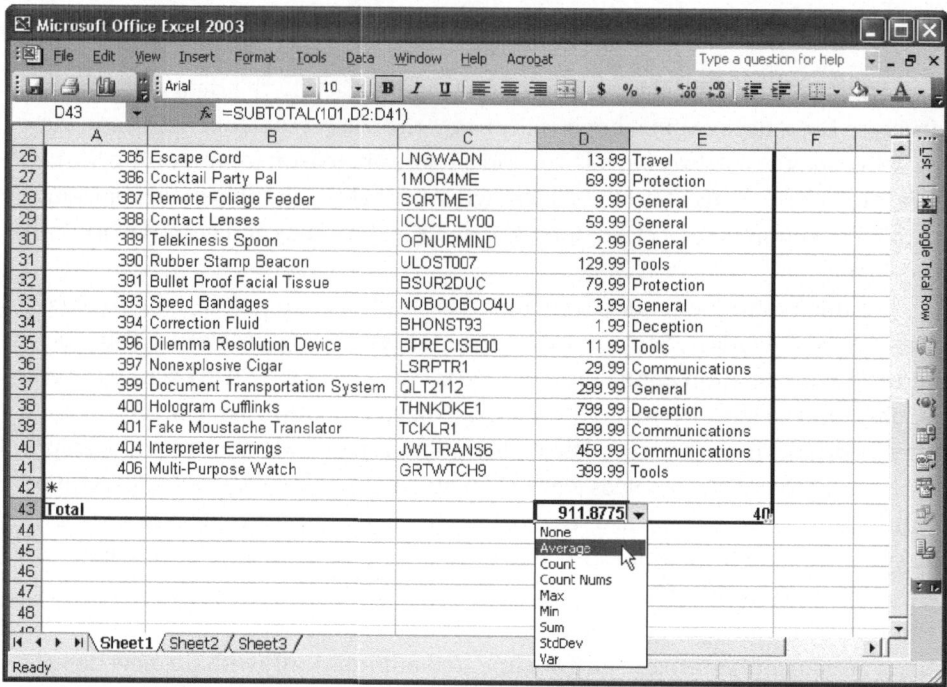

Figure 3-22. Caclulating the average price

The total row is simply a convenience for at-a-glance data analysis. It won't be included if you export the XML data.

Calculated Columns, Formulas, and Charts

For calculations that involve more than one column, you can easily extend an XML list with new calculated columns. Just right-click the list and choose Insert ➤ Column. As with the total row, calculated columns won't be exported to XML, because they aren't a part of the XML schema or workbook map.

You can also use the XML list data in calculations or graphs elsewhere on your spreadsheet. Best of all, if the list grows or shrinks as you edit it or import additional files, the formulas and chart ranges will be modified automatically to correspond. This makes it easy to calculate totals and other information that works with the whole list.

You can try a quick example with the online samples files. First, create a new spreadsheet. Add the ProductExpenses.xsd schema to the workbook maps. This contains the structure for a slightly different type of product list—one that defines the number of units in stock and on order. Map all the columns to one XML list at the top of the spreadsheet (starting at the first cell, A1).

Before actually importing any data, you can add these two calculated columns:

- ValueInStock calculates the value of the total inventory items. It multiplies the UnitPrice and UnitsInStock fields of the current row. Type the formula **=C2*D2** into the first cell under the header.

- ValueOnOrder calculates the value of the items that are on order. It multiplies the UnitPrice and UnitsOnOrder fields of the current row. Type the formula **=C2*E2** into the first cell under the header.

Figure 3-23 shows how the example should look, with the two calculated columns added to the far right of the XML list.

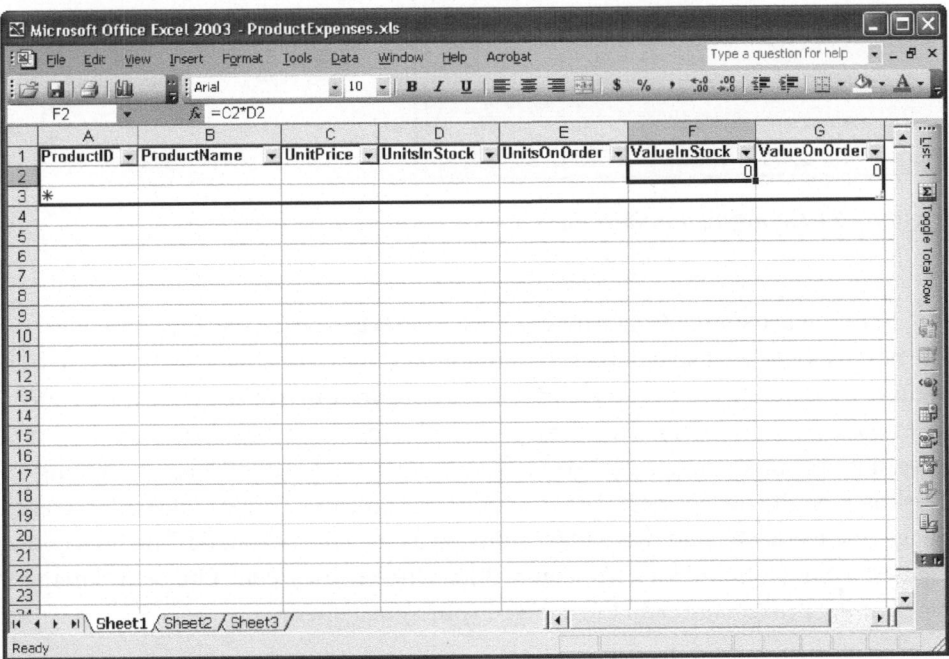

Figure 3-23. Adding calculated columns

Now, why not add a chart based on the ValueInStock and ValueOnOrder fields? Like the columns, the chart can be created after you've imported the data. But there's no harm in creating it immediately. The quickest approach is to click the Chart Wizard button in the List toolbar. When prompted to choose a type of chart, choose stacked column, as shown in Figure 3-24. Then click Next.

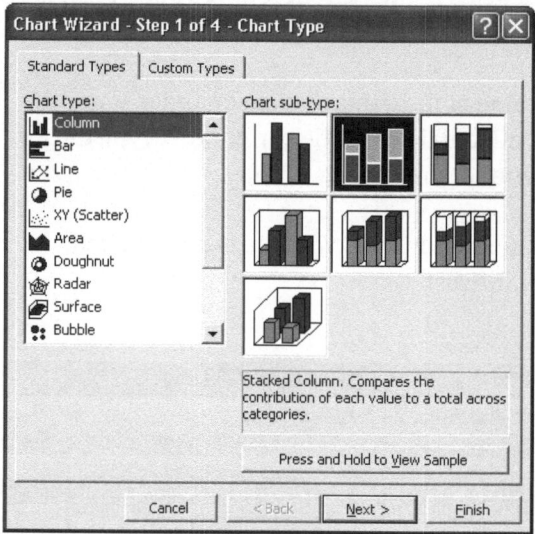

Figure 3-24. Choosing the chart type

In the Chart Source Data window, click the Series tab. In this case, the only data that should be displayed is the ValueInStock and ValueOnOrder fields, so remove all other items from the Series list box. (Click once to select the item, and then click the Remove button.) Next, you need to define the category axis. In this case, it makes sense to use the ProductID, because the ProductName is too long to be shown on the dense chart. The ProductID is column A. You can use the current range **=Sheet1!A2** and this will be adjusted as the chart expands. The final configured window should look like Figure 3-25. Once it does, click Finish to skip the fine-tuning process and add the chart to your spreadsheet.

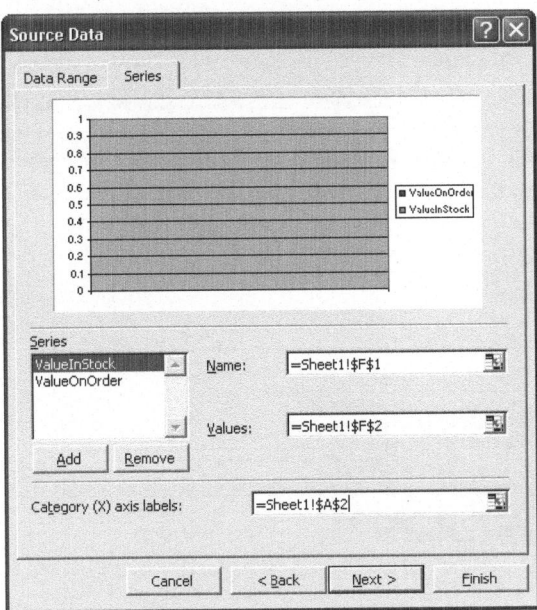

Figure 3-25. Configuring chart options

Now that you've created the Excel template for analyzing your data, you're ready to import it from the XML source. Click the list and select Data ➤ XML ➤ Import from the menu. Choose the ProductExpenses.xml file, which contains the full product list. The list will be expanded, the ValueInStock and ValueOnOrder columns will be calculated, and the chart will be refreshed with the new data. Looking at the chart, you can compare the value of the inventory on order against the value of the in-stock inventory for each product.

The next step is to reuse your editing template with other XML files that have the same structure. For a look at some different data, you can import CurrentProductExpenses.xml, which shows the catalog of currently offered items, or DiscontinuedProductExpenses.xml, which shows products that are no longer offered. You'll notice that the chart for the discontinued products looks quite a bit different, as there are no items on order (see Figure 3-26). But either way, you won't need to modify the structure of the spreadsheet or change your mapping. Your spreadsheet can analyze any XML data that fits the schema.

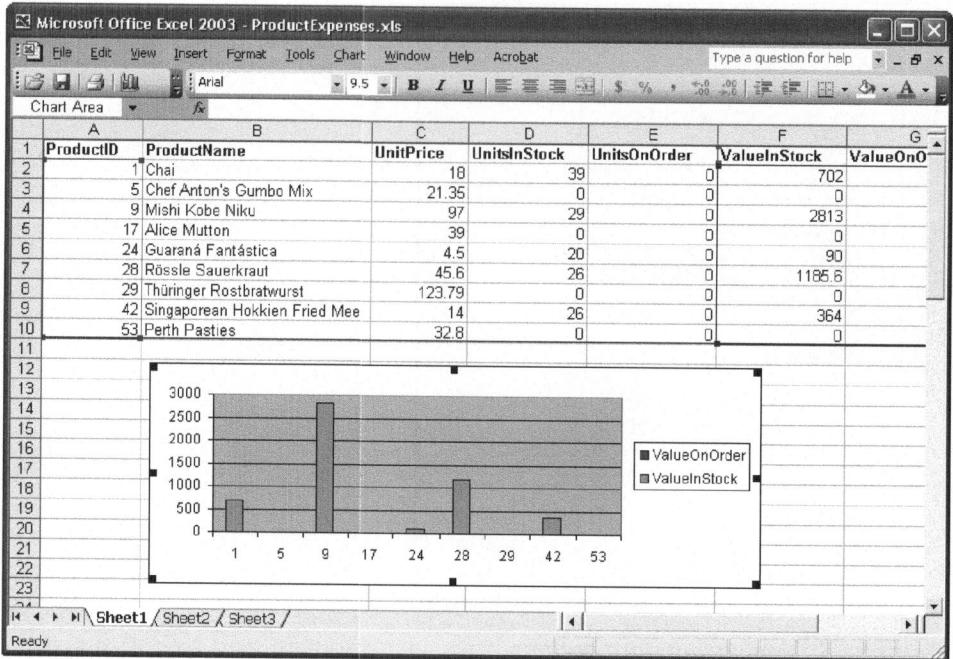

Figure 3-26. Analyzing the XML

> **TIP** *For examples of linked schemas, look in the AnalyzingXML subdirectory of the companion content for this chapter.*

Data Mining

So far, this chapter has focused on using XML mapping to analyze XML data with all the conveniences of XML. But there's another reason you might use these features: to let other applications gain access to the data stored in XML spreadsheets. For example, you might want to take an expense list, and feed it into an automated workflow application that understands XML. Currently, the only way you can read Excel data in another application is either to force the users to export their entire spreadsheets to a simple text-based format, or use the Office automation objects. The first approach requires additional manual steps, and the second one only works if the workflow application has Office installed (and even then it introduces a sizeable overhead). More importantly, both approaches are dangerously unreliable, because they force applications to make assumptions about where to find data using cell numbers. If the structure of the Excel spreadsheet is modified even slightly, the application reading it will generate an error—or worse yet, receive invalid information.

The solution is to map your existing templates to XML, and then export data to an XML-enabled application. We'll look at a quick example of this technique in this section.

Retrofitting Existing Templates

It's estimated that there is more data in Excel spreadsheets than all the world's relational databases combined. And while it's hard to tell if this estimate is accurate, it's undeniably true that a significant amount of important business information ends up trapped in Excel spreadsheets, where it's beyond the reach of any automated application. Even when Excel data is sent from one individual to another, the recipient needs to find the file, open it, and manually retrieve the relevant information, which can be time consuming.

Consider the example of an expense report. Usually, the form must be completed, printed, and then sent to the appropriate individual, who then copies the information into another spreadsheet or some type of custom software that writes it to a centralized database. These steps can be cut down dramatically with a little XML.

The next example shows how you can map an existing Excel spreadsheet to a schema you've defined. The process is essentially the same as that demonstrated throughout this chapter. The only difference is that you'll be mapping an existing file instead of starting from scratch with a new spreadsheet.

To run this test, you can use the source files included with this chapter. (You'll find these files in the TemplateRetrofit subdirectory.) Just take the following steps:

1. Open the UnmappedExpenseReport.xls spreadsheet file (shown in Figure 3-27).

2. Select Data ➤ XML ➤ XML Source.

3. Click the Workbook Maps button.

4. Click Add and select ExpenseSchema.xsd.

5. Click OK to close the dialog box. Now you're ready to start the mapping.

6. Click the Name element in the XML Source pane and drag it to the input cell for "Name:".

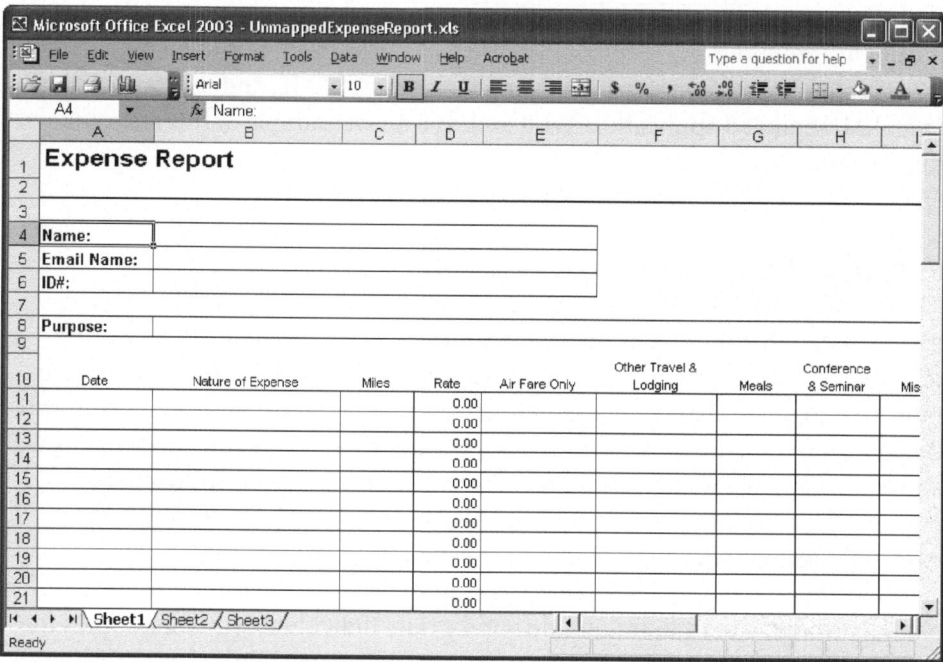

Figure 3-27. The original spreadsheet

7. Repeat step 6 for all the header data, which includes the Email, IDNumber, and Purpose elements.

8. Now you can map the repeating items. These are elements under the ExpenseItem branch, which will become an XML list. Map these elements one at a time by dragging elements onto the headers in the table. (In this case, you can actually select the whole ExpenseItem branch and drag it onto the spreadsheet in one operation. This only works because the order of the child elements happens to match the order of columns on the spreadsheet.)

9. The next step is to delete the empty rows in the expense list. Otherwise, these items will be exported as empty XML elements. Select the rows by clicking the row number on the left of the sheet. Select the rows 11 through 39, right-click the selection, and choose Delete. Be careful not to select the last row (the one with the asterisk), because it is used to insert new items into the list. If you select this row, the Delete option won't be available.

10. The Rate and Total columns are calculated based on other cells. You'll
    need to make sure each cell has the appropriate formula. The Rate for-
    mula for row 11 is **=C11*0.32** and the Total formula is **=SUM(D11:I11)**.
    You can add this to the first entry in the list, and it will automatically be
    copied into all the new rows you add.

11. You can also remove the summary row. Instead, this functionality is pro-
    vided through the totals row, as described earlier. Enable the totals row by
    selecting Data ➤ List ➤ Total Row, and then configure each numeric col-
    umn to show a sum total.

The retrofitted spreadsheet is now complete. To test it, fill out the general
report information, and add a few expense items. The XML list will grow dynamically as needed. Figure 3-28 shows an example expense report.

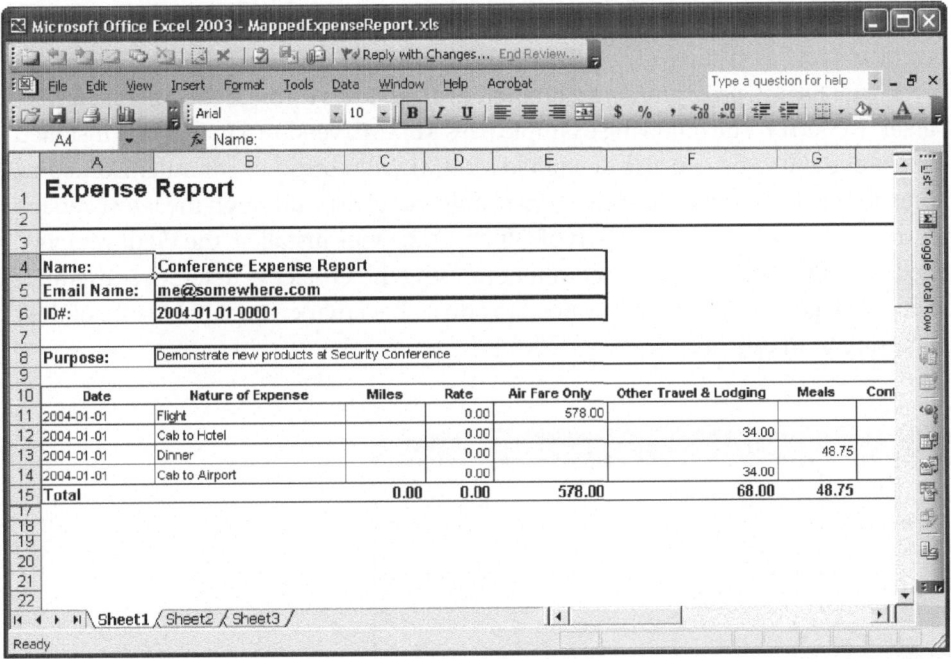

Figure 3-28. A sample spreadsheet with the mapped template

To export the expense report data, select Data ➤ Export ➤ XML and choose
a file.

Getting the Data in Visual Basic 6

So now that you have the data in an XML format, what do you do with it? Most programming languages—including Visual Basic, C#, C++, and Java—have built-in or separately installable components that can handle XML access. These components are able to read and validate XML in a standardized way, navigate through the branches of a document, retrieve values based on the element name, and more.

Serious XML programming is beyond the scope of this book (although I'll touch on it in Chapter 8). The approach and syntax you use to manipulate XML in code depends on the programming language and platform you want to use. However, reading XML is so easy that it's worth a quick digression to show you an example. In this case, I'll use the tried-and-true Visual Basic 6. If you want to create or open this project on your own computer, you'll need the Microsoft Visual Basic software installed. However, you can run the compiled .exe file even if you don't have it. In addition, if you're a budding .NET developer, you'll find a remarkably similar version of this application that's written in VB .NET code. This chapter, however, focuses exclusively on the VB 6 version.

Visual Basic 6 programmers gain their XML abilities through the Microsoft XML Parser (MSXML). The following example uses MSXML version 5.0, which is installed with Office 2003. You can also download MSXML from http://msdn.microsoft.com/library/default.asp?url=/downloads/list/xmlgeneral.asp, although the latest version (currently 5.0) is installed as a part of Office 2003. Once installed, the VB developer needs to add a reference to the component using the Project ➤ References menu, as shown in Figure 3-29. You simply need to add a checkmark next to the name of the component (in this case, Microsoft XML).

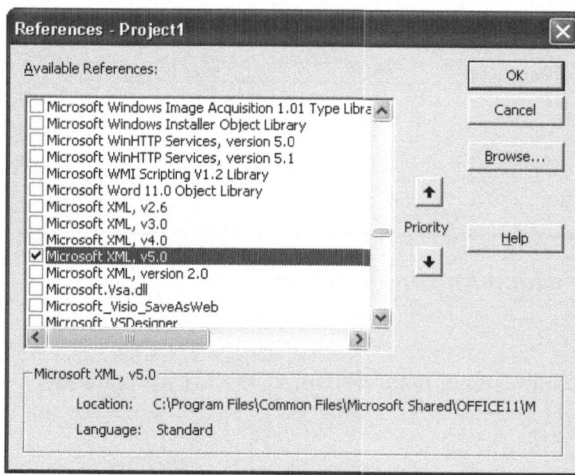

Figure 3-29. Adding a reference to the MSXML component

Now you can use two new objects to read and analyze the XML. The first of these is the DOMDocument object, which represents XML data that's been read into memory. Using this object, you can navigate through the XML structure and retrieve various pieces of information. Conceptually, the XML document is divided up into nodes, which are represented by the IXMLDOMNode interface. Types of nodes include attributes, elements, text content, and the document prolog.

Retrieving information from an XML document in code is just a matter of moving to the right node and reading its text. To find the root document element and start your exploration, you use the DOMDocument.documentElement property. Then, you can examine the nodes that are contained inside the document element using the DOMDocument.childNodes property. The following code snippet looks for specific nodes in the XML document, and copies them onto a form when it first loads:

```
Private Sub Form_Load()

    ' Create the DOMDocument object.
    Dim Doc As DOMDocument
    Set Doc = New DOMDocument

    ' Load the ExpenseData.xml file into memory.
    If Doc.Load(App.Path & "\ExpenseData.xml") Then

        ' Scan all the nodes under the root element.
        Dim Node As IXMLDOMNode
        For Each Node In Doc.documentElement.childNodes

            ' Check if the node contains the metadata (header) section.
            If Node.nodeName = "Meta" Then

                ' Retrieve information about the expense report.
                txtName.Text = Node.childNodes(0).Text
                txtID.Text = Node.childNodes(2).Text

            ' Check if the node contains the expense list.
            ElseIf Node.nodeName = "ExpenseItem" Then

                ' Get the description and total of each expense item.
                Dim Description As String
                Description = Node.childNodes(1).Text
                Dim Total As String
                Total = FormatCurrency(Node.childNodes(10).Text)
```

```
        ' Show this information in a list box.
        lstItems.AddItem (Description & " (" & Total & ")")
      End If
    Next
  End If

End Sub
```

The result is the form shown in Figure 3-30. The application can easily retrieve the data, without needing to start an Office application or even have it installed.

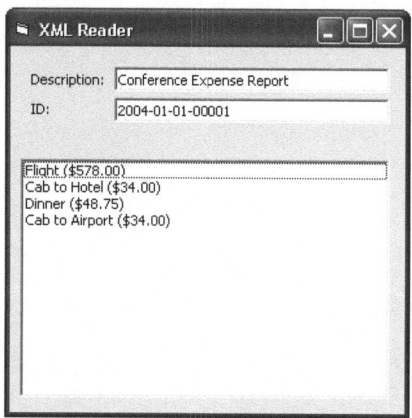

Figure 3-30. A simple VB 6 program for reading XML

Of course, the Excel approach isn't perfect. One key issue is the fact that someone still needs to export the data in the first place, and then send it to the data mining application. However, you can build automated solutions with a little effort. We'll look at how Web services, in conjunction with a little VB code, might make this process seamless in Chapter 8.

The Last Word

This chapter thoroughly explored the XML mapping features in Excel. You learned how you can import XML data into a spreadsheet to analyze it, and how you can export spreadsheet data so it can be used in another business process. This technique has the potential to dramatically change the way information travels through a business or organization. In today's world, information is trapped in spreadsheets, and can only be read, understood, and used by a human. But if the information is converted into XML, it can be read and used by an application, which can employ it as part of an automated process.

In order for this XML vision to become reality, you'll need to add a few more pieces to the puzzle. Using the approaches shown in this chapter, users still need to manually export and copy XML data files. However, a little VBScript code can automate the steps needed to get and submit information, allowing you to centralize data and glue together the individual pieces of a workflow. This approach is developed in Chapter 8. First, however, you need to consider the XML features provided in two other members of the Office family: Word and Access.

CHAPTER 4

Mapping XML in Word

OFFICE 2003 TURNS Microsoft Word into an XML heavyweight. But you won't find Word abandoning its rich documents for data-only XML. Instead, the majority of Word's XML features are designed to break down the boundary between XML data and the classic .doc format. Thanks to these new features, Word can now play a part in automated business processes, without needing to abandon any of its rich formatting, page layout, and editing features.

In Word, you'll find three levels of XML support:

- Limited support for opening, viewing, and editing XML files directly in Word.

- Strong support for creating and editing XML documents based on a schema. Best of all, Word uses IntelliSense to alert you when your document deviates from the schema rules.

- Strong support for exporting some or all of the information in Word documents to a custom XML markup. This allows you to create hybrid Word documents that use rich formatting, but can still be exported to data-only XML.

The last two points are the heart of Word's XML support. Both of these features are provided in Word through XML mapping, and they both require an XML schema document. Unlike Excel, there's very little you can do with XML data in Word unless you have a corresponding schema. This difference is the result of Word's loose document-oriented nature. Without the schema rules, it's impossible to impose any kind of order on the XML data in a Word document.

Word 2003 also introduces a new custom XML language it calls WordML. WordML allows you to save any Word document to XML without losing formatting information. This feature is entirely separate from XML mapping. Although it uses XML markup, it doesn't allow you to define the elements and structure for that XML. However, this feature does raise interesting possibilities, such as the ability to programmatically create Word documents, extract Word-specific information from a Word document, and transform ordinary XML into formatted WordML for specific display or printing purposes. You can even transform Word's custom WordML into another form of XML. These features are explored in Chapter 6 and Chapter 7.

Viewing an Ordinary XML File

To get started with Word's XML features, you can look at how Word treats an ordinary XML file. Consider the quotation list file first presented in Chapter 2. Figure 4-1 shows what happens when you try to open this format in an earlier version of Word (in this case, Word 2000). The file is opened as ordinary text, and you can freely modify tags, change the structure, and add illegal characters—just like you can in Notepad. Word 2000 also uses whatever structure is in the source file. If all the elements run into a single line with no whitespace or line breaks (as shown with the second quotation), that's how it will appear in the Word display.

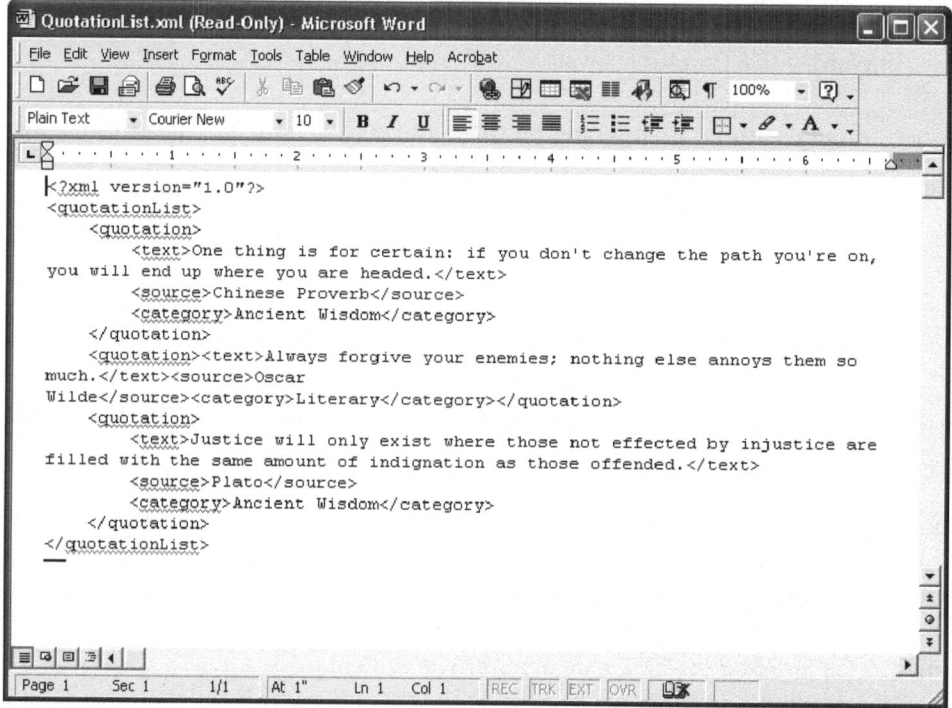

Figure 4-1. XML in Word 2000

Figure 4-2 shows the same file in Word 2003. Word 2003 automatically recognizes the XML format, and changes the tags into special pink boxes. It also formats the tags using standard indenting to show you the document structure. You can edit the data inside the tags, and you can delete, cut, and paste the tags themselves. However, you can't directly edit the tag content or insert new tags. Similarly, Word won't spell check the tag names.

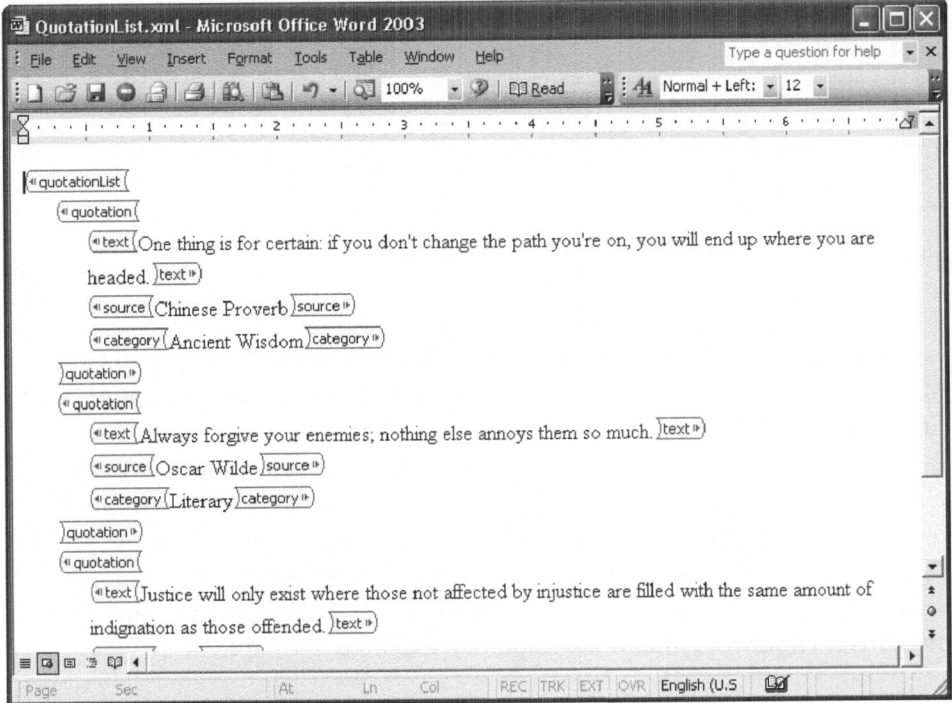

Figure 4-2. XML in Word 2003

In some respects, it might seem at first that the Word 2003 XML editing features are less powerful. For example, when opening a stand-alone XML file, Word won't allow you to create new tags! This limitation exists because Word 2003 isn't intended to be an all-purpose XML editing tool—instead, it's designed to work closely with XML schemas, as you'll see in the next section.

In several obvious respects, however, the Word 2003 XML support is already far better than it was in previous versions. First of all, the XML display is much easier to browse and understand. Spell checking and grammar checking also work as expected, because Word won't get distracted by the beginning and ending tags and flag them as errors. More importantly, because Word 2003 recognizes XML natively, it correctly handles the data when you save it. That means that special characters (like the angle brackets <>) are automatically replaced with the required character encodings. Similarly, Word will never split a tag over a line break, and by default it will prevent you from saving the XML unless it is well formed (for example, if the tags in your document aren't properly nested). The same validation is performed when opening an XML document. Figure 4-3 shows what happens if you attempt to open the ProductList_WithErrors.xml file from Chapter 1.

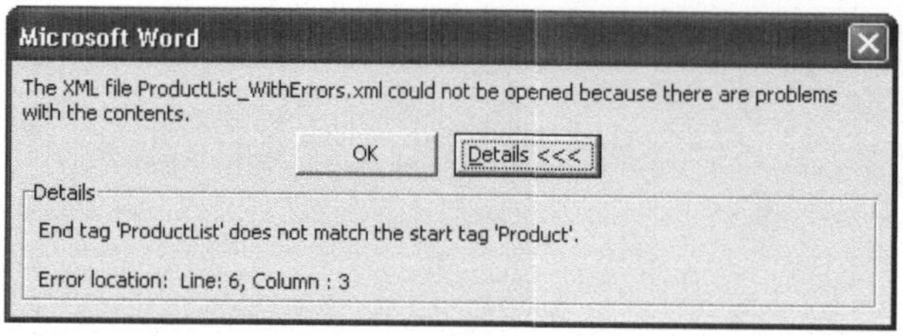

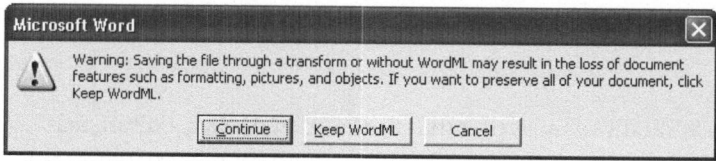

Figure 4-3. Attempting to import invalid XML

In fact, Word 2003 makes it difficult to even create XML that isn't well formed. For example, when you delete a start tag, the corresponding end tag is removed automatically.

When you save the XML document, you'll see a message informing you that you'll lose any formatting you've applied (shown in Figure 4-4). For example, if you've inserted an image or made some text bold, these details will be lost in the XML file. Click Continue to save the file. Word provides its own XML format that can resolve these problems, at the expense of changing the document into the proprietary WordML standard. This option is explored in Chapter 6.

Figure 4-4. Saving XML

Mapping XML with a Schema

To unlock Word's full XML support, you need to use XML schemas. Word 2003 treats schemas in a similar manner to the way it treats document templates. Every user has a unique schema library, with XML schemas that can be applied to Word documents. To attach a schema to a document, you must begin by importing the schema into the schema library. Once you've imported the schema, it can be used with any Word document, including existing files and new documents.

To view the schema library, follow these steps:

1. Select Tools ➤ Templates and Add-Ins from the menu.

2. Select the XML Schema tab.

You'll see a few schema-related options that control how Word performs validation, and a list of XML schemas. Figure 4-5 shows a schema library with two schemas (although if this is the first time you're using this feature, you'll probably see an empty list). If a schema appears in the schema library with a checkmark next to it, that schema has been applied to the current document.

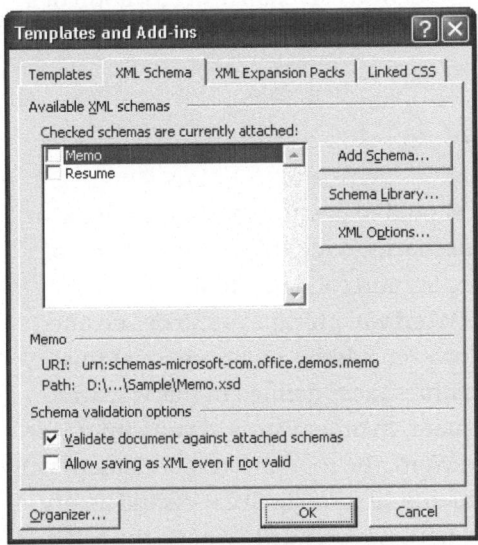

Figure 4-5. A list of installed schemas

Word tracks three pieces of information for each schema:

- *A namespace URI:* It's recommended that all your XML documents use a unique namespace. Otherwise, you'll be forced to define one when you import the schema into Word.

- *A friendly name:* This is a user-readable label that you assign when adding the schema to the library. For example, although the namespace http://mycompany/OrderML uniquely identifies order documents, the label "Order Record" is easier to understand and refer to at a glance.

- *A full file path:* This indicates where the schema document can be found. That means that if you change the location of a schema after you import it into the library (or just delete the file entirely), you'll receive an error.

When you click a schema in the list, the namespace URI and file path are shown at the bottom of the window.

Because Word stores the full path for each schema, organizations should consider deploying schemas in a centralized location on the network, and individuals may want to store all their schemas in a specific directory. One possibility is the user-specific directory Word uses for templates. This is typically C:\Documents and Settings\[UserName]\Application Data\Microsoft\Templates, or C:\Documents and Settings\All Users\Application Data\Microsoft\Templates if you want to share templates with all the users of a single computer. You can change the location of a schema after you add it, but the process must be performed one schema at a time.

Managing the Schema Library

Before adding a schema to the library, you should make sure that it specifies a target namespace. Word relies on unique namespaces to identify different types of XML documents, and determine how to display and validate them.

If you don't define a target namespace, Word will prompt you to define one when you add the schema to the library. However, adding a namespace at this point will complicate your life. First of all, namespaces defined in this way will only apply to the root element of the document. In other words, if you import the resume schema and assign a namespace in Word, the root <Resume> element will be placed into a namespace, but other elements, like <objective>, <workHistory>, and so on, will still be in the default, empty namespace. Furthermore, the original resume schema won't be modified, so you won't have any way to determine what the unique namespace URI is unless you load Word and dig through the schema library. For these reasons, it's recommended that before you use Word, you add target namespaces to your schemas (and use them in your XML documents).

The following steps outline the process for adding a new schema to the library:

1. Select Tools ➤ Templates and Add-Ins from the menu.

2. Select the XML Schema tab.

3. Click the Add Schema button.

4. Browse to the location of the XML schema file, and select it. As a test, find and select the QuotationList.xsd file originally introduced in Chapter 2. Use the version included with the download for this chapter, as it specifies a namespace (http://www.prosetech.com/Schemas/QuotationList).

> **TIP** *Word catalogs XML schemas based on their target namespace. If you import a schema that doesn't have a target namespace, you'll be asked to define one. For that reason, the XML files saved with Word are always placed in a namespace. To make life simple, define this namespace as early as possible, when you first create your schema. For a quick refresher on how you can define a target namespace in your schemas, just review the "Schemas and Namespaces" section toward the end of Chapter 2.*

5. Give the schema a friendly name, which will be displayed in the library. In this example, "Quotation List" works well (see in Figure 4-6).

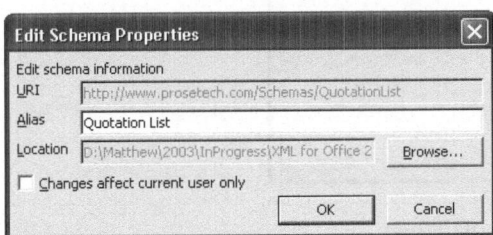

Figure 4-6. Adding a schema to the library

6. If you want the schema to be available only to the current user, select the "Changes affect current user only" checkbox. If you don't select this checkbox, the schema will be available to all users on this computer.

7. Click OK to add the schema. By default, the schema will appear with a checkmark next to it, indicating it will be applied to the current document. If this isn't what you want, clear the checkbox.

You can remove schema documents from the library just as easily as you add them. In this case, click the Schema Library button in the XML schema tab. A new window will appear, with the same list of schemas and a few additional buttons (see Figure 4-7).

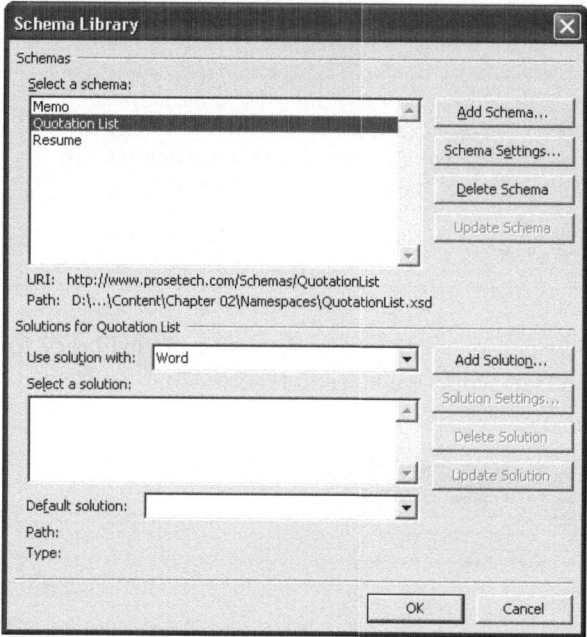

Figure 4-7. Modifying or deleting schemas

You can perform two useful tasks here:

- To delete a schema, select it and click the Delete Schema button. This removes the information from the schema library, but it doesn't actually delete the physical file.

- To specify a new location for a schema document, select the schema and click the Schema Settings button. This brings up the same configuration window that appears when adding the schema (shown in Figure 4-6).

Creating an XML Document with a Schema

Once you have a schema in the schema library, you can apply it to a new or existing document in much the same way that you would apply a template with a set of styles. As a simple test, you can use the product list schema to create a new product list document. First, create a blank document in Word. Then, choose Tools ➤ Templates and Add-Ins from the menu, and select the XML Schema tab. Finally, place a checkmark next to the product list schema, and click OK.

> **TIP** *If you receive an error when attempting to attach a schema to a document, the problem is probably caused by a moved or deleted schema file. Check the location that's specified for the schema file in the library. If necessary, modify it to set a valid location.*

When you complete these steps, the XML Structure pane will appear on the right of your document window. This window serves two purposes: It shows you a hierarchical view of the XML elements that are mapped to your document, and it allows you to apply new tags. When you first attach a schema, no elements will be mapped, so the top portion of the XML Structure pane will be empty. Figure 4-8 shows the XML Structure pane.

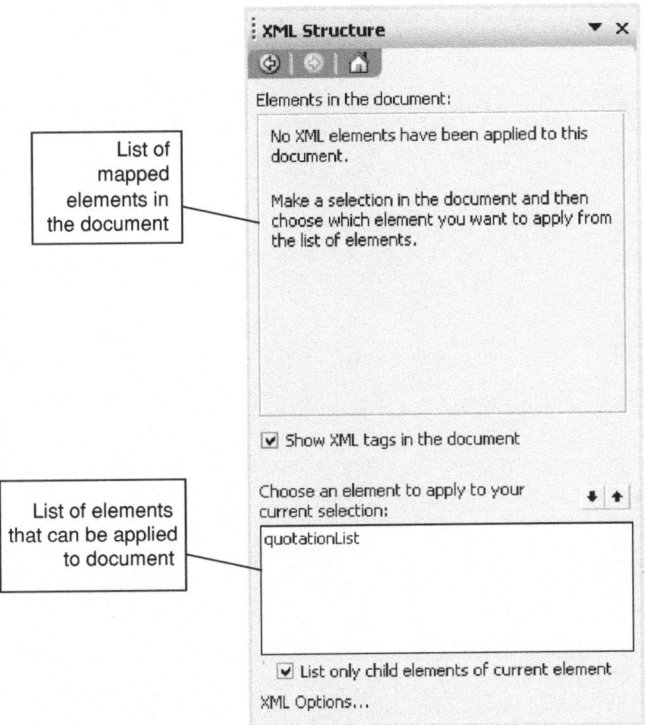

Figure 4-8. The XML Structure pane with the quotation list schema

TIP *If at any point the XML Structure pane disappears, you can show it by selecting View ➤ Task Pane from the menu. Then, click the heading of the Task pane, and choose XML Structure. Make sure the "Show XML tags in the document" checkbox is selected at all times, so that you can see the XML mapping tags you create.*

In the bottom of the XML Structure pane is a list box that shows the elements you can apply to the current selection in the document. For example, in the new document with the quotation list schema, only one element is shown: <quotationList>. This is because the other elements (like <quotation>, <category>, and <source>) must all be nested inside the <quotationList>. Until your document includes a <quotationList> element, there's nowhere to place these other elements.

Optionally, you can display the full list of schema-defined elements in the XML Structure pane, including those that can't be applied to the current selection, by clearing the "List only child elements of current element" checkbox. In this case, you'll see all the elements, but some will be marked with a special warning symbol to indicate they don't apply to the current selection. Figure 4-9 shows the XML Structure pane with the full list of elements. These elements are listed in the order they appear in the XML schema.

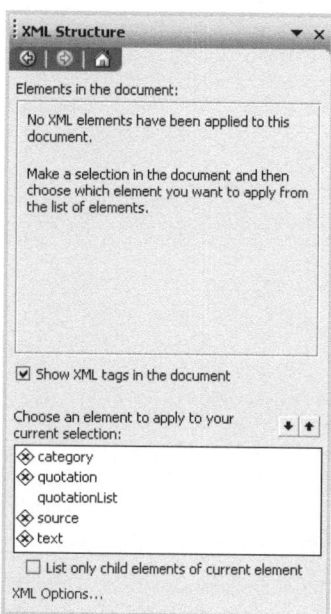

Figure 4-9. The XML Structure pane with the full list of elements

There are two ways to map a portion of a Word document to an element defined in the schema. The first approach is to simply click an item in the list of allowed elements. This inserts start and end tags around the currently selected text. If no text is selected, an empty pair of start and end tags is inserted at the current location. You can use this approach to insert the <quotationList> element. Then, if you position your cursor inside the <quotationList> element, the list of allowed items will enable you to insert a nested <quotation> element. If you move inside a <quotation> element, the list will be updated again to allow you to insert the <text>, <source>, and <category> elements.

The second approach that you can use to map XML tags is to right-click somewhere in the document, and choose Apply XML Element from the context menu. This shows a submenu that lists the elements that are valid for this location in the document (see Figure 4-10).

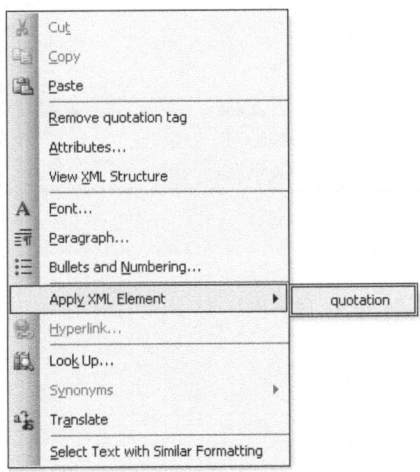

Figure 4-10. Mapping XML through the context menu

As you add elements, the XML Structure pane will display a hierarchical map of the elements in your document. You can jump quickly to a particular portion of the document by clicking an element in this map. Figure 4-11 shows a document that maps all the elements of the schema.

You'll notice that elements that allow text content, like <text>, <source>, and <category>, are displayed slightly differently from other elements. Namely, their beginning and ending tags are "filled in."

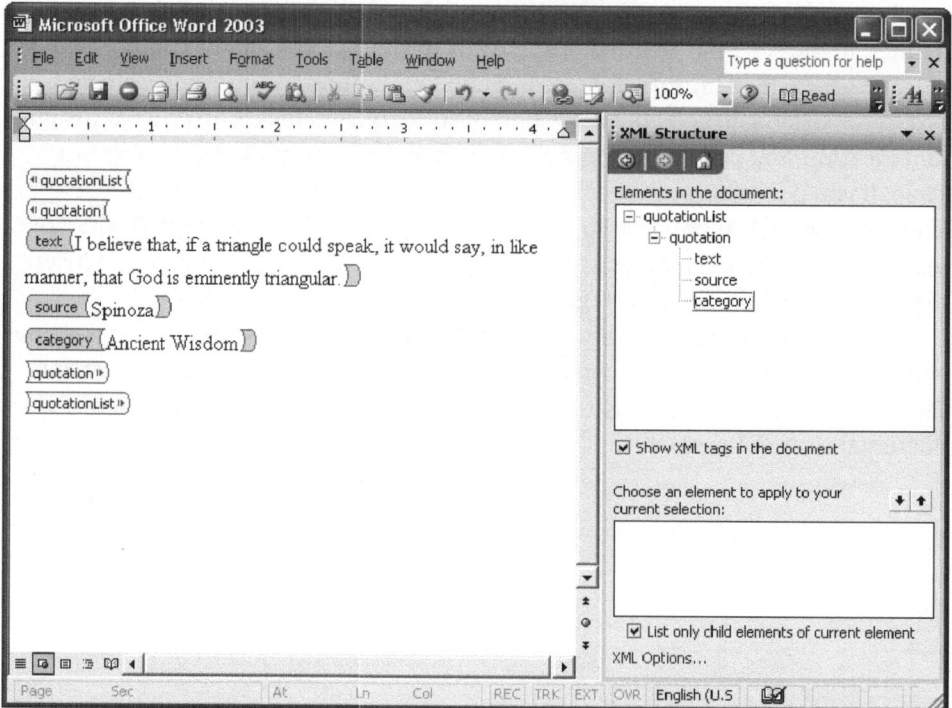

Figure 4-11. A simple mapped document

Saving Mapped XML

You have three choices for saving your mapped XML:

- *The classic .doc format:* When you save your work as an ordinary Word document, the mapping information will be retained. That means you can open
  your file in Word, and then export the XML data at any time.

- *WordML:* Word's proprietary XML format, called WordML, is effectively the
  same as using the .doc format, because your XML structure won't be preserved. As with .doc files, you can export your XML data later on using Word.
  WordML also adds a few interesting possibilities that let other applications
  read the file and interact with the Word-specific data (like versioning, comments, and so on). You'll get a chance to explore WordML in Chapter 6 and
  Chapter 7.

- *Data-only XML:* In this case, your XML markup is used, but you lose all formatting and rich Word content.

Often, you'll use more than one of these approaches. For example, you might create an ordinary Word document, and store it as a .doc file. In addition, you could use a macro to export the mapped XML data to some other business application, like a Web service.

To choose between the different data formats, make a selection from the "Save as type" drop-down list box in the Save or Save As dialog boxes. To save as rich WordML, simply choose XML Document, as shown in Figure 4-12. To export using your mapped XML markup, choose XML Document and select the "Save data only" checkbox to the right.

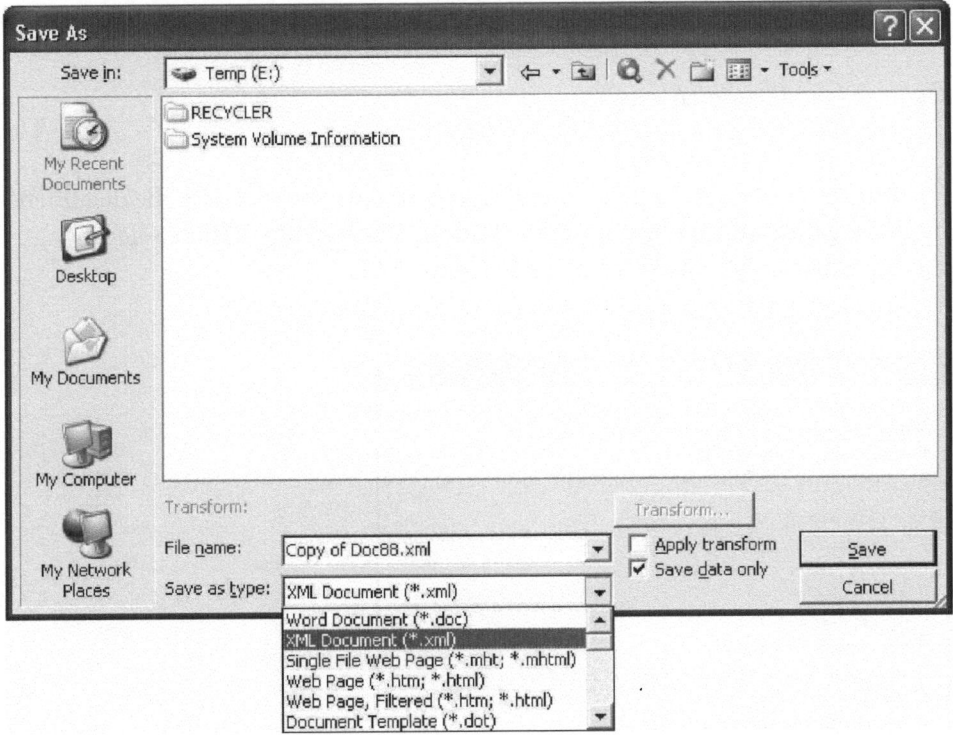

Figure 4-12. Saving Word XML

When you export a document as data only, you'll receive a warning message that informs you that any Word content (pictures, formatting, whitespace, and so on) will be stripped out of the document. If you need this information, make sure you save a copy using one of the rich Word formats, either WordML or .doc.

When you save a document as WordML, it will appear with a Word icon in Windows Explorer (see Figure 4-13). This is because Windows examines the header of XML files, and looks for special processing instructions. In the case of a WordML document, the following processing instruction is added to indicate that the file represents a Word document:

```
<?mso-application progid="Word.Document"?>
```

Thanks to this processing instruction, when you double-click a WordML file in Windows Explorer, the default XML viewer (usually Internet Explorer) isn't launched. Instead Word is launched to edit the file just as if it were a .doc file.

MyFile.xml

Figure 4-13. A WordML file

You can configure the default type of XML that will be saved for the document by clicking the XML Options link at the bottom of the window. Then, select or clear the "Save data only" checkbox shown in Figure 4-14.

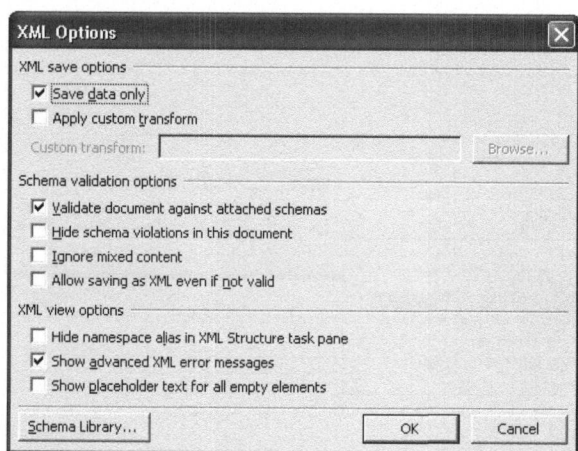

Figure 4-14. General XML options for a document

Opening Mapped XML

As you saw earlier, when you open an ordinary XML file, your editing options are limited because Word won't have the corresponding schema. However, the same restriction isn't true if you open a mapped XML file, because its schema is available in the schema library.

Essentially, Word goes through a few simple steps whenever you open a custom data-only XML file:

1. Word retrieves the namespace from the root element in the XML document. If no namespace is specified, it skips directly to step 3.

2. Word checks to see if a schema with the same namespace is in the schema library. If it is, this schema is loaded and made available through the XML Structure pane, allowing you to easily add new elements and validate the document.

3. If there is no matching schema in the schema library, Word attempts to find the schema using the schema location information in the XML file.

4. If still no schema can be found, Word opens the document in the limited editing mode described at the beginning of this chapter.

Unfortunately, Word doesn't interpret the schema location information in the same way that Excel does. Namely, it won't look for a schema file in the directory where the XML file is located. Instead, you must use a fully qualified file path, which is much less flexible. For that reason, it's usually easiest to add all the schemas you need to use to the schema library before opening any document.

When importing the document, Word chooses a default display that formats the content hierarchically with whitespace, as shown in Figure 4-2. However, this information is never saved with the file.

Schema Validation

Word uses the schema information to validate the document dynamically. When it discovers an error, it underlines the source of the problem (or the nearest relevant location) with a wavy pink line. You can right-click this area of the document to see detailed error information. However, the detailed error information can be a little overwhelming. For simpler messages, click the XML Options link at the bottom of the XML Structure pane, and then clear the "Show advanced XML error messages" checkbox.

Figure 4-15 shows the full error message you'll see if you enter text directly in the <quotationList> element, while Figure 4-16 shows the corresponding simple error message.

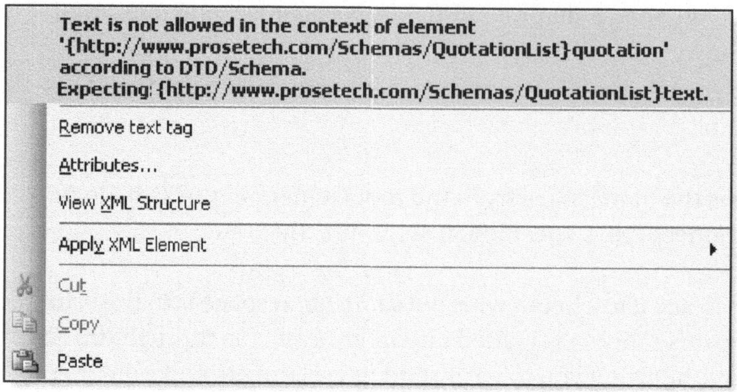

Text is not allowed in the context of element
'{http://www.prosetech.com/Schemas/QuotationList}quotation'
according to DTD/Schema.
Expecting: {http://www.prosetech.com/Schemas/QuotationList}text.
Remove text tag
Attributes...
View XML Structure
Apply XML Element
Cut
Copy
Paste

Figure 4-15. A full schema validation error message

Text is not allowed here.
Remove quotation tag
View XML Structure
Cut
Copy
Paste

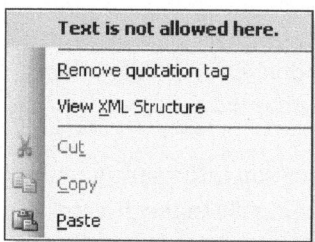

Figure 4-16. A simple schema validation error message

Word 2003 is a fully featured XML parser and schema validator. That means it catches all schema violations, including missing tags, duplicate or incorrectly ordered tags, incorrect data types, and violated constraints. Figure 4-17 shows a more complex sample document—the ProductCatalog_Invalid.xml file from Chapter 3—with several schema violations highlighted:

- The <expiryDate> element is out of place in the structure of the XML document. It's flagged using a circle with an "x" drawn in it.
- The <productPrice> element has incorrect content (because the decimal data type doesn't support the currency symbol). It's also flagged using a circle with an "x" drawn in it.
- The second <product> element has missing content. It's flagged with a question mark.

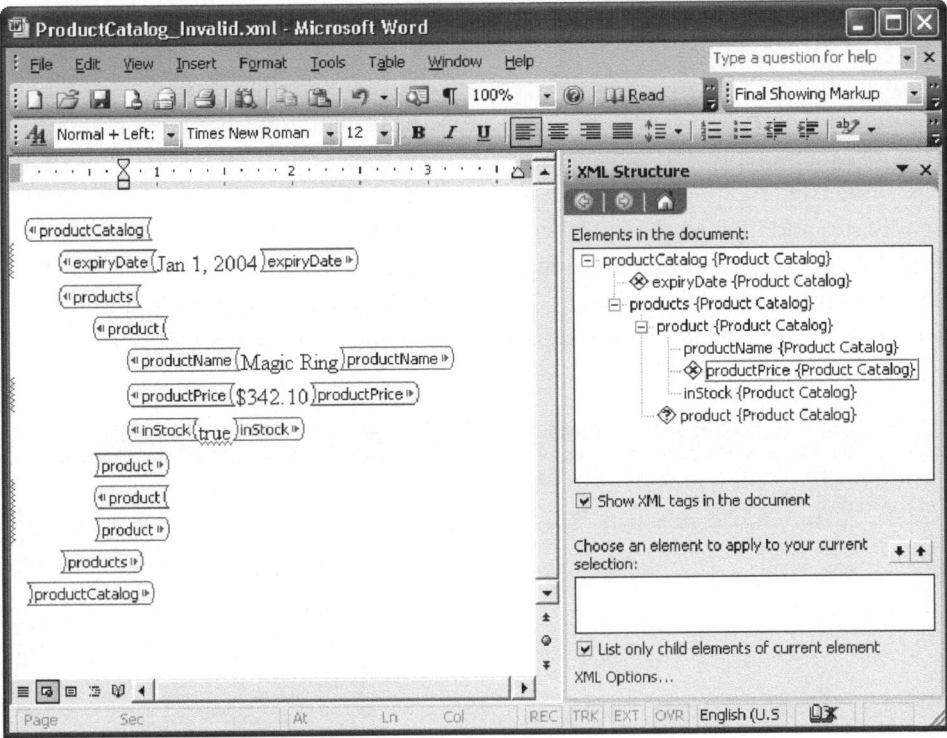

Figure 4-17. An invalid document

You can disable schema validation for your document. Just click the XML Options link at the bottom of the XML Structure pane, and then perform one of the following actions:

- Select the "Hide schema violations in this document" checkbox. Now, errors won't be underlined, although they'll still appear in the XML Structure pane.

- Clear the "Validate document against attached schemas" checkbox. Now, errors won't be underlined and won't appear in the XML Structure pane.

- Select the "Allow saving as XML even if not valid" checkbox if you want to be able to save your document as XML even if it contains schema violations.

Unlike Excel, Word won't stop you from opening invalid XML documents, as long as they're well formed. The schema violations will be flagged, but you can still load and edit the data.

Using Schemas with Mixed Mode

Word supports mixed mode elements (elements that contain text and nested tags) seamlessly. For example, consider the resume example from Chapter 2. It allowed resume candidates to write a paragraph detailing their education in the <education> tag, while flagging specific school names with the <school> tag. Similarly, resume candidates add their work history information in the <workHistory> element, while flagging every company using the <companyName> element. Figure 4-18 shows a sample resume document. Notice that the XML Structure window uses an element with ellipsis (. . .) to represent embedded text in mixed mode.

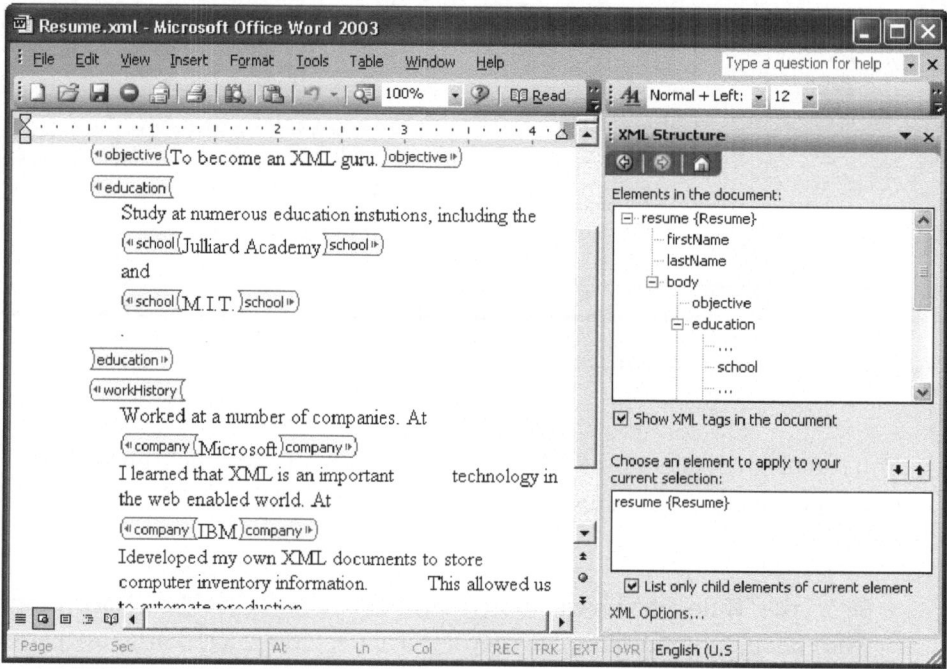

Figure 4-18. Mixed mode data in Word

Remember, if you want to create resume documents in Word, you'll need to first add the schema to the library. If you want to perform this test, use the versions of Resume.xml and Resume.xsd that use namespaces.

Elements with Attributes

Word forces you to go to a little more work to add attributes to an element. You can't enter them directly in the document. Instead, you must right-click the appropriate element tag, and select Attributes from the context menu. This displays a dialog box that allows you to view existing attributes and add new ones. Figure 4-19 shows an example with the Quotation_Attributes.xml file from Chapter 2.

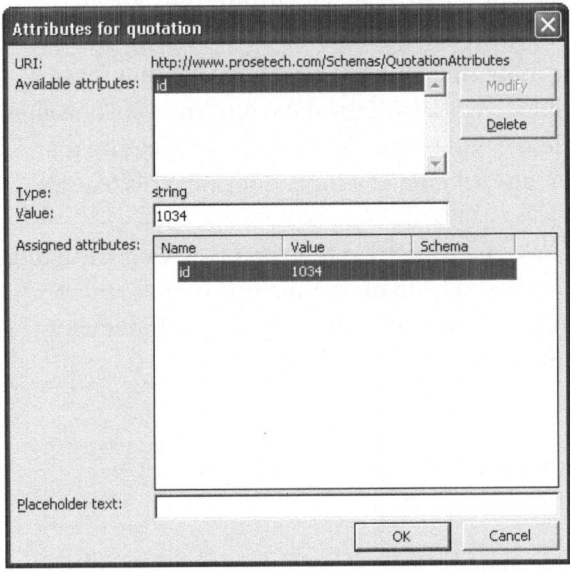

Figure 4-19. Assigning attributes from a schema

The top part of the window lists the attributes you can use with this element. As with elements, you can only insert attributes if they are defined in the schema. The schema for the Quotation_Attributes.xml file defines one allowed attribute for the <quotation> element, named id.

Using this window, you can perform three operations:

- To add an attribute to the element, select it from the available attributes list, type a value in the provided text box, and click Add. The attribute and value will then appear in the assigned attribute list.

- To change an attribute once it's been added, simply select it in the assigned attribute list, enter a new value, and click Modify.

- To delete an attribute once it's been added, simply select it in the assigned attribute list, and click Delete.

Unfortunately, you can't map attributes to a portion of your document. Instead, they must be entered manually. For that reason, Word works best when editing documents without attributes, or where attributes are optional.

Using Multiple Schemas

Microsoft Word allows you to attach multiple schemas to a document. Using this technique, you could map separate portions of the same document to different XML files. Unfortunately, this causes a problem when you export the data as XML. Word will allow the export operation (with a warning), but the resulting XML won't be well formed because it will have more than one root element. For that reason, no other XML application will be able to work with the data, and you won't be able to open the file in Word. This problem could be solved if Word had a feature that allowed you to export the data from one schema at a time, but sadly this feature doesn't exist.

However, using multiple schemas can be very useful when you're constructing a single XML document that uses XML data from more than one namespace. For example, consider the order document shown in Chapter 1 that combines client information with a list of order items:

```
<?xml version="1.0"?>
<ord:order xmlns:ord="http://mycompany/OrderML"
 xmlns:cli="http://mycompany/ClientML">
    <cli:client>
        <cli:firstName>Sally</cli:firstName>
        <cli:lastName>Samura</cli:lastName>
    </cli:client>

    <ord:orderItem>27" Television</ord:orderItem>
    <ord:orderItem>Leather Shoes</ord:orderItem>
</ord:order>
```

This document places its elements into two distinct namespaces, http://mycompany/OrderML and http://mycompany/ClientML. When you define the schema for this document, you'll probably want to separate these two types of markup. Here's the schema you would use to define the client information:

```
<?xml version="1.0"?>
<xsd:schema xmlns:xsd="http://www.w3.org/2001/XMLSchema"
 targetNamespace="http://mycompany/ClientML" elementFormDefault="qualified">

    <xsd:element name="client">
        <xsd:complexType>
            <xsd:sequence>
                <xsd:element name="firstName" type="xsd:string" />
                <xsd:element name="lastName" type="xsd:string" />
```

```
        </xsd:sequence>
      </xsd:complexType>
    </xsd:element>

</xsd:schema>
```

Using this schema, you can create stand-alone client XML documents. Here's the schema you could use to define the full order:

```
<?xml version="1.0"?>
<xsd:schema xmlns:xsd="http://www.w3.org/2001/XMLSchema"
 targetNamespace="http://mycompany/OrderML" elementFormDefault="qualified">

    <xsd:element name="order">
      <xsd:complexType>
        <xsd:sequence>
          <xsd:any />
          <xsd:element name="orderItem" type="xsd:string" minOccurs="1"
           maxOccurs="unbounded" />
        </xsd:sequence>
      </xsd:complexType>
    </xsd:element>

</xsd:schema>
```

This order schema defines an <any> element that can hold any single element from any namespace, followed by a list of products. This gives some much-needed flexibility when creating order documents. For example, the preceding order document is now valid, because the <client> element matches the <any> condition. You can validate the complete order document using both schemas.

Creating a compound order document in Word is easy. Begin by adding both the OrderML and ClientML schemas to the library. Then, attach both of these schemas to a document by selecting the Tools ➤ Templates and Add-Ins from the menu.

Now you can begin the XML mapping process. The XML Structure pane will allow you to assign elements from both namespaces. Start by adding the <order> element to your Word document. Then, add the root <client> element, and the nested <firstName> and <lastName> elements. You can finish the document by adding one or more <orderItem> elements. Alternatively, once you've imported the schemas, you can open an XML order document directly. Word will automatically attach the two required schemas based on the namespaces the order document uses.

Figure 4-20 shows a complete order document. Note that the XML Structure pane shows how the document uses elements from both namespaces, and indicates the friendly name of the namespace next to the element name.

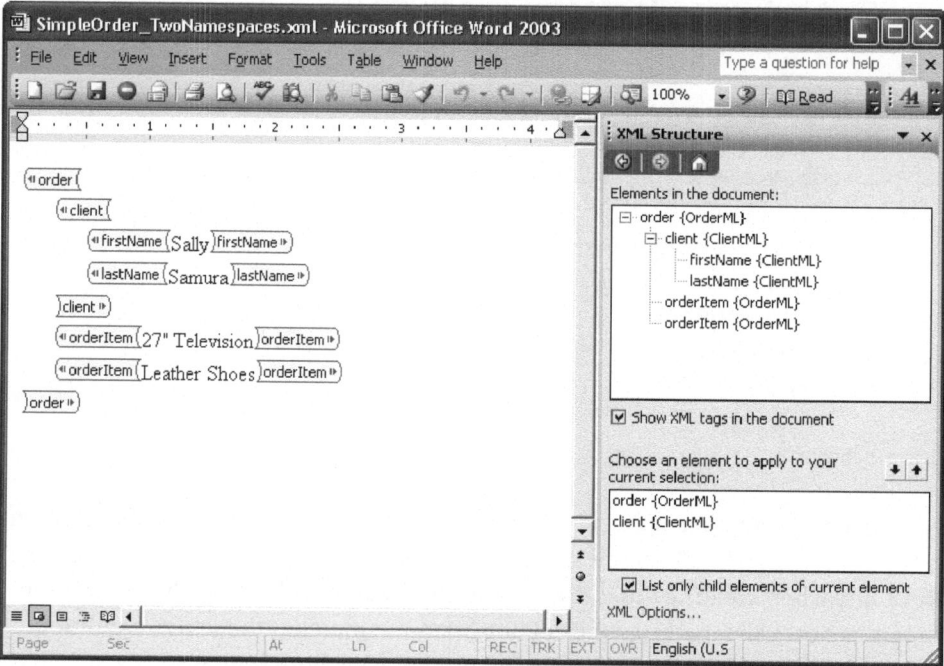

Figure 4-20. A mapped document with two namespaces

Hybrid Word XML Documents

In most cases, you won't map XML schemas directly to a blank document. Instead, you'll map the schema to an existing document or, even better, a document template. In this case, you might only be interested in mapping a portion of the document. The document will then be maintained in its rich Word format, but the data can be exported to XML when it needs to be used by another application.

For an interesting example, consider a standardized company memo written in Word. This memo might include formatting, a company logo, and various other Word-specific details. Memos are always printed and distributed directly—however, the organization that uses them decides to create a custom tracking application that will archive memo data and allow users to search it. This application needs the information to be submitted in a set XML format, as defined by a custom schema.

When implementing this solution, you don't want to map each individual memo document separately, because that process would be far too time consuming. A better solution is to create a Word template that defines the structure for all memo documents, and map that template to the XML schema. Because all other users will create memo documents based on that template, all memo documents will have the same mapping, and will have the ability to save data-only XML. The next section describes this process, using an example adapted from the Word 2003 XML Content Development Kit (CDK). You can download this kit from http://msdn.microsoft.com/downloads/list/office2k3.asp.

The Memo Template Solution

Word templates are, at their simplest, ordinary Word documents with the extension .dot. When you open a template, a new copy of the document is created. When you save your document, Word forces you to use a new filename. Best practices suggest that you make templates read-only, and install them in the user-specific template directory (which is typically something like C:\Documents and Settings\[UserName]\Application Data\Microsoft\Templates). That way, when the user chooses to create a new document, the user will see the option in the Template window under the General heading, as shown in Figure 4-21.

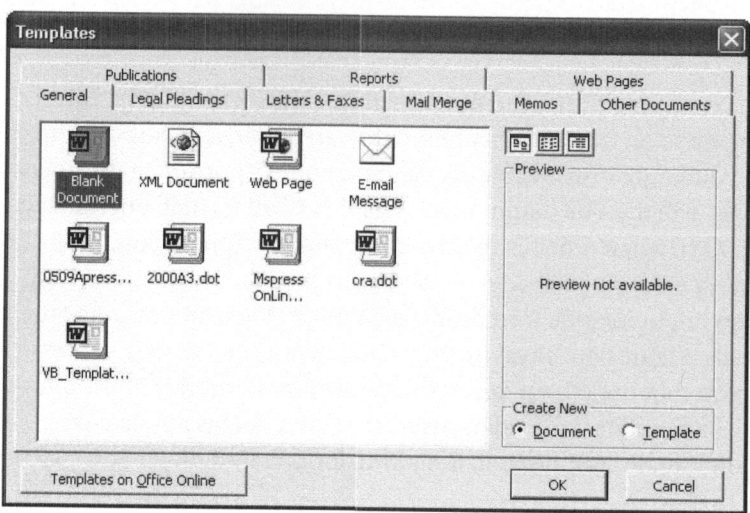

Figure 4-21. Creating a document from a template

To get started with the memo example, you can begin by opening the Memo.dot template included with the download for this chapter. It shows the basic memo display that appears in Figure 4-22.

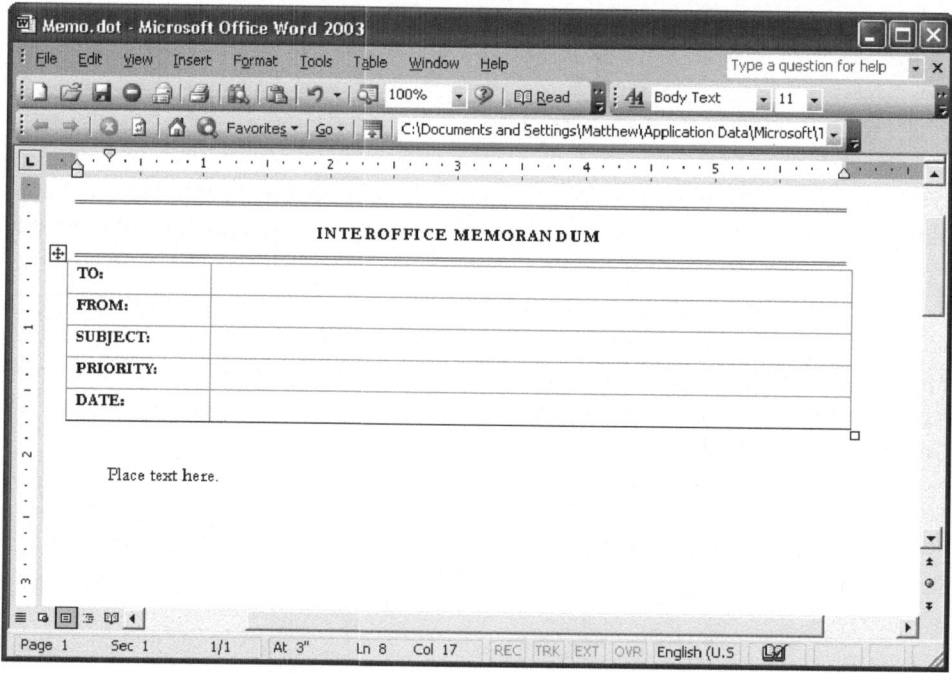

Figure 4-22. The unmapped memo

The memo schema follows this template closely. It's provided in the Memo.xsd file, and is shown here:

```xsd
<xsd:schema xmlns:xsd="http://www.w3.org/2001/XMLSchema"
 xmlns="urn:schemas-microsoft-com.office.demos.memo"
 targetNamespace="urn:schemas-microsoft-com.office.demos.memo"
 elementFormDefault="qualified">

    <xsd:simpleType name="priorityType">
        <xsd:restriction base="xsd:string">
            <xsd:enumeration value="Low"/>
            <xsd:enumeration value="Medium"/>
            <xsd:enumeration value="High"/>
        </xsd:restriction>
    </xsd:simpleType>

    <xsd:simpleType name="subjectType">
        <xsd:restriction base="xsd:string">
            <xsd:maxLength value="40"/>
        </xsd:restriction>
    </xsd:simpleType>

    <xsd:complexType name="memoType" mixed="true">
        <xsd:all>
            <xsd:element name="to" type="xsd:string"/>
            <xsd:element name="from" type="xsd:string"/>
            <xsd:element name="subject" type="subjectType"/>
            <xsd:element name="priority" type="priorityType"/>
            <xsd:element name="date" type="xsd:string"/>
            <xsd:element name="body" type="xsd:string"/>
        </xsd:all>
    </xsd:complexType>
    <xsd:element name="memo" type="memoType"/>
</xsd:schema>
```

Before continuing, add this memo to the schema library. Then, attach the memo schema to this document using the Tools ➤ Templates and Add-Ins dialog box. Finally, you can map the document by following these steps:

1. First, select the entire document (use Ctrl+A to do this quickly), and click the <memo> element located in the box at the bottom of the XML Structure pane. Click the Apply to Entire Document button when Word prompts you.

2. Map the cells in the table. Start by clicking inside the cell that is immediately to the right of the "To:" cell. Then, click the <to> element in the XML Structure pane.

3. Repeat step 2 for the <from>, <subject>, <priority>, and <date> cells.

4. Select the body text (the sentence "Place text here.") and then click the <body> element.

The final marked up document is shown in Figure 4-23. You can now save this document. Choose to save as a document template (.dot file) so that other users can use this to create mapped memos. Don't worry that the current file doesn't meet the schema requirements because it's missing data. You can still save it as a template. When users create memo documents, they'll need to supply the necessary memo data.

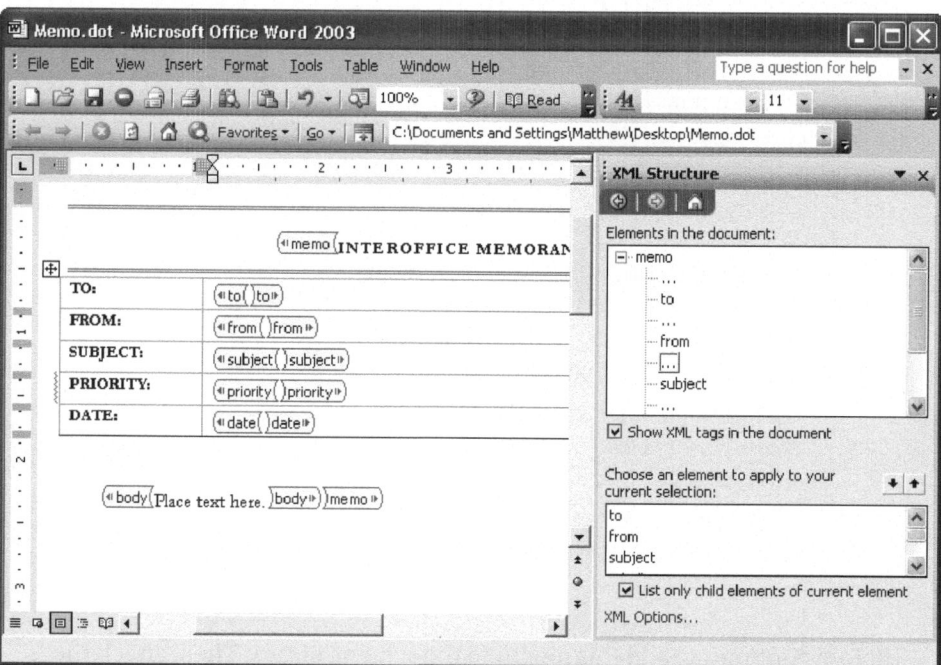

Figure 4-23. The mapped memo

You can now use this memo to create a memo document. You'll find that attaching the schema to the document hasn't just added the ability to export the memo data to XML, it's also added some basic validation. For example, the original schema defines an enumeration that restricts the <priority> element to one of three values: High, Low, or Medium. If the user enters anything else, that portion of the document will be highlighted, and a schema error will be shown. For example, if you enter the priority "Super High", you'll receive the error message "Super High violates enumeration constraint of Low Medium High."

Unfortunately, the memo XML document may contain some superfluous text. Even though you've carefully mapped the required portions of the document, the root <memo> element will contain all the text in the document, including the cell headings. Here's an example of a memo document that was created using the mapped template, and exported to XML:

```
<?xml version="1.0">
<memo xmlns="urn:schemas-microsoft-com.office.demos.memo">
interoffice memorandumTO:<to>John</to>
FROM:<from>Matthew</from>
SUBJECT:<subject>Sample Memo</subject>
PRIORITY:<priority>High</priority>
DATE:<date>2004-01-01</date>
<body>Place text here.</body></memo>
```

This document has the element text you want, but also includes additional text between the elements. Here's a version of the document that removes this unnecessary information:

```
<?xml version="1.0">
<memo xmlns="urn:schemas-microsoft-com.office.demos.memo">
<to>John</to>
<from>Matthew</from>
<subject>Sample Memo</subject>
<priority>High</priority>
<date>2004-01-01</date>
<body>Place text here.</body>
</memo>
```

Exporting this version is easy. Just click XML Options at the bottom of the XML Structure pane. Then, select "Ignore mixed content" in the settings window. This will strip out all the text between elements. You should also change the memo schema so that it won't allow mixed content.

```
<xsd:complexType name="memoType" mixed="false">
```

Sadly, there is no way to tell Word to ignore just certain portions of text. It's always an all-or-nothing affair. This is a major limitation if you need to retrofit existing templates to set schemas. Excel doesn't suffer from the same limitation, because it's much more structured, and maps based on specific cell ranges. Hopefully this much needed feature will appear in a future version of Word.

Placeholders and Tag View

In a perfect world, users would be able to work with XML-mapped templates without even being aware that XML mapping is being used. In fact, the user might never need to export the XML data directly. Instead, this extraction task might be taken care of by a VBScript macro or another application. Users would be completely shielded from the XML.

Word supports this idea by allowing you to hide the tags in a document. When tags are hidden, they remain in the document, but aren't shown to the user. To hide tags, simply clear the "Show XML tags" checkbox in the XML Structure pane. Or, you can use the shortcut Ctrl+Shift+X to turn tag view on or off.

Tag hiding simplifies the display, but it introduces two new potential problems:

- How will the user know where to type if the tag is empty?

- How can you make sure the tag won't be inadvertently deleted by the user, altering the structure of the document?

The first problem is solved using placeholder text, while the second is solved using Word's document protection feature.

To use placeholder text, click the XML Options link at the bottom of the XML Structure pane, and then select the "Show placeholder text for all empty elements" checkbox. The placeholders, by default, use the name of the element and appear between square brackets. The placeholders only appear when the element is empty and XML element view is off. Figure 4-24 shows the memo template with placeholder text. You'll notice that the priority field is still flagged with a wavy pink line because the priority field is empty, and a blank entry doesn't correspond to one of the allowed priority values.

You can also customize the placeholder text individually for each element. To do this, right-click the element you want to change in the XML Structure pane, and choose Attributes. At the bottom of the dialog box (shown earlier in Figure 4-19) is a text box where you can specify custom placeholder text. You'll have to include the square brackets if you want to use them. Once you've defined custom place-holder text, that text will always appear when the element is empty, even if the "Show placeholder text for all empty elements" option hasn't been selected.

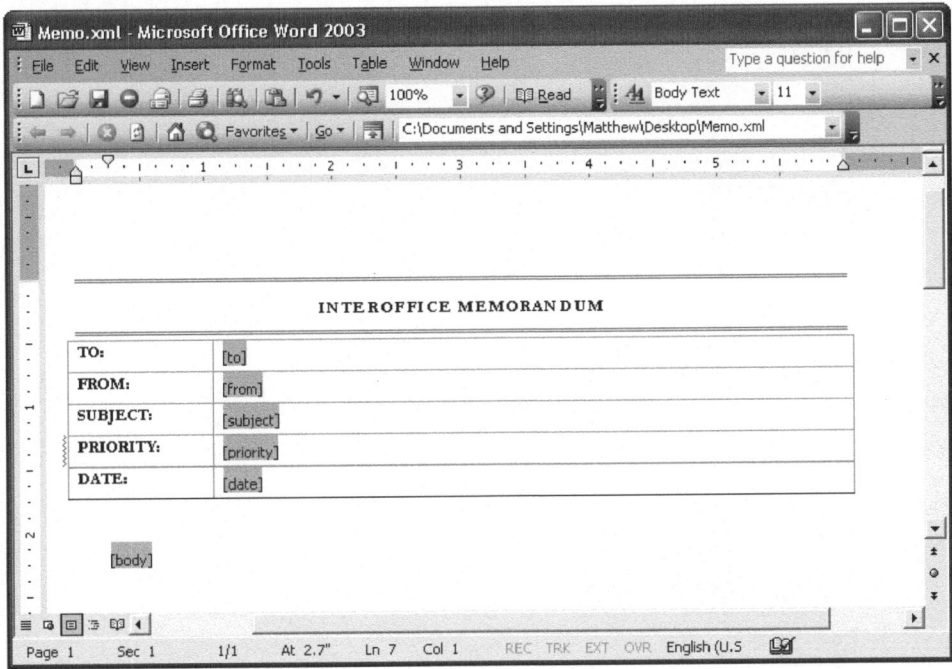

Figure 4-24. Placeholder text

Document Protection

Placeholder text doesn't solve the second problem. Namely, what happens if a user deletes a part of a document that contains a required element, or just unwittingly deletes the element tag from that portion of the document? If this happens, the document can no longer be exported to XML. To prevent this possibility, you can use document protection, which locks the document so that only specific areas are editable. The idea is to make it impossible to edit the portion of the document that contains the element tags, but still allow text to be inserted in the elements.

Before you begin applying document settings, you'll need to either insert default values in all the elements, or turn on tag view. This is because you need to precisely define the editable regions of the document so that they don't include the beginning and end tags, and in order to do that you need to be able to select the content between the tags.

To apply document protection, follow these steps:

1. Select Tools ➤ Protect Document from the menu. This shows the Protect Document pane on the right. You can use this window (shown in Figure 4-25) to restrict formatting changes and editing. In this case, you need to do the latter.

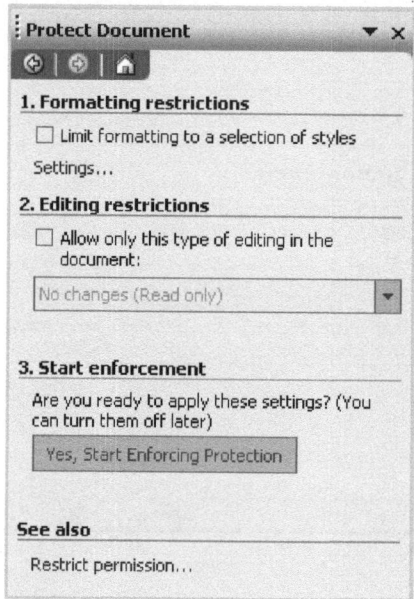

Figure 4-25. The Protect Document panel

2. Select the "Allow only this type of editing in the document" checkbox. In the drop-down list below the checkbox, choose "No changes (Read only)." This makes the entire document read-only.

3. Now you must define the portions of the document that can be edited. Begin with the <to> element. If it includes some default text, select that text. If it doesn't contain any text, make sure you are in tag view (so that the placeholder isn't displayed), and then click between the beginning and ending tag.

4. Select the Everyone checkbox in the Protect Document pane. This makes this portion of the document freely editable. However, users will only be able to change the content of the <to> element, not the tag itself.

5. Repeat steps 3 and 4 for all the other tags the user will need to enter. You should enable editing for the <from>, <subject>, <priority>, <date>, and <body> elements.

6. To start enforcing your document protection settings, click the Start Enforcing Protection button at the bottom of the Protect Document pane.

7. You'll be prompted for a password. If you enter one, users won't be able to turn off document protection unless they supply the correct password.

8. If you turned on tag view, you may want to turn it off now. Also, if you added default content in the tags, you may want to remove this content now so that only the placeholders will be shown.

9. To turn off document protection at any time, click the Stop Protection button and enter the required password.

Looking at the document, you'll see that editable portions are marked with a shaded yellow box (or just a yellow insertion mark if the content is empty).

This approach of defining XML mapping in a document template works best if your Word document has some obvious structure. For example, you can use this approach to map paragraphs or headings that have distinct styles, or separate cells in a table. It's much less suitable if the document has a free-flowing, document-oriented structure. For example, consider the resume document shown earlier. Because this document uses mixed mode to highlight a school and company names, there is no way to predefine the XML mapping. You just won't know where in the document this information will be entered (or even how many times it will be entered). In this case, users will need to use Word's XML features directly, and won't be able to safely switch off tag view.

Gaps in the Word 2003 XML Support

Word's XML features are a frustrating combination. On the one hand, they can be incredibly useful, allowing you to extract custom XML from the rich Word format with a couple of mouse clicks. But on the other hand, they bring some serious limitations and quirks that will challenge some projects.

We've already considered how Word won't let you map attributes, and how Word lacks any way to ignore sections of a mapped document. Another limitation is the absence of any type of import feature. That means that you can't import XML data into a Word template or document through XML mapping. This is in stark contrast to the more structured Excel, which supports both importing and exporting XML. One way to get around this limitation it to use custom XSLT transforms that convert your XML documents into WordML, as described in Chapter 7, but this task is far from easy.

Another limitation is the fact that Word's XML features don't integrate in any way with Word styles. This is unfortunate—if there were a way to map styles to XML elements, you could apply a custom style template to existing Word documents, and be able to extract the XML data immediately, without needing to perform any additional mapping. Unfortunately, this just isn't possible, because styles have no concept of structure. For example, you can apply styles in any order. Furthermore, styles are "flat." XML elements, on the other hand, overlap, and one element often contains other elements. These factors make a "styles-to-XML" feature extremely unlikely. Unfortunately, if you have existing Word documents and you want to extract the information they contain, you're in the unenviable position of needing to map each document separately.

The Last Word

This chapter outlined the XML features in Word 2003, which allow you to export portions of a rich Word document to your own custom XML formats. As in Excel, Word works using a feature called XML mapping, although it implements the concept in a different way, with a centralized schema library.

So which of the two Office heavyweights provides the best XML support? In all honesty, they both offer a few unique features and a few awkward tradeoffs. Excel has the best support for importing XML data. It allows you to create a single spreadsheet that can work with any XML document that has the same structure. Word XML lacks this ease-of-use for importing data, but it provides much better data validation by integrating schema rules into its IntelliSense feature. Excel, on the other hand, only performs schema validation when data is exported or imported.

In short, both Office applications have their strengths and weaknesses. In future versions of Office, you can expect to find increasingly better support for XML in both Word and Excel.

Exporting and Importing XML in Access

ACCESS, MICROSOFT'S DESKTOP database engine, has provided basic XML support since the Office XP release. This support remains in Office 2003, with a few enhancements.

So what can Access do with XML? Access provides two XML-related features: the ability to export data from a table or query to an XML file, and the ability to import XML data into an Access database. These features, while useful, aren't nearly as advanced as they are in Word or Excel. Access doesn't include any concept of "mapping" XML, which means you can't translate the XML generated by Access into your specific flavor of XML. Instead, the structure of the XML you import and export is rigidly determined by the structure of the Access database you're using. The names of the XML elements are determined by the table names and field names in the source database. There are some alternatives for customizing this XML (which this chapter explores), but they all require extra, manual steps. For that reason, it's easiest to use Access and its XML features when you can adjust other applications to expect the native Access XML format, or in conjunction with XSLT, the XML-based transformation standard described in Chapter 7.

One of the reasons that the XML features in Access are inherently limited is because relational databases and XML play different, complementary roles in the world of data storage. Relational databases break information into sets of linked, rectangular tables. This works well for storing and indexing large amounts of data, particularly for business applications. XML, on the other hand, uses a looser, hierarchical structure. As you've seen in Chapter 1 and Chapter 2, XML documents can be data-oriented or document-oriented, and both of these cases allow for almost unlimited variations in structure and organization. Overall, XML documents are more flexible and more portable, but relational databases are the most reliable and best-performing engines for the enterprise. For all these reasons, XML and Access aren't integrated. Instead, Access 2003 uses XML to share information with the rest of the world.

> **NOTE** *All the examples in this chapter use the sample Northwind database, which can be installed with the Access setup, and is available with the content download for this chapter.*

Exporting XML

In Access, you can export the following types of data to an XML file:

- An entire table

- A filtered or sorted table

- A set of linked tables (typically a parent and child table)

- The results of a query

- The data "behind" a form or report

In each case, you simply select the appropriate database object, and select File ➤ Export from the menu. For example, in Figure 5-1 the Orders table is selected. Choosing File ➤ Export now will export the full contents of that table to XML.

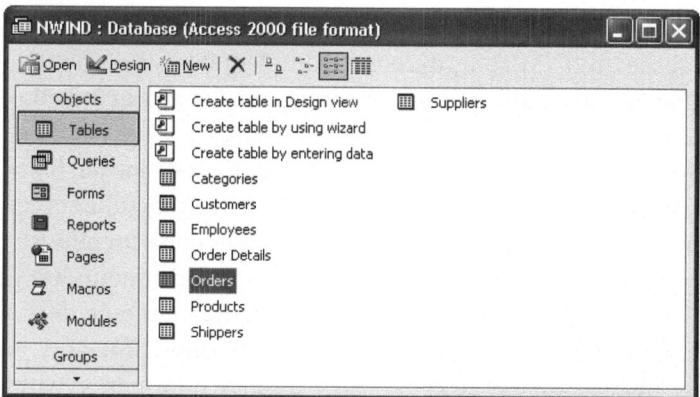

Figure 5-1. Tables in the Northwind database

When you start an export operation, Access will prompt you to specify a file-name and file type. Choose XML as your data type, and the filename will default to the name of the selected object (in this case, it will become Orders.xml). Then, click the Export button. At this point, Access will prompt you about what files it should create (see Figure 5-2). The XML data and schema will be selected by default.

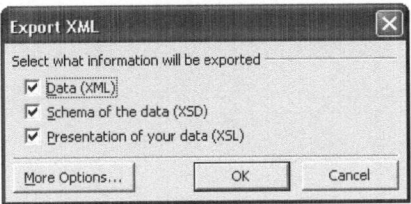

Figure 5-2. Exporting to XML

The More Options button allows you to specify some advanced options that are considered later in this chapter. For this test, simply select all three file types, and click OK. The following two sections dissect the generated files.

The Exported XML

All exported XML files use a root document element named <dataroot>. This element indicates the filename of the corresponding schema, and it doesn't apply a namespace. It also adds an attribute named generated, which provides the time that the data was exported (according to the clock of the computer that exported it). Inside the <dataroot> element are one or more row elements, which are named after the table. In this example, the table was named Orders, so each row element is also named <Orders>. Finally, each column is included as a separate element with the field name, so OrderID becomes <OrderID>, CustomerID becomes <CustomerID>, and so on.

Following is a fragment from the exported orders XML. It represents a single row.

```
<?xml version="1.0" encoding="UTF-8"?>
<dataroot xmlns:od="urn:schemas-microsoft-com:officedata"
 xmlns:xsi="http://www.w3.org/2001/XMLSchema-instance"
 xsi:noNamespaceSchemaLocation="Orders.xsd" generated="2003-06-12T15:02:24">
    <Orders>
        <OrderID>11077</OrderID>
```

```
        <CustomerID>RATTC</CustomerID>
        <EmployeeID>1</EmployeeID>
        <OrderDate>1996-06-05T00:00:00</OrderDate>
        <RequiredDate>1996-07-03T00:00:00</RequiredDate>
        <ShipVia>2</ShipVia>
        <Freight>8.53</Freight>
        <ShipName>Rattlesnake Canyon Grocery</ShipName>
        <ShipAddress>2817 Milton Dr.</ShipAddress>
        <ShipCity>Albuquerque</ShipCity>
        <ShipRegion>NM</ShipRegion>
        <ShipPostalCode>87110</ShipPostalCode>
        <ShipCountry>USA</ShipCountry>
    </Orders>

    <!-- Other Orders elements go here, one for each row. -->
</dataroot>
```

Figure 5-3 shows the corresponding order data in Access.

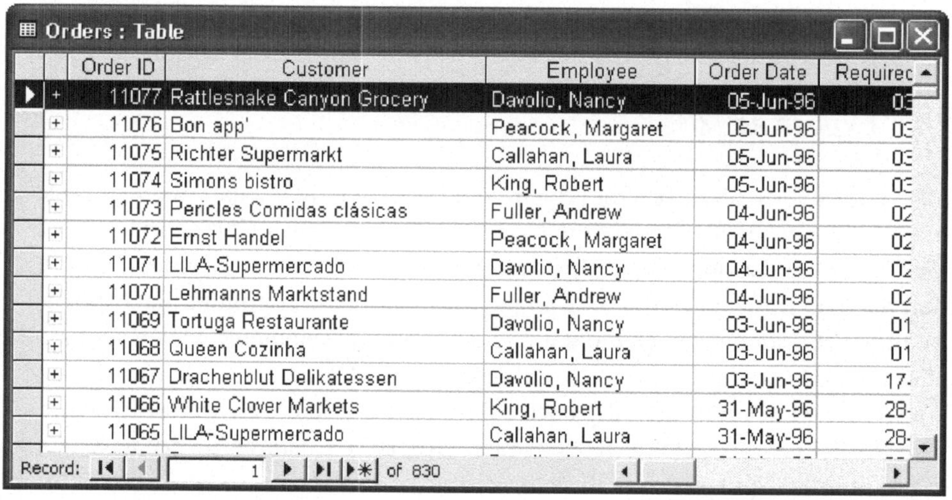

Figure 5-3. The table of orders

NOTE *If any of your table or column names have spaces, Access will replace the space with the character sequence _x0020_ when performing an export, because spaces aren't legal in XML tag names. That means an Order ID column would become the less attractive Order_x0020_ID element name.*

The XML Schema

The XML schema that Access generates defines the structure of the exported XML. A careful examination of the schema turns up some interesting details:

- The schema has two roots (two top-level <element> tags). The first <element> tag defines the <dataroot> element, and the second defines the table-specific <Orders> element. This means the schema can be used to validate the list of orders (using the first root) or an XML document representing a single order record (using the second root).

- The schema defines facets for several elements. This ensures that the element can only contain values that are valid according to the Access data type. The most common facet is the maximum length restriction on a text field.

- The schema includes additional information to define Access-specific field settings, like primary key information.

To get a better understanding of the schema, you can dissect it piece by piece. Here's the overall structure, which shows the two roots. The <dataroot> element is defined so that it contains an unlimited number of rows.

```
<xsd:schema xmlns:xsd="http://www.w3.org/2001/XMLSchema"
 xmlns:od="urn:schemas-microsoft-com:officedata">

    <xsd:element name="dataroot">
        <xsd:complexType>
            <xsd:sequence>
                <xsd:element ref="Orders" minOccurs="0" maxOccurs="unbounded"/>
            </xsd:sequence>
            <xsd:attribute name="generated" type="xsd:dateTime"/>
        </xsd:complexType>
    </xsd:element>

    <xsd:element name="Orders">
        <!-- Annotation with Access-specific information omitted. -->
        <xsd:complexType>
            <xsd:sequence>
                <!-- One element for field is defined here. -->
            </xsd:sequence>
        </xsd:complexType>
    </xsd:element>

</xsd:schema>
```

When declaring the <Orders> tag, Access inserts a special <annotation> element. The <annotation> element can be placed anywhere in a schema to indicate information that is read by a custom application, but isn't used by the XML parser when validating a document. In this case, Access uses the <annotation> element to store information about the defined indexes:

```
<xsd:annotation>
    <xsd:appinfo>
        <od:index index-name="PrimaryKey" index-key="OrderID " primary="yes"
          unique="yes" clustered="no"/>
        <od:index index-name="CustomerID" index-key="CustomerID " primary="no"
          unique="no" clustered="no"/>

        <!-- Other indexes omitted. -->
    </xsd:appinfo>
</xsd:annotation>
```

The final ingredient is the declaration for each field in the Orders table. These elements are declared as anonymous types, which means they are defined directly inside the <Orders> structure. Some types map easily to the XML schema data types, like the OrderID shown here:

```
<xsd:element name="OrderID" minOccurs="1" od:jetType="autonumber"
 od:sqlSType="int" od:autoUnique="yes" od:nonNullable="yes" type="xsd:int"/>
```

You'll notice that Access uses the od prefix (which is mapped to the urn:schemas-microsoft-com:officedata namespace) to include Access-specific information about the field. For example, the OrderID declaration includes attributes that map it to the Access int data type, identify it as a unique, nonnullable field, and specify that its value is generated automatically by the database on insert.

The CustomerID contains similar information, but it also adds a restriction limiting the length of the field to five characters.

```
<xsd:element name="CustomerID" minOccurs="0" od:jetType="text"
 od:sqlSType="nvarchar">
    <xsd:simpleType>
        <xsd:restriction base="xsd:string">
            <xsd:maxLength value="5"/>
        </xsd:restriction>
    </xsd:simpleType>
</xsd:element>
```

The XSL Transform

The export process can also create an XSLT document. This XSLT document (also known as an XSL transform) specifies how to convert the exported XML into another type of document.

The XSLT that Access creates has one goal in life: to transform the raw XML document into HTML suitable for display in a browser. Technically, the XSLT simply defines the rules for transforming the Orders.xml file into HTML. It can't be executed directly. To fill this gap, Access also generates another file, named Orders.htm. This file uses VBScript to load the exported XML and then use the XSLT stylesheet to transform it into an HTML table. To see the results, simply open the Orders.htm file in your browser. The whole process works seamlessly, assuming you use Internet Explorer (the only browser that supports VBScript). Figure 5-4 shows a partial view of the HTML table with the exported order data.

Order ID	Customer	Employee	Order Date	Required Date	Shipped Date	Ship Via	Freight	Ship Name
11077	RATTC	1	5-Jun-96	3-Jul-96		2	$8.53	Rattlesnake Canyon Grocery
11076	BONAP	4	5-Jun-96	3-Jul-96		2	$38.28	Bon app'
11075	RICSU	8	5-Jun-96	3-Jul-96		2	$6.19	Richter Supermarkt
11074	SIMOB	7	5-Jun-96	3-Jul-96		2	$18.44	Simons bistro
11073	PERIC	2	4-Jun-96	2-Jul-96		2	$24.95	Pericles Comidas clásicas
11072	ERNSH	4	4-Jun-96	2-Jul-96		2	$258.64	Ernst Handel
11071	LILAS	1	4-Jun-96	2-Jul-96		1	$0.93	LILA-Supermercado
11070	LEHMS	2	4-Jun-96	2-Jul-96		1	$136.00	Lehmanns Marktstand
11069	TORTU	1	3-Jun-96	1-Jul-96	5-Jun-96	2	$15.67	Tortuga Restaurante
11068	QUEEN	8	3-Jun-96	1-Jul-96		2	$81.75	Queen Cozinha
11067	DRACD	1	3-Jun-96	17-Jun-96	5-Jun-96	2	$7.98	Drachenblut Delikatessen
11066	WHITC	7	31-May-96	28-Jun-96	3-Jun-96	2	$44.72	White Clover Markets
11065	LILAS	8	31-May-96	28-Jun-96		1	$12.91	LILA-Supermercado
11064	SAVEA	1	31-May-96	28-Jun-96	3-Jun-96	1	$30.09	Save-a-lot Markets
11063	HUNGO	3	30-May-96	27-Jun-96	5-Jun-96	2	$81.73	Hungry Owl All-Night Grocers
11062	REGGC	4	30-May-96	27-Jun-96		2	$29.93	Reggiani Caseifici
11061	GREAL	4	30-May-96	11-Jul-96		3	$14.01	Great Lakes Food Market

Figure 5-4. Transforming the order information to HTML

The XSL transforms gets much more interesting when exporting a report. For example, if you export the Summary of Sales by Quarter report to XML with the

XSL file, you'll find that this transform attempts to replicate the rich report format. Figure 5-5 shows how the raw report data will appear in your browser.

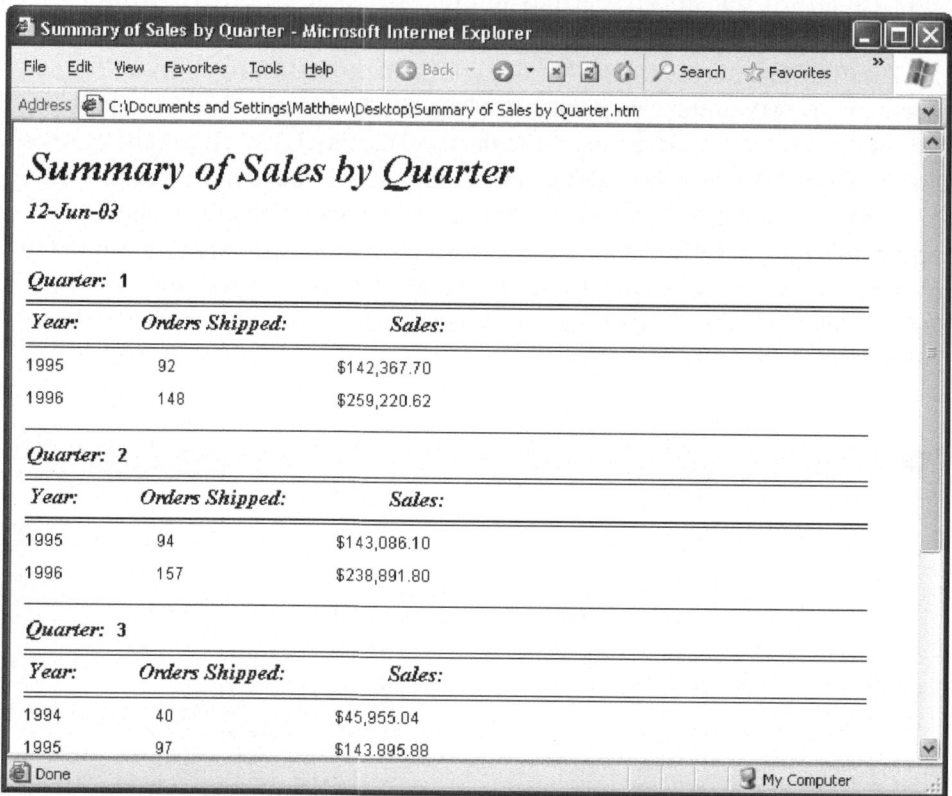

Figure 5-5. Transforming a report into HTML

XSL transforms are discussed in detail in Chapter 7.

Exporting Related Tables

The default export option copies all the data in a single table. In many data exchange scenarios, this won't provide enough information. For example, the Northwind database breaks down order information into several separate tables. The Order Details table includes line-by-line information about each product in an order. The Customers table includes information about the individual who made the order. The Shippers table includes information about the shipper sending the order. In a typical database, information is broken down into its component parts to ensure the least amount of duplication, which helps to avoid errors and optimize performance. In order to interpret that data in an application, however, it's often necessary to assemble details out of several related tables.

Fortunately, Access makes it easy to export a set of related tables—provided you're willing to accept the structure it uses. The first step is to make sure that the database has the appropriate relationships defined. You can select Tools ➤ Relationships from the menu to see how tables are linked. Figure 5-6 shows the full set of relationships defined for the Northwind database.

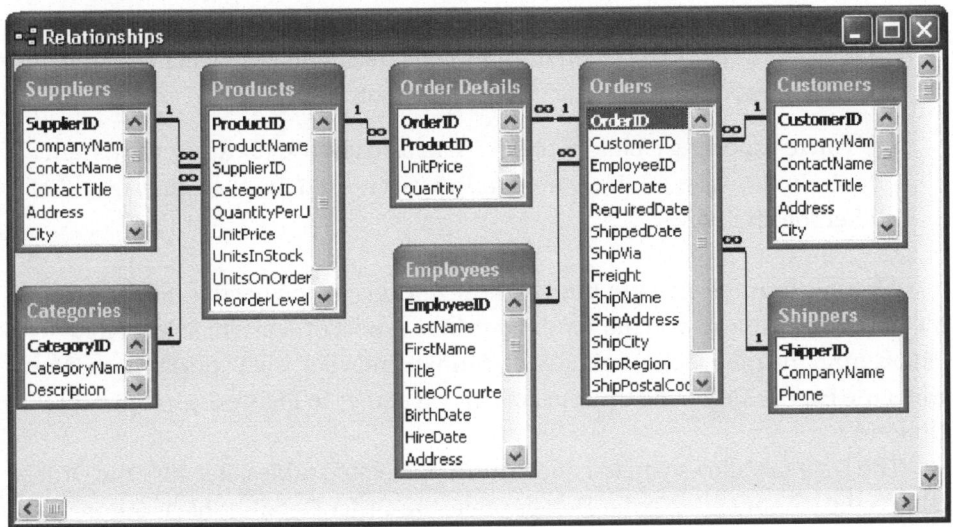

Figure 5-6. Relationships in the Northwind database

As you can see, the Orders table is linked to four other tables. The most important of these relationships is the *parent-child* relationship between the Orders and Order Details table. According to this relationship, for each order record there may be one or more detail records. In the other three relationships, the Orders table is on the receiving end: It's the child in the parent-child relationship. For example, in the relationship between Customers and Orders, one customer record may be linked to one or more orders.

It's important to understand which table is the parent and which table is the child in a parent-child relationship. That's because the child table is always the one that defines the relationship. The child table includes an additional foreign key field that links it to the parent. For example, the Order Details table includes a foreign key called OrderID. This makes it the child of the Orders table. Similarly, the Orders table includes a CustomerID field that links it to the Customers table.

> **NOTE** *Often, in Access you'll use lookup fields to simplify relationships. In the case of the relationship between the Orders and Customers table, the Orders table uses a lookup field on the CustomerID field. Technically, this link uses the unique CustomerID value. However, to make it easier to define this link while editing the database, Access can be configured so it shows other information, like the CompanyName.*

Using these relationships, you have two options when exporting XML:

- If you're exporting a parent table, you can also choose to export the child table. In this case, the elements for the related child rows will be nested inside the corresponding parent row element.

- If you're exporting a child table, you can also choose to export the parent table. In this case, all the related rows aren't nested. Instead, they're added after the child rows.

A simple example can put both of these options in perspective. Start by selecting the Orders table as you did for the previous export operation. Select File ➤ Export from the menu, choose the XML format, and click the Export button. Now, when the Export XML window appears (shown earlier in Figure 5-2), click More Options.

The Data tab allows you to choose multiple related tables. Because the Orders table is the parent of the Order Details table, the Order Details table is automatically added to the list. Click the checkbox next to the table name to include it in the export, as shown in Figure 5-7. Click OK to save the file.

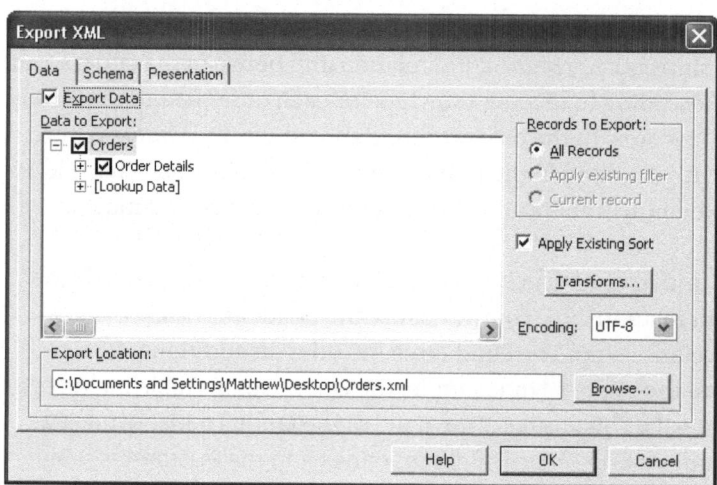

Figure 5-7. Exporting a linked child table

Now if you look at the XML document, you'll see the following nested structure. Each <Orders> element will contain one or more <Orders_x0020_Details> elements.

```xml
<?xml version="1.0" encoding="UTF-8"?>
<dataroot xmlns:od="urn:schemas-microsoft-com:officedata"
 xmlns:xsi="http://www.w3.org/2001/XMLSchema-instance"
 xsi:noNamespaceSchemaLocation="Orders.xsd" generated="2003-06-12T18:31:47">
    <Orders>
        <OrderID>11077</OrderID>
        <CustomerID>RATTC</CustomerID>
        <EmployeeID>1</EmployeeID>
        <OrderDate>1996-06-05T00:00:00</OrderDate>
        <RequiredDate>1996-07-03T00:00:00</RequiredDate>
        <ShipVia>2</ShipVia>
        <Freight>8.53</Freight>
        <ShipName>Rattlesnake Canyon Grocery</ShipName>
        <ShipAddress>2817 Milton Dr.</ShipAddress>
        <ShipCity>Albuquerque</ShipCity>
        <ShipRegion>NM</ShipRegion>
        <ShipPostalCode>87110</ShipPostalCode>
        <ShipCountry>USA</ShipCountry>

        <Order_x0020_Details>
            <OrderID>11077</OrderID>
            <ProductID>2</ProductID>
            <UnitPrice>19</UnitPrice>
            <Quantity>24</Quantity>
            <Discount>0.2</Discount>
        </Order_x0020_Details>

        <!-- Other order details omitted. -->
    </Orders>

    <!-- Other orders omitted. -->
</dataroot>
```

You can also export relationships that go multiple layers deep. For example, you can export the Customers table, include a nested list of orders for each customer, and include a nested list of order items for each order.

It's also sometimes useful to export related parent tables. For example, the Orders table includes a CustomerID field that indicates the customer who made the order. However, when processing the XML, it might be important to retrieve other customer information, like the customer name and address. This could be exported to a separate XML document, or included in the Orders XML.

To include the customer information in the Orders XML, you use the same window. You'll find the Customers table under the [Lookup Data] node. Figure 5-8 shows an export operation that includes the Orders and Customers tables.

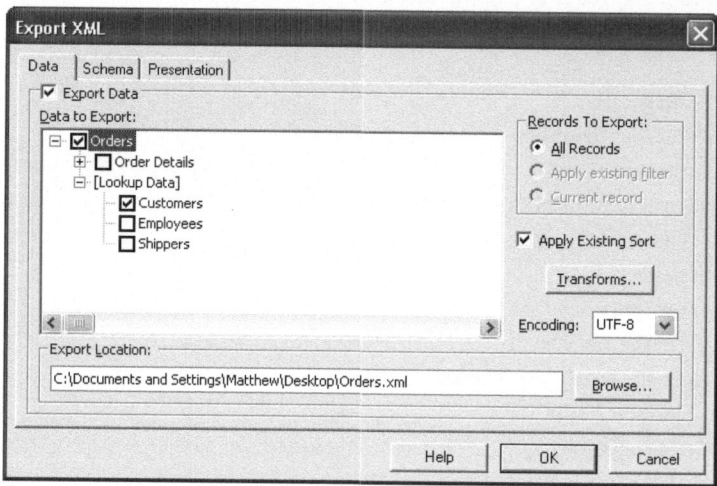

Figure 5-8. Exporting a linked parent table

In this case, the customer data won't be nested. Instead, it will be included after the order data. It's up to the application processing the XML to infer the relationship. Here's an example of the XML you'll see:

```xml
<?xml version="1.0" encoding="UTF-8"?>
<dataroot xmlns:od="urn:schemas-microsoft-com:officedata"
 xmlns:xsi="http://www.w3.org/2001/XMLSchema-instance"
 xsi:noNamespaceSchemaLocation="Orders.xsd" generated="2003-06-12T15:02:24">
    <Orders>
        <OrderID>11077</OrderID>
        <CustomerID>RATTC</CustomerID>
        <EmployeeID>1</EmployeeID>
        <OrderDate>1996-06-05T00:00:00</OrderDate>
        <RequiredDate>1996-07-03T00:00:00</RequiredDate>
        <ShipVia>2</ShipVia>
        <Freight>8.53</Freight>
        <ShipName>Rattlesnake Canyon Grocery</ShipName>
        <ShipAddress>2817 Milton Dr.</ShipAddress>
        <ShipCity>Albuquerque</ShipCity>
```

```
        <ShipRegion>NM</ShipRegion>
        <ShipPostalCode>87110</ShipPostalCode>
        <ShipCountry>USA</ShipCountry>
    </Orders>
    <!-- Other orders omitted. -->

    <Customers>
        <CustomerID>ALFKI</CustomerID>
        <CompanyName>Alfreds Futterkiste</CompanyName>
        <ContactName>Maria Anders</ContactName>
        <ContactTitle>Sales Representative</ContactTitle>
        <Address>Obere Str. 57</Address>
        <City>Berlin</City>
        <PostalCode>12209</PostalCode>
        <Country>Germany</Country>
        <Phone>030-0074321</Phone>
        <Fax>030-0076545</Fax>
    </Customers>
    <!-- Other customers omitted. -->
</dataroot>
```

You can export multiple parent tables, and they will all be added to the generated XML file separately. You can also mix related parent tables and child tables in the same XML document. However, none of these choices will affect the XSL transform that Access generates, which means you'll still see the same HTML table with only the order information.

> **TIP** *There's a reason that parent rows can't be nested inside child rows. More than one child may refer to the same parent. For example, one customer may have made multiple orders. If you nest customer information inside order information, you may have the same information duplicated in several locations of the document. Besides wasting space, this raises the possibility that the data could be changed in one place but not in another, leading to inconsistencies that can't be resolved.*

Other Export Options

There are a few other options that you can use when exporting data. These are all accessed by clicking the More Options button when exporting your XML.

In the Schema window (shown in Figure 5-9), you have two options of interest:

- Deselect the "Include primary key and index information" checkbox to leave the <annotation> element with Access-specific key information out of the schema.

- If you select the "Embed the schema in the XML document" checkbox, the generated XML will be placed inside a document element named <root>, which will contain both the <dataroot> and <schema> elements.

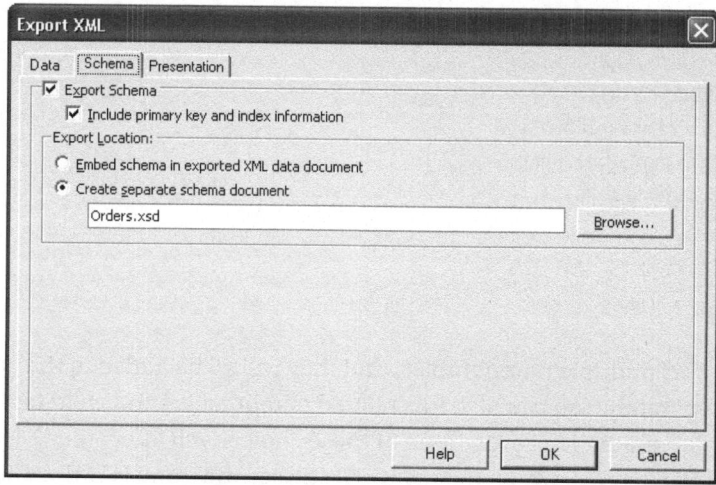

Figure 5-9. Schema export options

You also have the following two options that can affect how the presentation files are generated (see Figure 5-10):

- Select "Run from Server (ASP)" to generate server-side Active Server Page code for applying the XSL transform, instead of client-side VBScript code. Although ASP is outside the scope of this book, you'll see its successor, ASP.NET, in Chapter 8.

- When exporting a report, you can include linked images. The images will be used when you use the default XSL transform to show the report data in a browser.

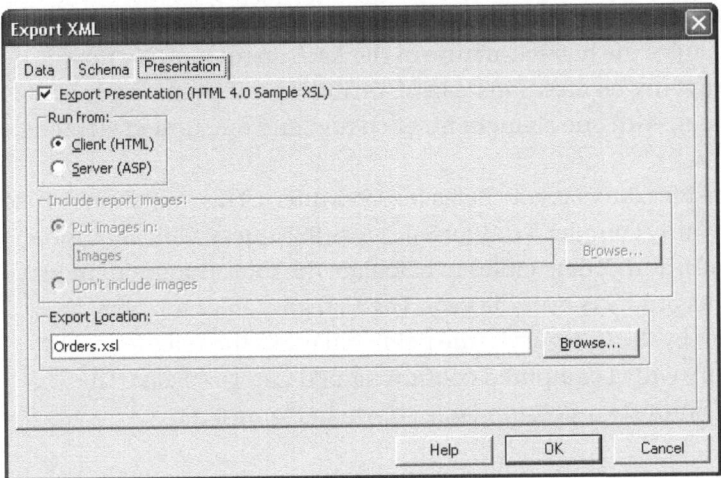

Figure 5-10. Presentation export options

Customizing Exported XML with a Query

The options for exporting XML in Access are somewhat inflexible. There is no way to rename an element name (or map a field name to a different element name). It's also impossible to select only some columns from a table for export. If you display the data before exporting it, you can apply two changes: a default sort order (right-click a column header and choose Sort Ascending or Sort Descending), and a filter condition (select Records ➤ Filter from the menu). Other than these two options, your choices are limited.

However, there is another way to customize your data before you export it: by using a custom query. In this case, you use your query to select the data you want and arrange it appropriately. Then you use the built-in XML export features in Access. Access won't give you any additional export options, but this extra layer gives you the chance to tweak the data.

Here are some changes you could apply using a query:

- Combine the data from multiple tables into one result set using a join query.

- Change the names of various columns using the AS keyword.

- Add computed columns using column expressions.

- Apply a custom sort order based on one or more fields.

- Filter the results to include only the relevant columns.

- Filter the results to include only the relevant rows.

On the other hand, there are a few things that you won't be able to modify with a query. This includes the basic structure of the XML document. No matter what, Access will always use elements instead of attributes, and enclose your data in a <dataroot> element, with one element for each row, and one nested element for each column.

For example, consider the Category Sales for 1995 query. This query makes use of another query, the fairly complex Product Sales for 1995 query, which joins the Products, Order Details, and Orders tables to calculate the total amount of money being made for various products over the year. The Category Sales for 1995 query then groups this result by the CategoryName field, and totals the sales for each product in the category with a computed column named CategorySales. The results appear in the simple two-column table shown in Figure 5-11.

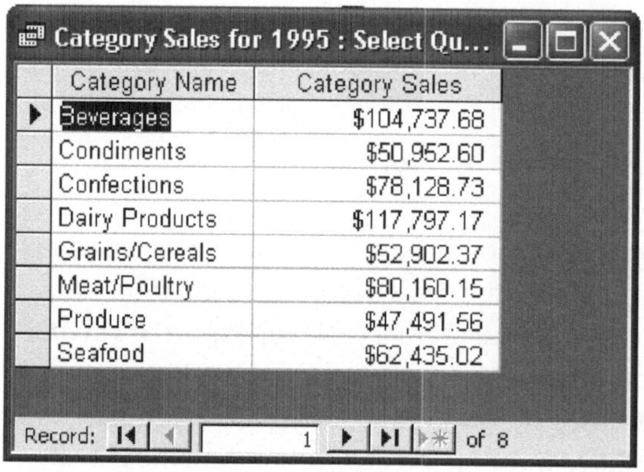

Category Name	Category Sales
Beverages	$104,737.68
Condiments	$50,952.60
Confections	$78,128.73
Dairy Products	$117,797.17
Grains/Cereals	$52,902.37
Meat/Poultry	$80,160.15
Produce	$47,491.56
Seafood	$62,435.02

Figure 5-11. Calculating category sales with a query

To export the XML for this query, simply select the query, and choose File ➤ Export. Select the XML data type as you choose a filename, as you did with the previous examples. The exported XML looks like this:

```
<?xml version="1.0" encoding="UTF-8"?>
<dataroot xmlns:od="urn:schemas-microsoft-com:officedata"
 xmlns:xsi="http://www.w3.org/2001/XMLSchema-instance"
 xsi:noNamespaceSchemaLocation="Category%20Sales%20for%201995.xsd"
 generated="2003-06-12T19:47:28">

    <Category_x0020_Sales_x0020_for_x0020_1995>
        <CategoryName>Beverages</CategoryName>
        <CategorySales>104737.68</CategorySales>
    </Category_x0020_Sales_x0020_for_x0020_1995>
```

```
    <Category_x0020_Sales_x0020_for_x0020_1995>
        <CategoryName>Condiments</CategoryName>
        <CategorySales>50952.6</CategorySales>
    </Category_x0020_Sales_x0020_for_x0020_1995>

    <!-- Other categories omitted. -->
</dataroot>
```

NOTE *Although you can export the results of an Access query to XML, you can't execute a query that directly returns an XML document. SQL Server 2000 includes this ability with the FOR XML clause that you can use with any SELECT query. FOR XML allows other applications to retrieve XML data directly from the database, without any manual conversion step.*

Importing XML

Importing XML works in much the same way as exporting XML, but it isn't nearly as useful. The XML import option is a simple way to dump a large amount of data into an Access table. However, there aren't any practical options for controlling version, merging duplicate information, or handling errors, which makes it a fairly crude solution for transferring data. That means the XML import option is most useful if you have external data (from another application or another database) that you want to analyze using Access queries or reports. Unfortunately, you must follow the Access XML format exactly in order for an import operation to work. That means that all your data must be contained in elements, not attributes, with element names based on the desired table and field names.

To start an import operation, select File ➤ Get External Data ➤ Import from the menu. Then, select the XML format, choose an XML file, and click OK. (You can also import just a schema file in order to create a table but not add any data.) Access then displays the window shown in Figure 5-12 with a preview of the tables it found in the source XML and the fields in each table. Access correctly finds all nested (child) tables and any consecutive (parent) tables. However, you don't have the option to limit the rows or tables that are imported.

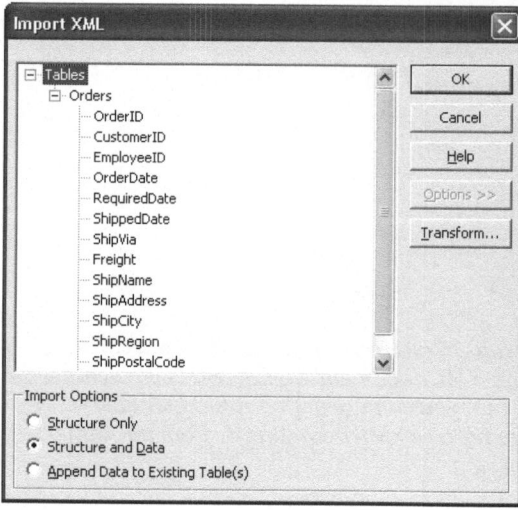

Figure 5-12. Importing XML

You can choose one of three import options. If these options aren't displayed, click the Options button.

- *Structure Only:* Access will infer the structure from the XML file, and use it to create a table (but not actually add any data).

- *Structure and Data:* Access will create a table and fill it with all the data.

- *Append Data to Existing Table(s):* Access will find the table with the same name, and add all the information in the XML file to this table.

If you choose either of the first two options, Access will always create a new table. If you're importing data and it includes element rows that have the same name as an existing table, Access will create a new table by adding a number to the end of the name. For example, importing the Orders XML file will create a new table called Orders1. Similarly, if you try to import the results from the Category Sales for 1995 query in this way, Access will create a new table named Category Sales 19951 with the query results, because it recognizes that there is already a database object (in this case, a query) with the same name.

If you choose the last option, Access will try to insert the rows in the table with the corresponding name, provided it exists. In this case, Access will attempt to insert *every* record, with no attempt to spot duplicates. Every time an insert operation fails, it will add a record to a table named ImportErrors, which is created as required. A typical error in the ImportErrors table records the XML text from the offending element, the result of the error, and an error message like "Microsoft JET Database Engine: The changes you requested to the table were not successful because they would create duplicate values in the index, primary key, or relationship."

Programmatic Importing and Exporting

If you need to use the importing and exporting features regularly, you can control them programmatically in Access VBScript. Access includes this ability in two methods of the Application object: ExportXML() and ImportXML().

To export XML, you use the Application.ExportXML() method with the following parameters:

```
Application.ExportXML ObjectType, DataSource, DataTarget, SchemaTarget, _
  PresentationTarget, ImageTarget, Encoding, OtherFlags
```

- **ObjectType:** A constant that identifies the type of object you're exporting. Usually it will be acExportTable, acExportQuery, or acExportReport.

- **DataSource:** A string with the name of the Access object.

- **DataTarget:** A string that contains the path for the XML file you want to create. Omit this if you don't want to export the XML.

- **SchemaTarget:** A string that contains the path for the XML schema file you want to create. Omit this if you don't want to export the schema.

- **PresentationTarget:** A string that contains the path for the XSL transform file you want to create. Omit this if you don't want to export the transform.

- **ImageTarget:** A string that contains the path that will be used for exporting report images.

- **Encoding:** Specifies the encoding of the text files. This can be acUTF16 (for full Unicode encoding) or acUTF8 (for UTF-8 encoding, which is the default).

- **OtherFlags:** A number that's a combination of other constants. Use 1 to embed the schema inside the XML file, 2 to leave index information out of the schema, and 4 to create an ASP presentation file instead of an HTML file.

For example, you can add this code to a macro to export the Customers table and schema:

```
Application.ExportXML _
    ObjectType := acExportTable, _
    DataSource := "Customers", _
    DataTarget := "C:\Customers.xml", _
    SchemaTarget := "C:\CustomersSchema.xml"
```

The corresponding Application.ImportXML() method takes only two parameters:

```
Application.ImportXML DataSource, ImportOptions
```

- **DataSource:** A string containing the XML file you want to import.

- **ImportOptions:** Can be one of three constants that configure how the import will be performed (acStructureOnly, acStructureAndData, and acAppendData). The default is acStructureAndData, which imports all the information and creates a new table if the XML file specifies a table that already exists.

The Last Word

The XML features in Access are most useful when your data needs to travel. For example, using the XML export feature and a query in the Northwind database, you could export detailed sales information as an XML file, and then attach it to an e-mail. The recipient of the e-mail could use the XML data in conjunction with another application, like Excel, to analyze market trends and make sales projections. This scenario wouldn't make nearly as much sense in a single-user environment, because Excel includes the ability to query information directly from a data source like an Access database. However, if the recipient doesn't have the original Access database, or doesn't have Access installed, the XML solution makes perfect sense.

The XML export is also an excellent option if you need to take data across platform boundaries. For example, you could send XML data to a user running an XML application on a Linux platform. This is the real niche of XML and Access: extending the reach of your data to other computers and platforms.

WordML and SpreadsheetML

CHAPTER 3 AND CHAPTER 4 focused on XML mapping, a remarkable new feature that lets you write and read XML documents in your own custom XML format with Word and Excel. The XML mapping features are at the heart of Office 2003 XML, but they don't solve every problem. One limitation is that the users who are working with the mapped documents need to take additional steps to import or export the XML data. In some cases, users will also need to understand how to work with the rich Office format (.doc or .xls), *and* the data-only XML that's sent to other applications. And though you can hide the XML mapping information (for example, by turning off Word's tag display and using placeholder text), you can't hide the fact that there are two ways to save an Office document—in its proprietary Office format, or in more limited, but fully customizable, XML.

To a certain extent, these problems are unavoidable. They are a result of the evolution of Office, which created its .doc and .xls file formats long before XML and the Internet even existed. Microsoft is well aware of these challenges, and is hard at work laying the groundwork for future solutions. To help break down the barriers between Office formats and XML, Microsoft has equipped both Word and Excel with new, native XML formats. These formats preserve all the information and formatting in a document (with a few minor exceptions), but use a custom set of XML elements designed for Word and Excel. In this chapter, we'll consider this compromise, and explore a few of the options it gives you for mining Office data and programmatically creating Office documents.

The Role of WordML and SpreadsheetML

Before you dive into the Word XML format (WordML) and the Excel XML format (SpreadsheetML), it's worth considering what these formats offer.

Although WordML and SpreadsheetML don't give you the same flexibility as your own custom XML format, they can make your Office data much more portable. Because an XML document consists of ordinary text, it's easy to transport to another platform or store in any storage medium. For example, you could store a portion of a Word document in a text field in a database record, and extract it into a local document as required. The same magic is possible with the proprietary Office formats (.doc and .xls), but it isn't nearly as easy.

Perhaps the most interesting part of the Office XML formats is the potential they offer for creating custom applications that work with Office documents. For example, you could create an application that searches Word documents for specific text. This task is fairly easy with the WordML format (just ignore all the tag names and search the element content), but it would be a serious challenge with the proprietary .doc format. Furthermore, if you know a little bit about the structures used in WordML and SpreadsheetML, you can quickly extract details like the document author and creation date. As an example, a developer could build a customized cataloguing application that stores a collection of Office documents and indexes them based on a few document properties. These applications can be written in any programming language that includes an XML parser, even on non-Microsoft operating systems and on computers where Office isn't installed.

The Office XML format isn't just limited to data mining; it also comes in handy if you want to create Word or Excel documents programmatically. For example, a hospital might use an application that requests some information about a patient exam, and then generates a complete report document. Or, a job seeker might enter resume information using an online web page, and receive a complete formatted Word file. Depending on how ambitious these applications are, they can be fairly trivial, or quite complicated. The WordML standard is particularly difficult to master, and it isn't trivial to generate rich Word documents. However, no matter how ambitious you are, the Office XML formats broaden your possibilities. At the end of this chapter, you'll see some sample code that works with the Office XML formats.

How the Office XML Formats Work

WordML and SpreadsheetML documents are 100 percent pure XML, which should come as no surprise. The XML format is so flexible that there's no need for Microsoft to add any type of proprietary ingredients. And unlike an XML export operation, saving a document using the Office XML formats guarantees that no information will be lost. The next time you save the document or spreadsheet, the XML format will be used automatically. Of course, you can choose to take a SpreadsheetML or WordML document and save it as a traditional .xls or .doc file. One reason you might need to take this step is if you want to allow users with an earlier version of Office to open and edit the documents.

Saving SpreadsheetML and WordML documents is easy. Just follow these tips:

- To save a SpreadsheetML document in Excel, choose File ➤ Save As from the menu. Then choose XML Spreadsheet from the "Save file as type" drop-down list box.

- To save a WordML document in Word, choose File ➤ Save As from the menu. Then choose XML Document from the "Save file as type" drop-down list box. Make sure that the "Save data only" checkbox is not selected before you click the Save button.

WordML and SpreadsheetML files use the .xml file extension. However, when you double-click a WordML or SpreadsheetML file, Windows will automatically load the file into Word or Excel, provided Office 2003 is installed. (Windows will even indicate the registered application using a special Word or Excel icon when you view the document in Windows Explorer.) That's because the Office XML formats include a processing instruction that indicates the program that was used to create them. This processing instruction appears immediately after the XML declaration at the start of the document. Here's the processing instruction for a SpreadsheetML file:

```
<?mso-application progid="Excel.Sheet"?>
```

And here's the processing instruction for a WordML file:

```
<?mso-application progid="Word.Document"?>
```

Of course, you can still open these files in other applications. If you want to look at the raw XML, you can drag and drop the file into Internet Explorer, or open it manually in an XML editor.

> **TIP** *Interestingly, the processing instruction doesn't indicate the version of Word or Excel that the document requires. That means if you take this file to a computer that only has an earlier version of Word installed (like Word 2000 or Word XP), you can still launch Word and use it to open this file. However, because these versions of Word don't support XML mapping, the file will be converted to plain text, which makes it very difficult to edit. For that reason, you won't use WordML or SpreadsheetML unless you're certain that the file doesn't need to be opened by users with earlier versions of Office.*

Dissecting SpreadsheetML

SpreadsheetML is the simpler of the Office XML formats. It lays out the document out as a series of rows and columns, along with additional information about document properties and styles. Figure 6-1 shows a simplified picture of the SpreadsheetML format.

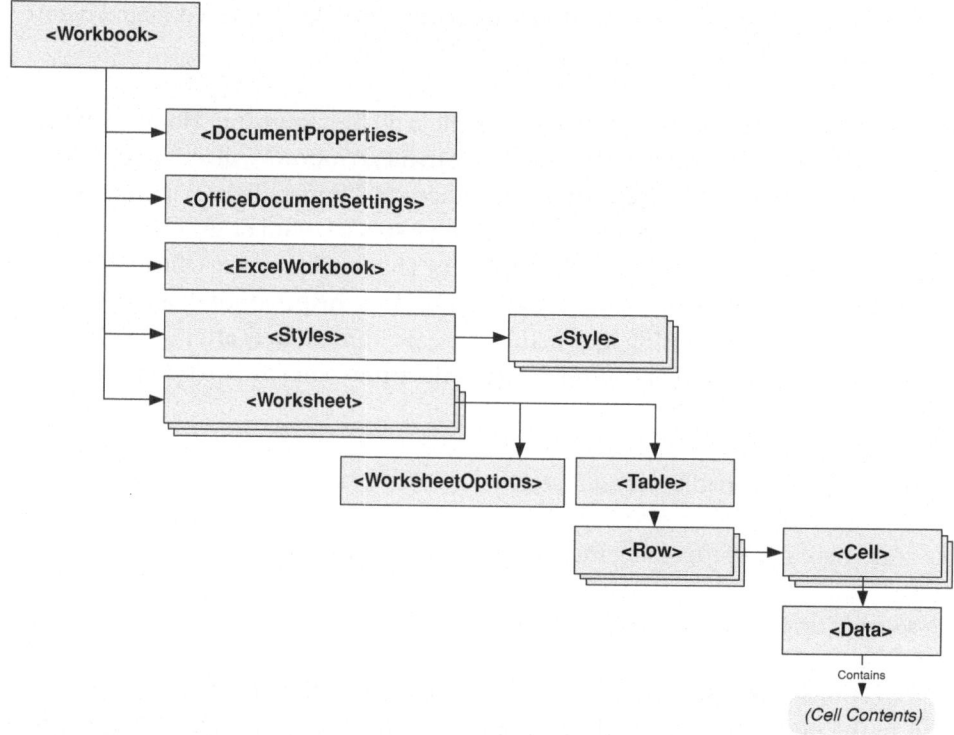

Figure 6-1. Elements in a typical SpreadsheetML document

The root element of a SpreadsheetML document is named <Workbook>. The actual data is divided into one or more <Worksheet> elements. A typical <Worksheet> contains a <Table> with multiple <Row> elements. Every <Row> consists of columns represented by individual <Cell> elements. However, the <Cell> element doesn't contain the data directly. Instead, the <Cell> element contains a <Data> element that identifies the type of data. The actual text content of the cell is placed inside the <Data> element.

The following sections dissect the XML produced for some typical Excel spreadsheets.

A Simple SpreadsheetML Document

Consider the simple spreadsheet shown in Figure 6-2. It contains four unformatted cell values.

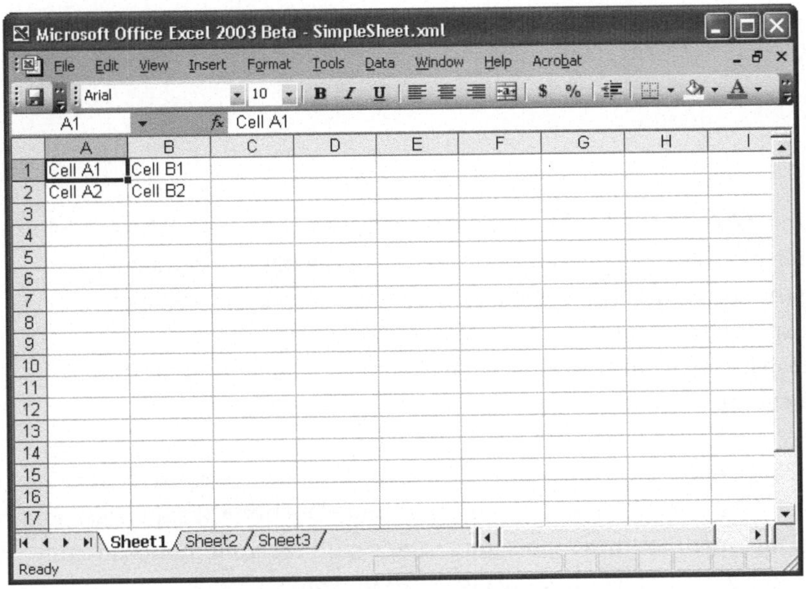

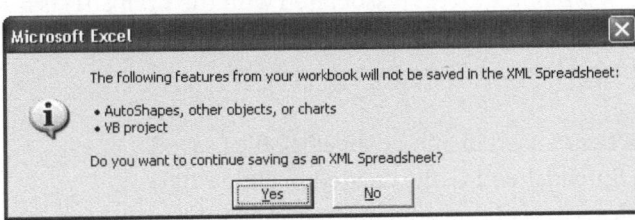

Figure 6-2. A simple spreadsheet with four values

To export this spreadsheet to SpreadsheetML, select File ➤ Save As. Choose XML Spreadsheet in the "Save as type" list box. Excel can save almost any spreadsheet to XML without losing data. Two exceptions are charts and VBScript code, neither of which can be persisted in XML. If your spreadsheet contains any ingredients that can't be saved to XML, you'll be warned when you attempt to save the file, as shown in Figure 6-3.

Figure 6-3. Saving a SpreadsheetML document with unsupported content

The SpreadsheetML document will have the following basic structure:

```
<Workbook>
    <DocumentProperties>...</DocumentProperties>
    <OfficeDocumentSettings>...</OfficeDocumentSettings>
    <ExcelWorkbook>...</ExcelWorkbook>
    <Styles>...</Styles>
    <Worksheet>...</Worksheet>
    <Worksheet>...</Worksheet>
    <Worksheet>...</Worksheet>
</Workbook>
```

By default, a new spreadsheet is created with three worksheets, which is why you'll find three <Worksheet> elements. If you delete the unused worksheets before saving the spreadsheet, there will only be one <Worksheet> element.

You can explore the namespaces in this document using the GetXMLNamespaces.exe utility presented in Chapter 1. You'll find that three core namespaces are used in SpreadsheetML:

- *urn:schemas-microsoft-com:office:office* (associated with the prefix o) is used for Office-specific information, including <DocumentProperties> and <OfficeDocumentSettings>. This namespace (and these elements) are not specific to Excel—in fact, they are also used in WordML.

- *urn:schemas-microsoft-com:office:excel* (associated with the prefix x) is used for Excel-specific information. This includes information about window settings and document protection settings.

- *urn:schemas-microsoft-com:office:spreadsheet* (associated with the prefix ss, and used as the default namespace) is the most heavily used namespace in a SpreadsheetML document. It's used for all the elements that correspond to spreadsheet structures, like <Style>, <Worksheet>, and <Data>.

- *urn:schemas-microsoft-com:office:excel2* (associated with the prefix u1) is a new namespace added in Office 2003. This namespace is used for XML mapping information when saving a mapped worksheet.

The first three namespaces are used in SpreadsheetML files saved with Office XP. If you open a SpreadsheetML file created in Office 2003 using Office XP, it's reasonable to expect that any information in the new urn:schemas-microsoft-com:office:excel2 namespace will be ignored.

To get a better feel for the SpreadsheetML format, it helps to dissect the simple spreadsheet piece by piece. First of all, the root <Workbook> element defines all the namespaces that are used in the document. The default namespace (urn:schemas-microsoft-com:office:spreadsheet) is also declared.

```
<Workbook xmlns="urn:schemas-microsoft-com:office:spreadsheet"   ·
 xmlns:o="urn:schemas-microsoft-com:office:office"
 xmlns:x="urn:schemas-microsoft-com:office:excel"
 xmlns:ss="urn:schemas-microsoft-com:office:spreadsheet"
 xmlns:html="http://www.w3.org/TR/REC-html40">
```

You'll notice that if your document doesn't use XML mapping, the urn:schemas-microsoft-com:office:excel2 namespace won't be defined or used.

Next, the <DocumentProperties> element contains information about the user who created the document, when the document was created, and what version of Excel was used.

```
<DocumentProperties xmlns="urn:schemas-microsoft-com:office:office">
    <Author>Matthew MacDonald</Author>
    <LastAuthor>Matthew MacDonald</LastAuthor>
    <Created>2003-06-16T18:15:25Z</Created>
    <Version>11.4920</Version>
</DocumentProperties>
```

After this, <OfficeDocumentSettings> defines some application-specific information, including the installation path (which will be used to install new features if required).

```
<OfficeDocumentSettings xmlns="urn:schemas-microsoft-com:office:office">
    <DownloadComponents/>
    <LocationOfComponents HRef="file:///G:\"/>
</OfficeDocumentSettings>
```

The next element, <ExcelWorkbook>, defines some global settings that apply to the entire workbook. These settings include the positioning of the window in the Excel interface, and any document protection options.

```
<ExcelWorkbook xmlns="urn:schemas-microsoft-com:office:excel">
    <WindowHeight>4260</WindowHeight>
    <WindowWidth>6795</WindowWidth>
    <WindowTopX>0</WindowTopX>
    <WindowTopY>0</WindowTopY>
    <ProtectStructure>False</ProtectStructure>
```

```
        <ProtectWindows>False</ProtectWindows>
    </ExcelWorkbook>
```

The location of the window isn't usually of much interest, because in most cases the Excel document window will be maximized inside the Excel main window, and these settings will be ignored. The window location settings will be applied if you are in the habit of editing multiple spreadsheets side-by-side in the same window.

Document protection is an Excel feature that allows you to disable other users from changing portions of an Excel spreadsheet. Document protection can be applied at several different levels, including globally, to individual worksheets, and to specific cell ranges, so you'll see these elements appear elsewhere in the document.

The next element, <Styles>, contains one <Style> element for each style that is used in the document. Styles can include font, formatting, cell type, and protection settings. In this simple spreadsheet example, only the default style is saved to the spreadsheet.

```
<Styles>
    <Style ss:ID="Default" ss:Name="Normal">
        <Alignment ss:Vertical="Bottom"/>
        <Borders/>
        <Font/>
        <Interior/>
        <NumberFormat/>
        <Protection/>
    </Style>
</Styles>
```

Empty tags (like <Font/>) indicate that no settings are applied for this part of the style.

Finally, we move into the heart of the document, with the <Worksheet> elements. The Worksheet element contains two portions. Data is contained inside a <Table> element. Settings (like document protection) are contained inside a <WorksheetOptions> element). The first worksheet in this simple example contains a 2-by-2 table and no important settings.

```
<Worksheet ss:Name="Sheet1">
    <Table ss:ExpandedColumnCount="2" ss:ExpandedRowCount="2" x:FullColumns="1"
    x:FullRows="1">
        <Row>
            <Cell><Data ss:Type="String">Cell A1</Data></Cell>
```

```
        <Cell><Data ss:Type="String">Cell B1</Data></Cell>
    </Row>
    <Row>
        <Cell><Data ss:Type="String">Cell A2</Data></Cell>
        <Cell><Data ss:Type="String">Cell B2</Data></Cell>
    </Row>
    </Table>
  <WorksheetOptions xmlns="urn:schemas-microsoft-com:office:excel">
      <Selected/>
      <ProtectObjects>False</ProtectObjects>
      <ProtectScenarios>False</ProtectScenarios>
  </WorksheetOptions>
 </Worksheet>
```

As you can see, the data is laid out in a grid using <Row> and <Cell> elements. Because this document contains two rows, the preceding example shows two <Row> tags. Each row contains two columns, and thus each <Row> element contains two <Cell> elements. Inside the actual cell is a <Data> tag that indicates spreadsheet content. In this example, the <Data> tag identifies its content as a simple string using the Type attribute. The ExpandedColumnCount and ExpandedRowCount attributes of the <Table> element indicate the full size of the table.

If any row other than A1 is selected when you save the spreadsheet, Excel will add a <Panes> element to the <WorksheetOptions> element. The <Panes> element indicates the cell that was selected when you saved the file. This cell will receive the focus the next time the document is opened.

```
<Panes>
    <Pane>
        <Number>3</Number>
        <ActiveRow>2</ActiveRow>
    </Pane>
</Panes>
```

The other two worksheets in the document don't contain any information, because no cell content has been entered. They simply reflect the default worksheet options:

```
<Worksheet ss:Name="Sheet2">
    <WorksheetOptions xmlns="urn:schemas-microsoft-com:office:excel">
        <ProtectObjects>False</ProtectObjects>
        <ProtectScenarios>False</ProtectScenarios>
    </WorksheetOptions>
</Worksheet>
```

```
<Worksheet ss:Name="Sheet3">
    <WorksheetOptions xmlns="urn:schemas-microsoft-com:office:excel">
        <ProtectObjects>False</ProtectObjects>
        <ProtectScenarios>False</ProtectScenarios>
    </WorksheetOptions>
</Worksheet>
```

Spreadsheets with Noncontiguous Ranges

The previous example showed a neat grid of data. But what happens if you spread your information over the spreadsheet instead of using a rectangular table? You might expect that Excel would insert empty <Row> and <Cell> elements in the SpreadsheetML file to serve as placeholders. This actually isn't the case. For example, consider the spreadsheet in Figure 6-4.

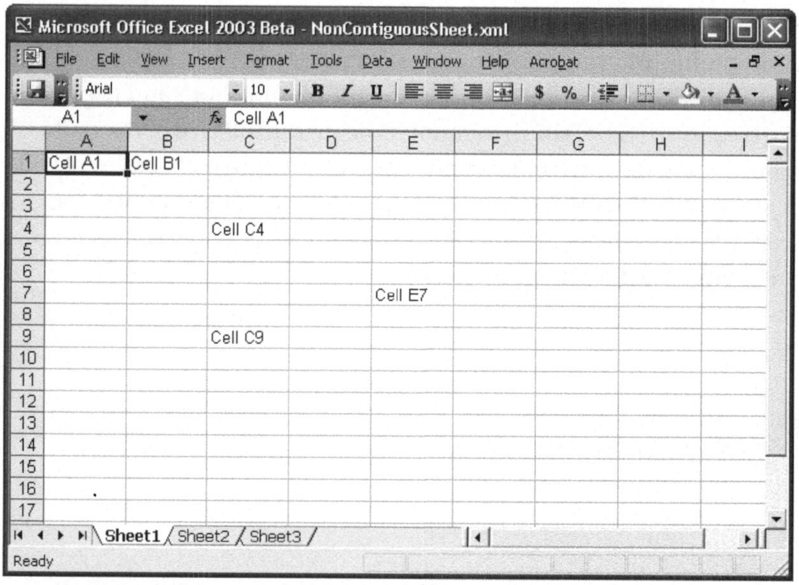

Figure 6-4. A noncontiguous spreadsheet

Excel measures the full size of the table using the furthest outlying data. In this case, the maximum row number is 9 (taken by the value in C9), and the maximum column number is 5 (taken by the value in E7). Thus, it determines that the maximum size of the table is 9 by 5, and it enters this information in ExpandedColumnCount and ExpandedRowCount attributes of the <Table> element.

```
<Table ss:ExpandedColumnCount="5" ss:ExpandedRowCount="9" x:FullColumns="1">
```

Next, Excel specifies the location of all noncontiguous rows and cells using an Index attribute. For example, consider cell E7. To put this value in the table, Excel creates a <Row> element with an index of 7, and adds to it a <Cell> element with an index of 5.

```
<Row ss:Index="7">
    <Cell ss:Index="5"><Data ss:Type="String">Cell E7</Data></Cell>
</Row>
```

Following is the complete <Table> element for this spreadsheet. Note that the Index attribute is not used with contiguous cells.

```
<Table ss:ExpandedColumnCount="5" ss:ExpandedRowCount="9" x:FullColumns="1"
 x:FullRows="1">
    <Row>
        <Cell><Data ss:Type="String">Cell A1</Data></Cell>
        <Cell><Data ss:Type="String">Cell B1</Data></Cell>
    </Row>
    <Row ss:Index="4">
        <Cell ss:Index="3"><Data ss:Type="String">Cell C4</Data></Cell>
    </Row>
    <Row ss:Index="7">
        <Cell ss:Index="5"><Data ss:Type="String">Cell E7</Data></Cell>
    </Row>
    <Row ss:Index="9">
        <Cell ss:Index="3"><Data ss:Type="String">Cell C9</Data></Cell>
    </Row>
 </Table>
```

The end result is that if you want to create an application that can process SpreadsheetML files, you'll need to first determine the total size of the table using the ExpandedColumnCount and ExpandedRowCount attributes. Then, you'll need to fill the table by examining each <Row> and <Cell>. When adding cell content, you'll need to first check whether an explicit index number was specified for the row and column. Otherwise, use the next available row and column.

Numbers and Formulas

The first two examples were spreadsheets with simple text. Excel distinguishes between text and other types of cell content, namely numbers, formulas, and dates. All these types of data are added to a SpreadsheetML document in much the same way.

Figure 6-5 shows a spreadsheet with two numeric cells and a formula that adds them together.

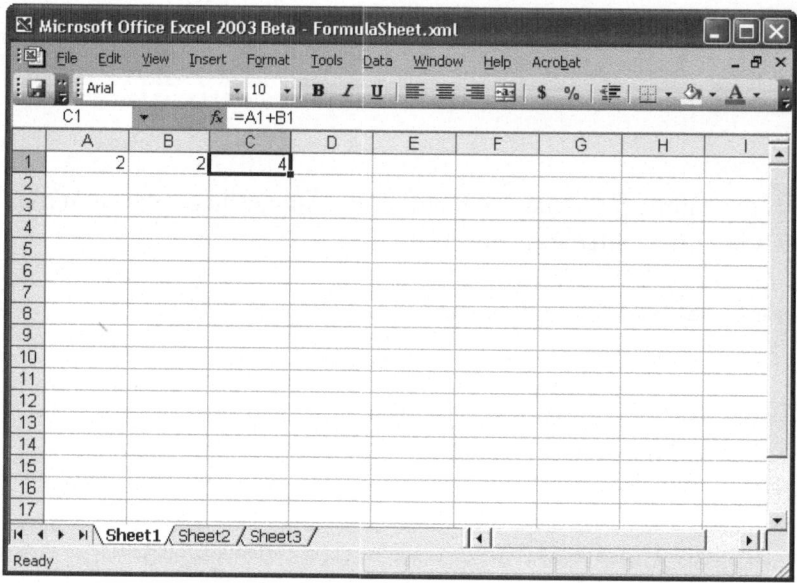

Figure 6-5. A spreadsheet with a formula

The <Table> element for this spreadsheet looks like this:

```
<Table ss:ExpandedColumnCount="3" ss:ExpandedRowCount="1" x:FullColumns="1"
 x:FullRows="1">
    <Row>
        <Cell><Data ss:Type="Number">2</Data></Cell>
        <Cell><Data ss:Type="Number">2</Data></Cell>
        <Cell ss:Formula="=RC[-2]+RC[-1]"><Data ss:Type="Number">4</Data></Cell>
    </Row>
</Table>
```

The two numeric cells contain a <Data> element with the value. The Type attribute of the <Data> element indicates that this value should be treated as a number. Incidentally, the supported types are all Excel-specific. There is no relationship between the full set of types defined in the XML Schema standard and the types that Excel uses. Excel's set of types is smaller, and simpler, which means the end user doesn't need to think about maximum sizes for specific data types, allowable ranges, and so on. However, this also forces Excel to take a couple of extra steps when working with mapped XML, which is why Excel only performs schema validation when exporting or importing data.

The cell with the formula looks a little different. It contains the computed value in a <Data> element, and it defines the formula that can be used to recalculate the value using a Formula attribute in the <Cell> element. The formula itself is less intuitive. It specifies other cells in the spreadsheet based on how they relate to the current cell, using the following syntax:

```
R[NumericOffset]C[NumericOffSet]
```

The R stands for row, while the C stands for column. The expression RC translates into "the cell at the current row and column." On the other hand, the expression R[1]C[2] means "find the cell one row down, and two columns to the right." The formula in the example spreadsheet, =RC[-2]+RC[-1], translates to "get the value two cells to the left, and add it to the value one cell to the left."

> **TIP** *The formula format you see in a SpreadsheetML document closely matches Excel's internal formula representation format (called R1C1 style). You'll notice that formulas are almost always based on relative references (i.e., get the value two cells to the left) rather than absolute references (i.e., get the value in cell A1). That's why when you cut and paste formulas in Excel, the references change automatically.*

Keeping this in mind, it's not too hard to interpret most Excel formulas. However, if you wanted to create an application that could examine a SpreadsheetML document and recalculate a formula, it would probably have to construct the complete table first.

Formatted Spreadsheets

The SpreadsheetML format handles formatting particularly well. As you format cells and cell ranges, Excel creates new styles that represent your formatting, and then applies these styles to the appropriate cells. This results in a fairly readable XML document, because most of the formatting information is stored separately in the <Styles> element, not directly in the <Table> element.

As an example, consider the spreadsheet shown in Figure 6-6. It applies two types of formatting. Cells A1 and B1 are formatted in bold. Cells B2 to B13 are formatted in the currency format, which means the numeric values appear with two decimal places and a preceding dollar sign.

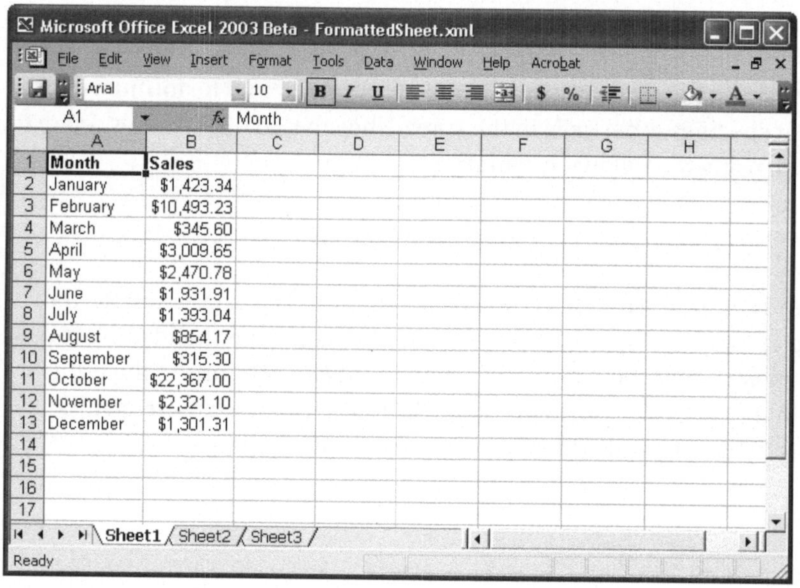

Figure 6-6. A formatted spreadsheet

The SpreadsheetML document defines both of these styles with distinct <Style> elements, and it assigns them dynamically created unique names. In this example, s23 becomes the style used for the bold font. Because this style only contains font information, the corresponding <Style> element contains a single child <Font> element. The s22 style is used for the currency formatting of the numeric cells. It contains a single <NumberFormat> child element, and no font information.

Here's the complete content for the <Styles> element in the resulting document:

```
<Styles>
    <Style ss:ID="Default" ss:Name="Normal">
        <Alignment ss:Vertical="Bottom"/>
        <Borders/>
        <Font/>
        <Interior/>
        <NumberFormat/>
        <Protection/>
    </Style>
    <Style ss:ID="s22">
        <NumberFormat ss:Format="&quot;$&quot;#,##0.00"/>
    </Style>
    <Style ss:ID="s23">
```

```
        <Font x:Family="Swiss" ss:Bold="1"/>
    </Style>
</Styles>
```

Other child elements are used to represent different types of formatting. The empty elements in the default style show your six options: <Alignment>, <Borders>, <Font>, <Interior> (fill patterns), <NumberFormat>, and <Protection>.

Once these styles are defined, they simply need to be applied to the appropriate cells through the StyleID attribute of the <Cell> element. For example, here's the bold row used for the column headings:

```
<Row>
    <Cell ss:StyleID="s23"><Data ss:Type="String">Month</Data></Cell>
    <Cell ss:StyleID="s23"><Data ss:Type="String">Sales</Data></Cell>
</Row>
```

And here's a single row of data, with a currency-formatted cell:

```
<Row>
    <Cell><Data ss:Type="String">January</Data></Cell>
    <Cell ss:StyleID="s22"><Data ss:Type="Number">1423.34</Data></Cell>
</Row>
```

In addition, if you resize columns in your spreadsheet, Excel inserts this information by adding <Column> elements before the <Row> elements in the <Table>. Here's an example:

```
<Column ss:Width="53.25"/>
```

Mapped Spreadsheets

If you export a mapped spreadsheet, your document will contain two additional elements at the very end, after all <Worksheet> elements: <MapInfo> and <Binding>. These elements will be explicitly placed in the urn:schemas-microsoft-com:office:excel2 namespace.

The <MapInfo> element contains the related schema (inserted inside a <Schema> element) and the cell-to-element mapping information in a <Map> element. This information is quite lengthy, and isn't shown here.

The <Binding> element specifies a linked data source for the mapping (which will usually be a fully qualified file path to the source XML document). When you refresh the data in your spreadsheet, Excel queries the location specified in the <Binding> element. Here's an example:

```
<u1:Binding u1:ID="Binding1" u1:LoadMode="normal">
    <u1:MapID>Products_Map</u1:MapID>
    <udc:DataSource MajorVersion="1" MinorVersion="0"
     xmlns:udc="http://schemas.microsoft.com/data/udc">
        <udc:Type Type="XMLFile" MajorVersion="1" MinorVersion="0"/>
        <udc:Name>Binding1</udc:Name>
        <udc:ConnectionInfo Purpose="Query">
        <udcxf:File xmlns:udcxf="http://schemas.microsoft.com/data/udc/xmlfile">
          C:\ProductList.xml</udcxf:File>
    </udc:ConnectionInfo>
    </udc:DataSource>
</u1:Binding>
```

Dissecting WordML

WordML is a much more verbose format than SpreadsheetML, and WordML documents are more difficult to understand and work with. There are three factors that contribute to this difference:

- WordML has a much larger vocabulary than SpreadsheetML, with separate elements to define all sorts of structures from frames to tables to bulleted lists.

- WordML uses a more deeply nested structure. To get to the actual content of a document, you need to drill down through sections, paragraphs, and runs. In addition, it's not always clear where text will be, because of the different layers of formatting that can be applied.

- WordML doesn't have the clear separation of formatting and data that you find in SpreadsheetML. Although you can use styles in a document, you can also apply formatting directly inline, which complicates the generated XML.

Figure 6-7 shows a simplified picture of the WordML format.

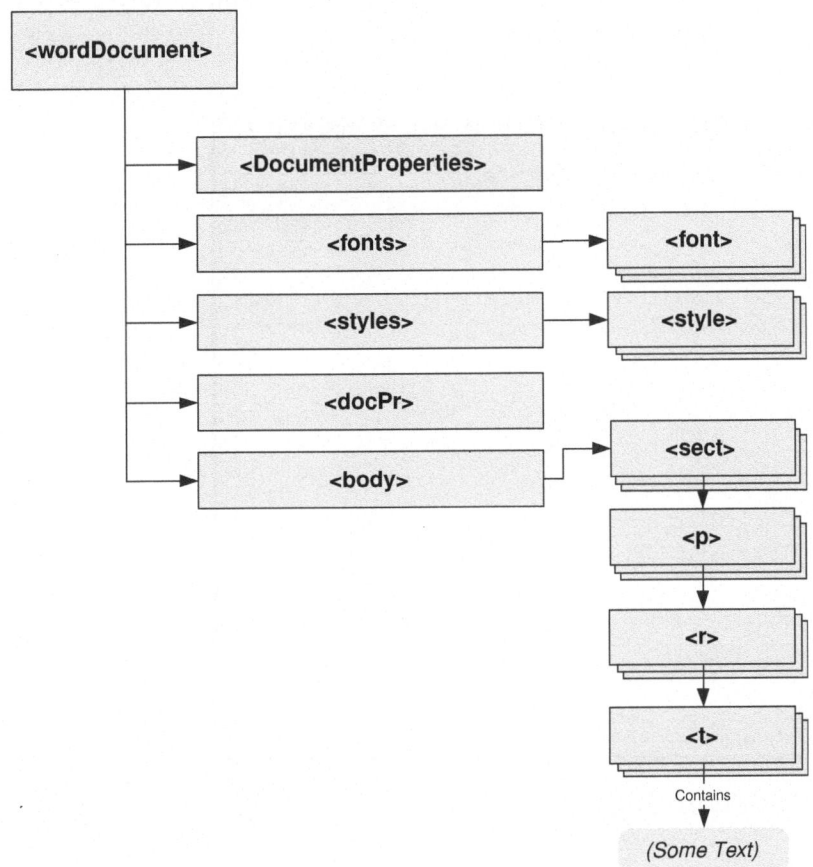

Figure 6-7. Elements in a typical WordML document

The root element of a WordML document is named <wordDocument>. The actual content of the document is found in the <body> element. The <body> element is subdivided into more elements, including paragraphs (<p>), runs (<r>), and text segments (<t>). It's the final <t> elements that actually contain the text. In addition, styled documents are further divided with <sect> and <sub-section> elements, which aren't shown in Figure 6-7.

The following sections dissect the XML produced for some typical Word documents.

A Simple WordML Document

Consider the simple Word document shown in Figure 6-8. It contains two lines of text using the default style and formatting.

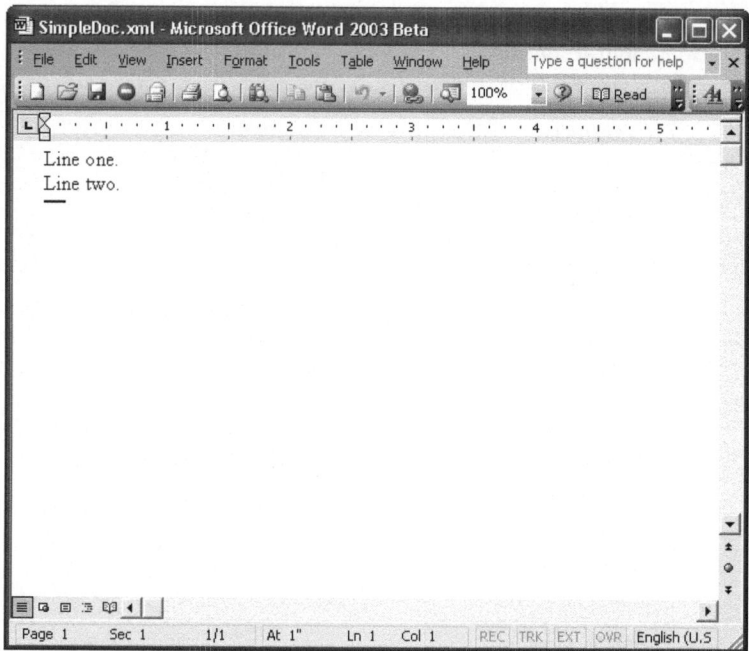

Figure 6-8. A simple Word document

To export this spreadsheet to WordML, select File ➤ Save As. Choose XML Document in the "Save as type" list box, and make sure that the "Data only" checkbox is *not* selected. The WordML format supports everything the .doc format supports, including graphics, macros, and even embedded objects.

The WordML document will have the following basic structure:

```
<wordDocument>
    <DocumentProperties>...</DocumentProperties>
    <fonts>...</fonts>
    <styles>...</styles>
    <docPr>...</docPr>
    <body>...</body>
</wordDocument >
```

The root <wordDocument> defines several namespaces. These include the following:

- *http://schemas.microsoft.com/office/word/2003/wordml* (associated with the prefix w) represents the core WordML standard, and it's used for the large majority of elements in the document, including all basic Word structures (styles, fonts, paragraphs, and so on).

- *urn:schemas-microsoft-com:office:office* (associated with the prefix o) is used for Office-specific information, like document properties. This information is used in WordML and SpreadsheetML.

- *urn:schemas-microsoft-com:office:word* (associated with the prefix w10) is used for Word-specific application information. This namespace is not used in a basic document.

- *urn:schemas-microsoft-com:vml* (associated with the prefix v) is used to store vector graphics inside the Word document using Vector Markup Language (VML).

To get a better feel for the WordML format, it helps to dissect the simple spreadsheet piece by piece. First of all, the root <wordDocument> element defines all the namespaces that are used in the document.

```
<w:wordDocument xmlns:w="http://schemas.microsoft.com/office/word/2003/wordml"
 xmlns:v="urn:schemas-microsoft-com:vml"
 xmlns:w10="urn:schemas-microsoft-com:office:word"
 xmlns:sl="http://schemas.microsoft.com/schemaLibrary/2003/core"
 xmlns:aml="http://schemas.microsoft.com/aml/2001/core"
 xmlns:wx="http://schemas.microsoft.com/office/word/2003/auxHint"
 xmlns:o="urn:schemas-microsoft-com:office:office"
 xmlns:dt="uuid:C2F41010-65B3-11d1-A29F-00AA00C14882" xml:space="preserve">
```

The final attribute in the <wordDocument> element, xml:space, indicates that whitespace should not be collapsed. That means that a document can contain a series of multiple spaces without your worrying that the XML parser will ignore this information. In fact, there are no superfluous spaces or even line breaks separating most of the XML elements in a WordML file, although the code listings in this chapter include some whitespace to make them easier to read.

The first element in <wordDocument> is <DocumentProperties>, which provides some general information about the document and when it was created. This is the same element that's used in a SpreadsheetML document, and it includes the same information about the author, creation date, and application version. In addition, it includes Word-specific information like the number of pages, words, and characters.

```
<o:DocumentProperties>
    <o:Author>Matthew MacDonald</o:Author>
    <o:LastAuthor>Matthew MacDonald</o:LastAuthor>
    <o:Revision>2</o:Revision>
    <o:TotalTime>1</o:TotalTime>
    <o:Created>2003-06-17T22:26:00Z</o:Created>
    <o:LastSaved>2003-06-17T22:27:00Z</o:LastSaved>
    <o:Pages>1</o:Pages>
    <o:Words>2</o:Words>
    <o:Characters>18</o:Characters>
    <o:Company></o:Company>
    <o:Lines>1</o:Lines>
    <o:Paragraphs>1</o:Paragraphs>
    <o:CharactersWithSpaces>19</o:CharactersWithSpaces>
    <o:Version>11.4920</o:Version>
</o:DocumentProperties>
```

The next element, <fonts>, lists the fonts that are used in the document, or are used in one of the nondefault styles in the document. This font information includes the font name, and some additional details that Word can use to choose a substitute typeface if the document is opened on a computer that doesn't have the original font.

Here's the slightly shortened font information from the sample document:

```
<w:fonts>
    <w:font w:name="Tahoma">
        <w:panose-1 w:val="020B0604030504040204" />
        <w:charset w:val="00" />
        <w:family w:val="Swiss" />
        <w:pitch w:val="variable" />
    </w:font>
</w:fonts>
```

The <styles> element presents all the styles used in the document. This section includes all the styles from attached templates. It also includes the default styles (Heading1, Heading2, and so on), if they are used in the document. Each style is identified by a separate <style> element. The <style> element includes a <name> element that indicates the name of the style, followed by a combination of elements indicating the formatting that it uses. These tags can include information like font, paragraph spacing, language settings, and much more.

Following is a partial list of the styles you'll find in the default document. Note that the first two tags actually indicate how the default styles will be treated. The current document is using "version 3" of the built-in Word styles.

```
<w:styles>
    <w:versionOfBuiltInStylenames w:val="3" />
    <w:latentStyles w:defLockedState="off" w:latentStyleCount="156" />

    <w:style w:type="paragraph" w:default="on" w:styleId="Normal">
        <w:name w:val="Normal" />
        <w:rPr>
            <wx:font wx:val="Times New Roman" />
            <w:sz w:val="24" />
            <w:sz-cs w:val="24" />
            <w:lang w:val="EN-US" w:fareast="EN-US" w:bidi="AR-SA" />
        </w:rPr>
    </w:style>

    <w:style w:type="character" w:default="on" w:styleId="DefaultParagraphFont">
        <w:name w:val="Default Paragraph Font" />
        <w:semiHidden />
    </w:style>

    <! -- Other styles omitted. -->
</w:styles>
```

The next section is <docPr>, which provides information about the presentation of the document. This includes the view setting, zoom percentage, use of placeholder text, and so on.

```
<w:docPr>
    <w:view w:val="normal" />
    <w:zoom w:percent="100" />
    <w:doNotEmbedSystemFonts />
    <w:attachedTemplate w:val="" />
    <w:defaultTabStop w:val="720" />
    <w:characterSpacingControl w:val="DontCompress" />
    <w:optimizeForBrowser />
    <w:validateAgainstSchema />
    <w:saveInvalidXML w:val="off" />
    <w:ignoreMixedContent w:val="off" />
    <w:alwaysShowPlaceholderText w:val="off" />
    <w:compat>
```

```
        <w:dontAllowFieldEndSelect />
        <w:useWord2002TableStyleRules />
        </w:compat>
    </w:docPr>
```

The most important part of the document is the <body> section, which wraps the content of the document. The first child of the <body> is a <sect> element, or section. Sections aren't a core part of the WordML standard—instead, they are designed to help convert the document to HTML. The WordML document also includes some section information in a <sectPr> element. However, because neither of these elements are used by Word, this chapter won't consider them.

Inside the section is one or more paragraphs (<p> elements). Paragraphs can include runs (<r> elements), which enclose a section of text with the same formatting. If a paragraph includes more than one type of formatting, it will be divided into separate runs. The actual content always appears as text inside a nested <t> element.

With these ingredients in mind, here's the body of the simple document example:

```
<w:body>
    <wx:sect>
        <w:p>
            <w:r><w:t>Line one.</w:t></w:r>
        </w:p>
        <w:p>
            <w:r><w:t>Line two.</w:t></w:r>
        </w:p>

        <!-- sectPr tag omitted. -->
    </wx:sect>
</w:body>
```

Formatted Documents

The simple WordML document considered in the previous example is already more complex than a typical SpreadsheetML document. The XML becomes more tangled when you apply formatting.

For a simple test, you can create a document like the one shown in Figure 6-9. This document also contains two lines of text, but with formatting. The first line is formatted using the Heading1 style. The second line is formatted with a combination of bold and italic formatting. The bold format is applied to the entire line, while the italic format is only applied to the bracketed portion at the end of the sentence.

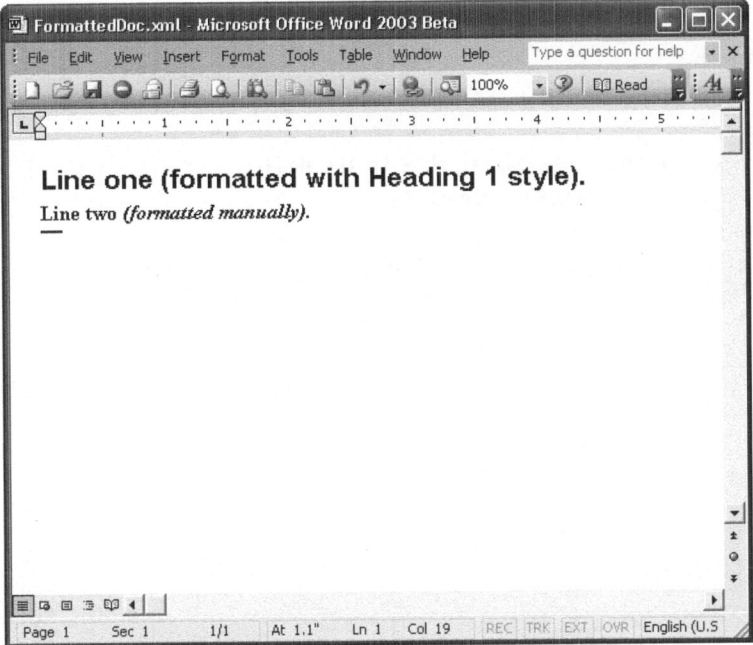

Figure 6-9. A formatted Word document

Looking at the WordML document, you'll find several changes. First of all, the Heading1 style will be added to the <styles> element. The Arial font that it uses will be added to the <fonts> element.

The body of the document is also changed. WordML uses a two-part structure to identify formatting. For example, if you format a paragraph, the formatting information will be added to a <pPr> paragraph presentation element inside the <p> paragraph element. If you format a section of text, a <rPr> run presentation element will be added inside the <r> run element. This model allows formatting to be applied to any of the Word structures in the document, without altering the element that contains the content.

As an example, consider the <body> element in the formatted document that follows. The Heading1 style is applied to the first paragraph using the <pStyle> element. The bold and italic formatting is indicated with <b> and <i> tags, and applied both to the second paragraph and to individual runs in the second paragraph. (You'll notice that the paragraph is split into two runs because it contains two "blocks" with different formatting.) To make the WordML easier to understand, all formatting information is highlighted in bold, and some comments are added inline.

```
<w:body>
    <wx:sect>
        <wx:sub-section>
            <w:p>
                <w:pPr>
                    <!-- Format this paragraph with the Heading1 style. -->
                    <w:pStyle w:val="Heading1" />
                </w:pPr>
                <w:r><w:t>Line one (formatted with Heading 1 style).</w:t></w:r>
            </w:p>
            <w:p>
                <w:pPr>
                    <w:rPr>
                        <!-- Apply bold and italic defaults to the paragraph. -->
                        <w:b />
                        <w:i />
                    </w:rPr>
                </w:pPr>
                <w:r>
                    <w:rPr>
                        <!-- Apply only bold to the first text run. -->
                        <w:b />
                    </w:rPr>
                <w:t>Line two</w:t>
                </w:r>
                <w:r>
                    <w:rPr>
                        <!-- Apply bold and italic to the second text run. -->
                        <w:b />
                        <w:i />
                    </w:rPr>
                    <w:t>(formatted manually).</w:t>
                </w:r>
            </w:p>

            <!-- sectPr tag omitted -->
        </wx:sub-section>
    </wx:sect>
</w:body>
```

This code segment shows the fundamentals for WordML formatting. Of course, as layers of different types of formatting are applied and combined with style information, the <body> element can become quite confusing.

Documents with Graphics

WordML can include any type of graphical content, from WordArt to embedded bitmaps. To test what the generated XML will look like, you can use a Word document like the one shown in Figure 6-10.

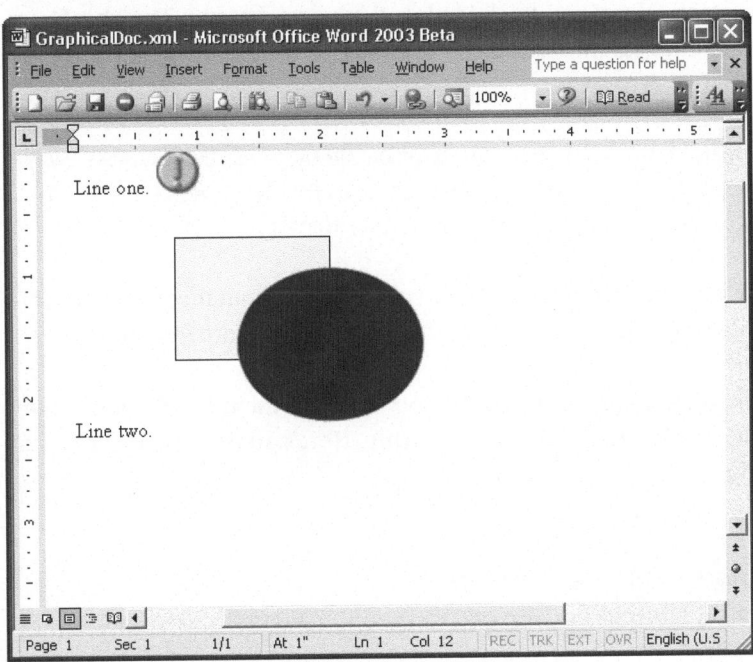

Figure 6-10. A Word document with graphics

This example includes two graphics. The first is an exclamation icon inserted from a GIF file. The second is a vector image that was drawn using the Word AutoShapes feature.

> **TIP** *Vector images and bitmaps are completely different. A bitmap description describes a graphic as a grid with thousands or millions of pixels. It stores information about the color of each individual pixel. A vector graphic uses a language to describe the graphic in geometric terms. For example, a vector description of a square might say, "Draw a 100 by 100 pixel square at the point (10, 10), and fill it with blue." Unlike bitmaps, vector images can be enlarged without losing quality, and the constituent objects in a vector image can be manipulated individually. Vector images also require much less space for storage.*

In the WordML, you'll find both the bitmap and vector graphic. Both are inserted using the <pict> element, which is placed inside a <r> run. The <binData> element includes the image data as a block of Base64-encoded binary information. It looks like this:

```
<w:binData w:name="http://01000001.gif">R0lGODlhGQAXAPcAAP///5SUlKV7a6VzWpSEe6V7Y
61zUrVrQv97Meeca7VzSr1zQt6ESsZrMf+Eb1jKedzKfd7Kc5jIe9zIfdzIZyEc71rMe+EOed7MfeEMf+
EMd5zKe97KcZjIdZrIedzId5rGNZj EKWEa6V7WrVzQrVrMe...</binData>
```

This is also the way that other types of embedded objects that contain binary data, like sounds, files, or documents from other applications, are inserted into a WordML document.

On the other hand, the <pict> tag for the vector image includes elements like <shape>, <fill>, and <path> that define the drawing. Here's an excerpted version of the sample drawing:

```
<w:pict>
    <v:shape id="_x0000_s1026" type="#_x0000_t75"
     style="position:absolute;left:1785;top:382;width:2700;height:2160"
     o:preferrelative="f">
        <v:fill o:detectmouseclick="t" />
        <v:path o:extrusionok="t" o:connecttype="none" />
    </v:shape>

    <v:rect id="_x0000_s1028"
     style="position:absolute;left:1935;top:536;width:1500;height:1234"
     fillcolor="yellow" />
    <v:oval id="_x0000_s1029"
     style="position:absolute;left:2535;top:845;width:1800;height:1543"
     fillcolor="purple" strokecolor="#f90" />
</w:pict>
```

In theory, another application could reconstruct both of these images. In the first case, it could translate the Base64 encoded data to a binary image, if it knows the expected format. In the second case, it would need to natively understand the Vector Markup Language (VML).

Mapped Documents

WordML treats mapped documents differently than SpreadsheetML. In SpreadsheetML, the mapping information is stored in a separate element in the document. Unfortunately, that means there's no easy way to convert a mapped SpreadsheetML into your custom XML structure. In order to do so, you'd need a custom program that could read the <MapInfo> element, reconstruct the spreadsheet table, extract the values from the mapped ranges, and then write the XML file. In WordML, however, your XML tags are used in the document—in fact, they're embedded directly in the <body> element.

For example, consider the quotation example from Chapter 4. If you save this document to WordML, you'll find that your namespace is declared in the root <wordDocument> element. It assigns a prefix of ns0. If there is more than one mapped schema, the prefix will be incremented as needed to ns1, ns2, and so on.

```
<w:wordDocument xmlns:w="http://schemas.microsoft.com/office/word/2003/wordml"
 xmlns:v="urn:schemas-microsoft-com:vml"
 xmlns:w10="urn:schemas-microsoft-com:office:word"
 xmlns:sl="http://schemas.microsoft.com/schemaLibrary/2003/core"
 xmlns:aml="http://schemas.microsoft.com/aml/2001/core"
 xmlns:wx="http://schemas.microsoft.com/office/word/2003/auxHint"
 xmlns:o="urn:schemas-microsoft-com:office:office"
 xmlns:dt="uuid:C2F41010-65B3-11d1-A29F-00AA00C14882"
 xmlns:ns1="http://www.w3.org/2001/XMLSchema-instance"
 xmlns:ns0="http://www.prosetech.com/Schemas/QuotationAttributes"
 xml:space="preserve">
```

In the body of the document, the quotation elements are mingled with the native WordML elements. For example, you can find a <category> tag that contains nested WordML paragraph, paragraph presentation, and run tags. Inside the run is the actual category data.

```
<ns0:category>
    <w:p>
        <w:pPr>
            <w:ind w:left="360" />
```

```
            </w:pPr>
            <w:r>
                <w:t>Ancient Wisdom</w:t>
            </w:r>
        </w:p>
    </ns0:category>
```

The full body content is shown here, with the quotation elements highlighted. You can see that the structure of the quotation elements is preserved perfectly. The only difference is the addition of the WordML elements, which are interspersed throughout the document.

```
<w:body>
    <wx:sect>
        <ns0:quotation id="1034">
            <w:p />
            <ns0:text>
                <w:p>
                    <w:pPr>
                        <w:ind w:left="360" />
                    </w:pPr>
                    <w:r>
                        <w:t>One thing is for certain: if you don't change the
                        path you're on, you will end up where you are headed.</w:t>
                    </w:r>
                </w:p>
            </ns0:text>

            <ns0:source>
                <w:p>
                    <w:pPr>
                        <w:ind w:left="360" />
                    </w:pPr>
                    <w:r>
                        <w:t>Chinese Proverb</w:t>
                    </w:r>
                </w:p>
            </ns0:source>

            <ns0:category>
                <w:p>
                    <w:pPr>
                        <w:ind w:left="360" />
```

```
                    </w:pPr>
                    <w:r>
                        <w:t>Ancient Wisdom</w:t>
                    </w:r>
                </w:p>
            </ns0:category>
        <w:p />
        </ns0:quotation>
        <!-- sectPr tag omitted -->
    </wx:sect>
</w:body>
```

In this example, it might look difficult to isolate the WordML elements from the quotation elements, but in fact it's not. Because the quotation elements are placed in a separate namespace, an XML application can filter them out easily. That means you can extract your custom XML data from a full WordML file. In fact, you can even use an XSL transform (as described in the next chapter) to change a rich WordML document into your custom data-only XML format. This flexibility raises a number of possibilities that aren't found with SpreadsheetML. For example, an organization could standardize on the WordML format for storing all documents. Then, assuming Word documents are stored in some centralized location (like a file share on a network server), you could create a custom application that could scan these WordML files, and extract the information it needs directly. You wouldn't need to perform any conversion, and users wouldn't have to give up their ability to use rich formatting!

Getting More Information About WordML Structures

The examples in this chapter only scratch the surface of the WordML language. Some of the structures that haven't been considered are those used for lists, tables, comments, change tracking, headers and footers, smart tags, and much more. For detailed information and the WordML schema, you can download the Word XML Content Development Kit (CDK). Be warned—the very terse reference information spans more than 100 pages, demonstrating that mastering WordML is no easy feat! You can download the Word XML CDK from http://msdn.microsoft.com/downloads/list/office2k3.asp. Unfortunately, you need to install the CDK to view the documentation. At the time of this writing, Microsoft doesn't provide any online reference information.

Programming with the Office XML Formats

Now that you've delved into the Office XML formats, it's worth asking what you can gain by using them. The key benefit is the way that Office data can be opened up to other applications, without forcing them to install Office or use the cumbersome Office objects.

Of course, this portability isn't without its own costs. Using the Office XML formats can be complicated, especially if you need to read formatted Word documents that use the dense WordML language. Microsoft product managers admit that the WordML and SpreadsheetML formats won't allow you to create your own spreadsheet or word processing application, but they will allow you to extract or modify some pieces of key data. In this section, you'll see a couple of simple examples that show how much work you'll need to really unlock Office data.

The examples in this section use Visual Basic 6, which is still the world's most popular programming language. The example won't use VBScript (the scaled-down version of Visual Basic 6 that's built into Office), because VBScript code only runs inside an Office document. If you're using VBScript code, it's easier to simply extract the information through the built-in Office objects. If you don't have a copy of Visual Basic 6 handy, you may still want to look over the code and try out the compiled application included with the content for this chapter, although you won't be able to modify it. And if you're working with the latest version of Visual Basic—VB .NET—be sure to check out the .NET versions of these applications, which are provided with the online chapter content.

The Visual Basic 6 applications use the Microsoft XML component (also called MSXML), which is included with Office 2003. In addition, these examples also use the File Scripting Model built into the Windows operating system to access files and folders on the hard drive. You can add a reference to this component in a VB 6 project by selecting Project ➤ References from the menu, and then placing a checkmark next to the Microsoft Scripting Runtime entry.

Mining Data

The most obvious use of the WordML and SpreadsheetML formats is to allow data mining. Users can save their Word documents and spreadsheets as XML without losing any data, and an application can scan these files to retrieve information when needed.

In principle, you can retrieve any information from a WordML or SpreadsheetML document, depending on how much work you want to go to. This example will demonstrate two common tasks: retrieving general document information from any Office document, and retrieving the entire text-only data. Figure 6-11 shows the application (called GetOfficeProperties.exe) when it first starts.

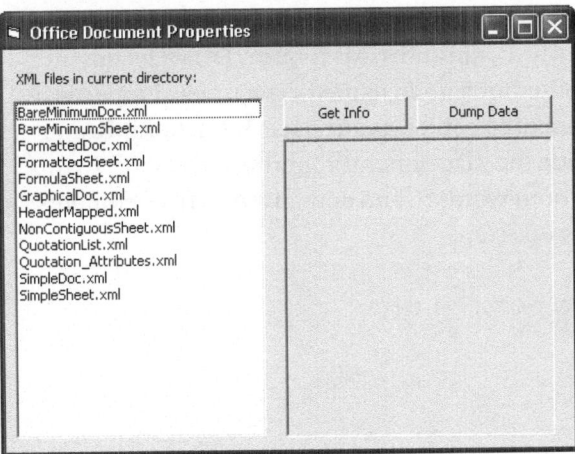

Figure 6-11. An application for mining Office data

When the GetOfficeProperties application starts up, it examines the current directory for XML files. Every time it finds an XML file of any kind, it adds it to the list, using this code:

```
Private Sub Form_Load()

    ' Create the FileSystemObject for accessing files and directories.
    Dim fso As Scripting.FileSystemObject
    Set fso = New FileSystemObject

    ' Get the startup folder.
    Dim Dir As Scripting.Folder
    Set Dir = fso.GetFolder(App.Path)

    ' Check all the files in the startup folder.
    Dim File As Scripting.File
    For Each File In Dir.Files
        ' If the file has the extension ".xml", add it to the list.
        If fso.GetExtensionName(File.Name) = "xml" Then
            lstFiles.AddItem (File.Name)
        End If
    Next

End Sub
```

You have two options with this application. If you click the Get Info button, the application opens the selected XML file and loads it into a DOMDocument object. The application then searches for a node named <DocumentProperties> in the urn:schemas-microsoft-com:office:office namespace. Both WordML and SpreadsheetML documents include the <DocumentProperties> element, so this code will find the information in both WordML and SpreadsheetML documents.

Here's the code that performs this step:

```
' Create the DOMDocument object for accessing the XML.
Dim Doc As DOMDocument
Set Doc = New DOMDocument


' Load the selected file into memory.
If Doc.Load(App.Path & "\" & lstFiles.Text) Then


' Define the node objects that will be used to retrieve information.
Dim PropertiesNode As IXMLDOMNode
Dim PropertyNode As IXMLDOMNode


' Before performing the search, you must map the namespace that
' you will use. In this case, it's the Office namespace, which is
' mapped to the prefix "o". The prefix used here does NOT need to
' match the mapping used in the XML document, as long as the namespace
' URI is the same.
Call Doc.setProperty("SelectionNamespaces", _
  "xmlns:o='urn:schemas-microsoft-com:office:office'")


' Search for a <DocumentProperties> node in the Office namespace.
Set PropertiesNode = _
  Doc.documentElement.selectSingleNode("//o:DocumentProperties")
```

In this case, the code uses the selectSingleNode() method to find the specific XML element. (Technically, the selectSingleNode() method uses an XPath expression, a standard explored in more detail in the next chapter.) Before performing the search, the code must call the setProperty() method to map the Office namespace to a prefix. It's then able to use the prefix with the selectSingleNode() search expression. If this step wasn't taken, the <DocumentProperties> element wouldn't be found, because the search wouldn't be performed in the correct namespace.

The selectSingleNode() method never generates an error, but it will return a null reference (identified by the keyword Nothing) if it can't find a match. Before continuing, the code needs to check whether the search was successful. Depending on the result, it sets a string named Info with some information that will be displayed to the user once the whole operation is complete.

```
' Use this string to store all the information you can retrieve.
Dim Info As String

' Check if you found it.
If PropertiesNode Is Nothing Then
    Info = " This file is not an Office XML document."
Else
    ' (Rest of code goes here.)
End If

' Display all the retrieved data in a label.
lblInfo.Caption = Info
```

If the search was successful, the code examines the root document to determine what type of Office document it's working with.

```
' Get the name of the root node to determine the type of document
' being read. Excel uses <Workbook> and Word uses <wordDocument>.
If Doc.documentElement.baseName = "Workbook" Then
    Info = " SpreadsheetML document." & vbNewLine
ElseIf Doc.documentElement.baseName = "wordDocument" Then
    Info = " WordML document." & vbNewLine
Else
    Info = " Unrecognizable Office document." & vbNewLine
End If
```

Finally, the code extracts multiple pieces of information from the <DocumentProperties> element, like the author and creation date. These child elements are also retrieved using the selectSingleNode() method. Each time this method is used, the code checks for a null reference, because not all Office documents will include all these pieces of document information. All the retrieved information is added to the Info string that is copied to the label at the end of the operation.

```
' Drill down in the <DocumentProperties> node to get additional
' information, like the author, creation date, etc.
' Every time a piece of informatio is successfully retrieved,
' add it to the Info string.
Set PropertyNode = PropertiesNode.selectSingleNode("//o:Author")
If Not PropertyNode Is Nothing Then
    Info = Info & "  Author: " & PropertyNode.Text & vbNewLine
End If

Set PropertyNode = PropertiesNode.selectSingleNode("//o:Created")
```

```
If Not PropertyNode Is Nothing Then
    Info = Info & "  Created Date: " & Left(PropertyNode.Text, 10) & vbNewLine
    Info = Info & "  Created Time: " & Mid(PropertyNode.Text, 12, 8) & vbNewLine
End If


Set PropertyNode = PropertiesNode.selectSingleNode("//o:Version")
If Not PropertyNode Is Nothing Then
    Info = Info & "  App Version: " & PropertyNode.Text & vbNewLine
End If


Set PropertyNode = PropertiesNode.selectSingleNode("//o:Pages")
If Not PropertyNode Is Nothing Then
    Info = Info & "  Pages: " & PropertyNode.Text & vbNewLine
End If
```

Figure 6-12 shows the retrieved information for a sample Word document.

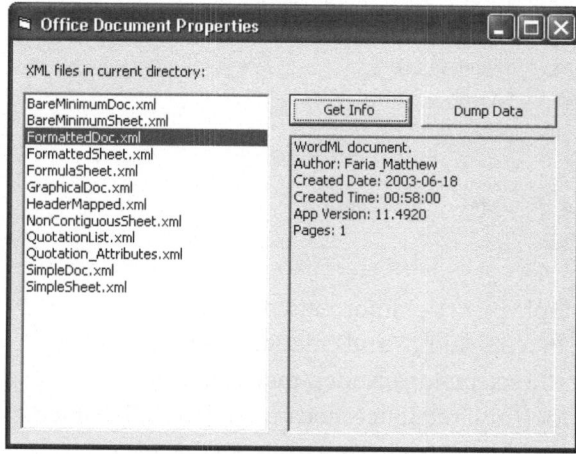

Figure 6-12. Getting the document properties of a Word document

The other button in the application, Dump Data, performs a slightly different task. It simply moves to the document data (the <body> element in a WordML document, or the <Worksheet> elements in a SpreadsheetML document), and extracts all the inner text. Because all the formatting information is contained in attributes and element names, it won't be included in the output.

In this case, WordML and SpreadsheetML documents need to be treated differently. The code will use selectSingleNode() to get the <body> elements in a Word file, and selectNodes() to get all the <Worksheet> elements in an Excel file (as there can be more than one). To distinguish the two types of documents, the code checks the name of the document element.

Here's the complete code:

```
Private Sub cmdDumpData_Click()
    ' Use this string to store all the information you can retrieve.
    Dim Info As String

    ' Create the DOMDocument object for accessing the XML.
    Dim Doc As DOMDocument
    Set Doc = New DOMDocument
    Dim ContentNode As IXMLDOMNode

    ' Load the selected file into memory.
    If Doc.Load(App.Path & "\" & lstFiles.Text) Then

        ' Get the name of the root node to determine the type of document
        ' being read. Excel uses <Workbook> and Word uses <wordDocument>.
        If Doc.documentElement.baseName = "Workbook" Then
            ' Before performing the search, you must map the namespace that
            ' you will use. In this case, it's the spreadsheet namespace, which
            ' is mapped to the prefix "ss".
            Call Doc.setProperty("SelectionNamespaces", _
                "xmlns:ss='urn:schemas-microsoft-com:office:spreadsheet'")

            ' Search for all tabular data.
            Dim ContentNodes As IXMLDOMNodeList
            Set ContentNodes = _
                Doc.documentElement.selectNodes("//ss:Worksheet/ss:Table")

            ' Ignore all the elements, and just get the text.
            For Each ContentNode In ContentNodes
                If Not ContentNode Is Nothing Then
                    Info = Info & ContentNode.Text
                End If
            Next

        ElseIf Doc.documentElement.baseName = "wordDocument" Then
            ' Before performing the search, you must map the namespace that
            ' you will use. In this case, it's the WordML namespace, which is
            ' mapped to the prefix "w".
            Call Doc.setProperty("SelectionNamespaces", _
                "xmlns:w='http://schemas.microsoft.com/office/word/2003/wordml'")

            ' Search for a <body> node.
```

```
            Set ContentNode = Doc.documentElement.selectSingleNode("//w:body")

            ' Ignore all the elements, and just get the text.
            If Not ContentNode Is Nothing Then
                Info = Info & ContentNode.Text
            End If

        Else
            Info = " Unrecognizable document." & vbNewLine
        End If
    End If


    ' Display all the retrieved data in a label.
    lblInfo.Caption = Info

End Sub
```

Figure 6-13 shows the data extracted from the formatted Word document shown earlier in this chapter.

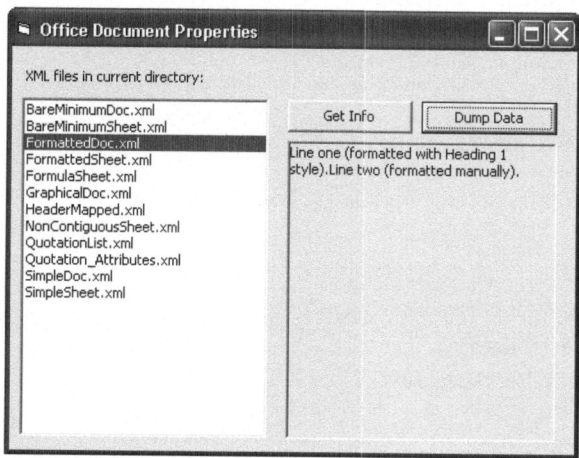

Figure 6-13. Getting data only from a Word document

This simple application demonstrates the approach you can use to get at information in Office XML documents. You simply need to search for the appropriate elements and get the text content. Similar applications can be developed to extract style and font information, comments, revision information, and more.

Creating Documents

The XML Office formats also make it possible to programmatically create Word or Excel documents. For example, an insurance application that adds a new customer into a policy database might want to generate a welcome letter or some other type of standardized form, with client information already filled in.

Generating WordML and SpreadsheetML can be tedious, because the average document is quite long. However, much of the WordML and SpreadsheetML information can be left out without causing a problem. For example, if you aren't using special formatting, the styles and fonts sections can be removed completely.

Here's an example of the bare minimum XML you need for an Excel spreadsheet that only contains data:

```xml
<?xml version="1.0"?>
<?mso-application progid="Excel.Sheet"?>
<Workbook xmlns="urn:schemas-microsoft-com:office:spreadsheet"
 xmlns:ss="urn:schemas-microsoft-com:office:spreadsheet">

 <Worksheet ss:Name="Sheet1">
  <Table ss:ExpandedColumnCount="2" ss:ExpandedRowCount="2">
   <Row>
    <Cell><Data ss:Type="String">Cell A1</Data></Cell>
    <Cell><Data ss:Type="String">Cell B1</Data></Cell>
   </Row>
   <Row>
    <Cell><Data ss:Type="String">Cell A2</Data></Cell>
    <Cell><Data ss:Type="String">Cell B2</Data></Cell>
   </Row>
  </Table>
 </Worksheet>
</Workbook>
```

And here's the bare minimum XML for a simple two-line Word document:

```xml
<?xml version="1.0" encoding="UTF-8" standalone="yes"?>
<?mso-application progid="Word.Document"?>
<w:wordDocument
 xmlns:w="http://schemas.microsoft.com/office/word/2003/wordml"
 xml:space="preserve">
    <w:body>
        <w:p><w:r><w:t>Line one.</w:t></w:r></w:p>
        <w:p><w:r><w:t>Line two.</w:t></w:r></w:p>
    </w:body>
</w:wordDocument>
```

When you resave either of these documents after opening them, you'll find that Word reinserts the additional information about styles, fonts, and document properties.

Generally, rather than trying to create a WordML or SpreadsheetML document that leaves out some information, it's easier to simply create an XML file to use as a starting point. You can create the starting point Word or Excel document using Word or Excel, and then modify the relevant portions of the document in your application.

For example, consider an application that needs to programmatically generate memo documents. (Perhaps it also takes on some additional responsibilities like logging memos in a database or sending them immediately via e-mail.) You can begin this solution by opening the Professional Memo template included with Word. Replace all the placeholder text with dummy values that your program will expect, as shown in Figure 6-14. (This document shouldn't be confused with the memo example, in Chapter 4, which uses XML mapping.)

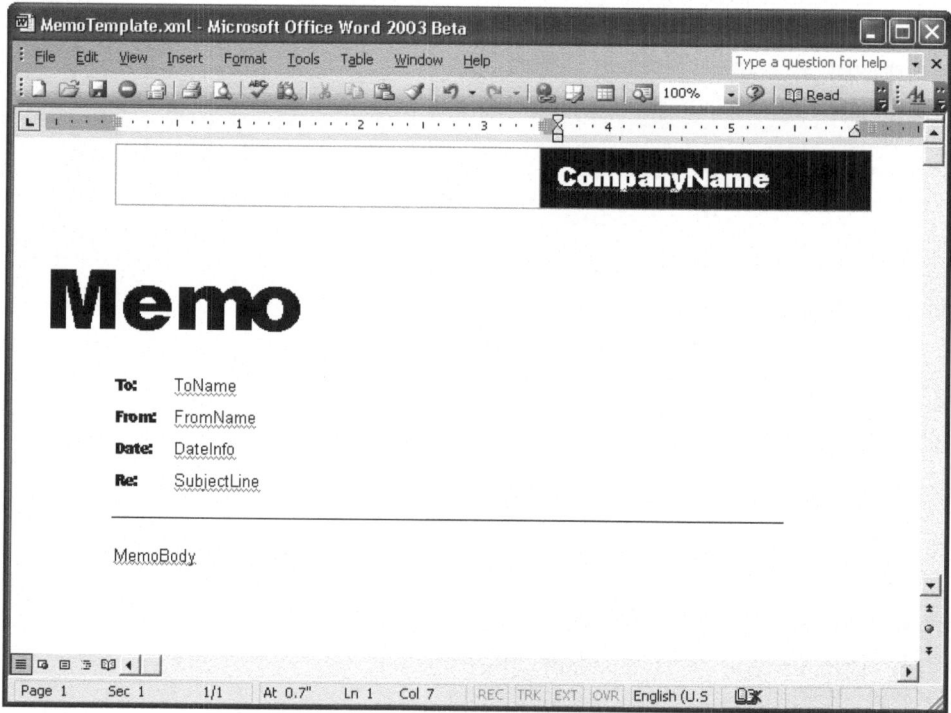

Figure 6-14. A Word document that will be modified programmatically

Save this document as a Word XML file. In this case, the filename is Memo-Template.xml. Next, you create an application that will use this XML template. An example is shown in Figure 6-15. In this sample (named CreateOfficeDoc.exe), the user enters memo information using the onscreen controls, and then clicks Generate to make the file.

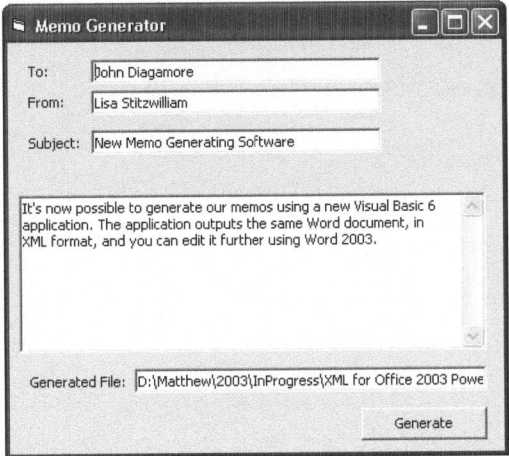

Figure 6-15. The memo-generating application

The code performs a few simple steps:

1. It loads the MemoTemplate.xml file into memory.

2. It searches for all the <t> text nodes in the whole document using the selectNodes() method.

3. It examines the content of each text node, and checks whether it matches one of the values that should be replaced. If it does, the substitution is performed.

4. When all the nodes have been examined, the file is saved with the new name.

Here's the complete code:

```
Private Sub cmdGenerate_Click()

    ' Create the DOMDocument object for accessing the XML.
    Dim Doc As DOMDocument
    Set Doc = New DOMDocument

    ' Load the selected file into memory.
    If Doc.Load(App.Path & "\MemoTemplate.xml") Then

        Call Doc.setProperty("SelectionNamespaces", _
          "xmlns:w='http://schemas.microsoft.com/office/word/2003/wordml'")

        Dim TextNodes As IXMLDOMNodeList
        Set TextNodes = Doc.documentElement.selectNodes("//w:t")

        Dim TextNode As IXMLDOMNode
        For Each TextNode In TextNodes
            Select Case TextNode.Text
                Case "CompanyName"
                    TextNode.Text = "ProseTech"
                Case "ToName"
                    TextNode.Text = txtTo.Text
                Case "FromName"
                    TextNode.Text = txtFrom.Text
                Case "DateInfo"
                    TextNode.Text = Now
                Case "SubjectLine"
                    TextNode.Text = txtSubject.Text
                Case "MemoBody"
                    TextNode.Text = txtBody.Text
            End Select
        Next

        Doc.save txtFileName.Text
        MsgBox "File saved."
    End If

End Sub
```

Figure 6-16 shows the newly generated document.

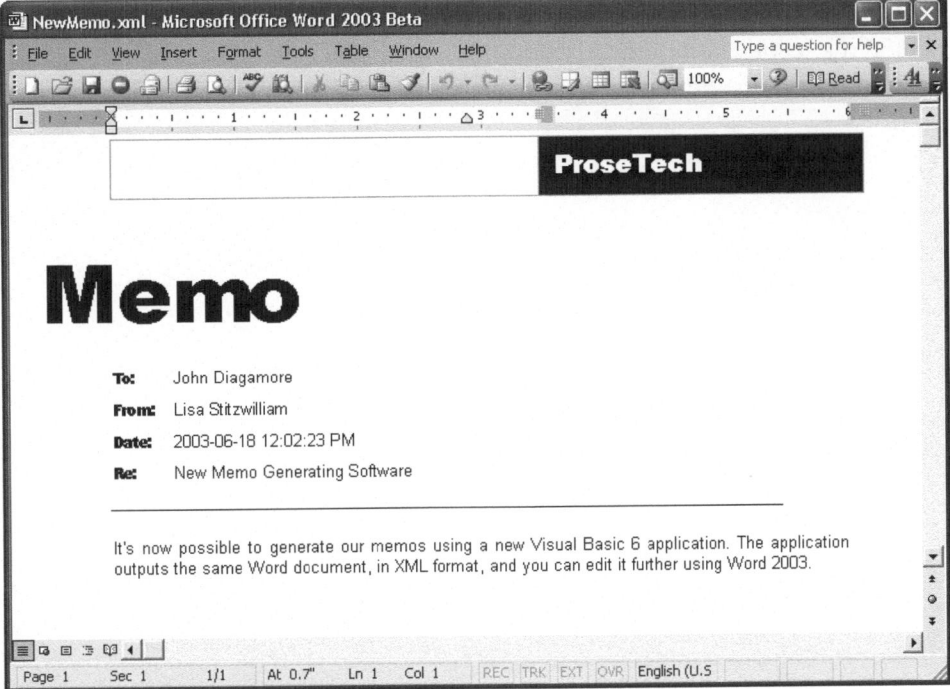

Figure 6-16. The generated memo

The Last Word

In this chapter you've seen a detailed look at the two Office XML formats—WordML and SpreadsheetML—and some of the ways that other applications can interact with these types of documents. But just how open are the Office XML formats? Clearly, they use XML, which makes them portable across platforms, applications, and businesses. However, although WordML and SpreadsheetML are based on XML, they are Microsoft-specific. No other software uses these formats natively, and they aren't easy to master. By comparison, OpenOffice.org, a Microsoft competitor, is working with the open source community to develop a truly standardized XML document format that it would use natively. OpenOffice doesn't currently include any sort of XML mapping features, but its use of native XML has broader support than SpreadsheetML or WordML. Only time will tell whether the Office XML formats will gain widespread use.

In any case, WordML and SpreadsheetML raise some interesting possibilities for businesses. If you're able to ignore older versions of Office, you can standardize on the XML Office formats, and gain easier access to features like data mining and programmatic document creation. Best of all, these features can be integrated behind the scenes, and they can work with native Office files. That means that the user won't need to understand anything about XML or even know that it's being used.

CHAPTER 7

Transforming XML

So **FAR, YOU'VE LEARNED** how you can extract XML data from the Office 2003 applications using XML mapping, exporting, and the custom WordML and SpreadsheetML languages. In this chapter, you'll see how you can take that XML a little further using another XML-based standard: Extensible Stylesheet Language Transformations (or XSLT).

XSLT is an XML-based language for creating stylesheets. *Stylesheets* are special documents that can be used (with the help of an XSLT processor) to convert your XML documents into other documents. For example, you can use an XSLT stylesheet to transform one type of XML to a different XML structure. Or, you could use a stylesheet to convert your data-only XML into one of the Office XML formats, or filter out just part of a WordML or SpreadsheetML document. XSLT stylesheets can also be used to transform XML documents into other types of text-based documents, like HTML pages. One of the most common uses of XSLT is to transform a data-only XML into a web page that you can serve directly to a browser, with little or no custom code. In this chapter, you'll see examples of all of these approaches.

> **TIP** *XSLT, like XML and XML Schema, is a W3C standard, and it isn't Microsoft-specific or Office-specific. While XSLT isn't required, it is useful in many Office 2003 scenarios, because it allows you to bridge the gaps between different types of XML. In that way, it often works like the "glue" between different XML-enabled applications.*

The XSL Standard

XSLT is actually part of a larger specification, called Extensible Stylesheet Language, or XSL. XSL was designed to allow XML documents to be transformed into presentation documents. As you learned in Chapter 1, XML doesn't include any display-related information—it's just a package for data. (In fact, even if you create an XML document that does include display-related information, you would need to create a custom application that reads this information and uses it to display the data. This is completely different from HTML, which is recognized natively by all Web browsers.)

XSL is intended to fill the gap between XML data and printed or onscreen documents. But as XSL was developed, it became clear that the standard was really dealing with more than one problem. In particular, the problem of changing XML into another form of text-based document is different from the challenge of creating a binary document with exact formatting specifications. For that reason, XSL was split into two pieces:

- XSLT, the focus of this chapter, is a language for transforming XML documents into other XML or text-based documents (provided they don't break the rules of valid XML).

- XSL Formatting Objects (XSL-FO) is a more complex standard for generating documents like PDFs or PostScript files based on XML content.

XSL-FO is the more complex piece, because formatted documents usually contain a great deal of intricate detail. For that reason, XSL-FO hasn't been adopted and integrated into other tools nearly as quickly as XSLT. XSL-FO also targets a more specific problem domain, whereas XSLT is a generic solution that is indispensable for many types of problems. None of the Office applications support XSL-FO directly. This chapter deals exclusively with XSLT.

Even though XSLT is more straightforward than XSL-FO, it's still a remarkably powerful and full-featured standard, and this chapter will only begin to touch on some of its more advanced features. An expert XSLT guru can create stylesheets that incorporate many of the elements of a programming language, such as conditional logic, loops, branching structures, and variables. On the other hand, even an XSLT novice can create a simple stylesheet that changes an XML document to a web page.

XSLT 1.0 was released in its final stage as a W3C recommendation in 1999. A second version, XSLT 2.0, is currently in a working draft stage, and hasn't been incorporated into many tools yet. You can read the current XSLT 1.0 specification at http://www.w3.org/TR/xslt, and you'll find information about the upcoming

XSLT 2.0 at http://www.w3.org/TR/xslt20. And for information about the whole XSL standard, which includes XSL-FO, try http://www.w3.org/TR/xsl.

The Role of XSLT

As you've seen in the previous chapter, once your data is in an XML format, there's no limit to what you can do with it in a custom application. For example, you can build an application in nearly any programming language that reads an XML document and writes the data to a different type of XML document or even an HTML file. The problem is that you need to write all the code on your own. And not only do you have to create this application from scratch, you'll also need to make sure you run it at the appropriate time (which might involve deploying the application to other computers), and you'll probably need to tweak the code or even create an entirely new application for each conversion task you want to perform. In other words, though you have unlimited flexibility with custom code and XML data, you'll need a developer with a lot of free time and a healthy degree of patience.

On the other hand, if you work with XSLT for these types of tasks, you can specify the rules for converting XML documents without writing any custom code. And though this approach is simpler, it isn't any less powerful. XSLT stylesheets have a wide range of abilities: They can select a portion of the source document, add new data to the source document, or change the structure of the overall document. They can even apply HTML tags to format the document as a web page.

Of course, all the XSLT stylesheet does is specify the *rules* for transforming one type of XML into another. In order to actually execute these rules on an XML document and create your new document, you'll need an XSLT processor. Figure 7-1 shows the role the XSLT processor plays. It's analogous to the role that an XML validating parser plays with a schema file.

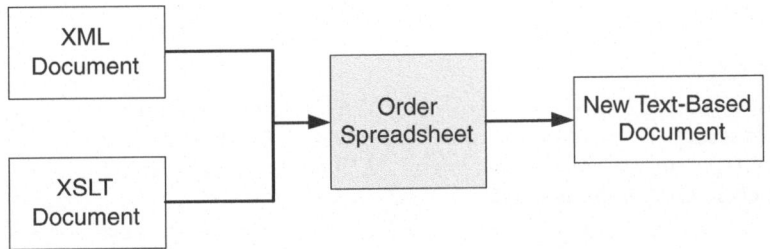

Figure 7-1. Using an XSLT to transform a document

With XML schema documents, you had several choices of XML validating readers. You can use the Office 2003 applications themselves, Internet Explorer (if the schema is linked to the XML document), or a stand-alone application. With XSLT, you have a similar choice of XSLT processors. You can use those built into Office, Internet Explorer (version 6.0 or later), or just about any programming platform.

XSLT Basics

An XSLT document (also known as a stylesheet) is made up of one or more *templates*. Each template describes the formatting for a portion of the XML document. For example, a template might describe how to transform a single element into the appropriate HTML markup.

To better understand XSLT, you'll need to consider a few simple sample documents. You'll study these in the next sections.

The Empty Stylesheet

XSLT, like XML Schema, is an XML-based language. This means that when you create an XSLT document, you are just creating a special type of XML document—one that uses a specific set of elements. These elements must be a part of the XSLT namespace http://www.w3.org/1999/XSL/Transform.

The root element of an XSLT document can be <stylesheet> or <transform>. Both are equivalent. Here is the simplest possible XSLT document:

```
<?xml version="1.0"?>
<xsl:stylesheet version="1.0" xmlns:xsl="http://www.w3.org/1999/XSL/Transform">
</xsl:stylesheet>
```

> **NOTE** *When using the XSLT namespace, you must also include the attribute version="1.0" to specify that you're using the first version of the XSLT standard. At the time of this writing, the second version of XSLT, which boasts a slew of minor refinements, hasn't been released.*

Inside the <stylesheet> element, you can place an <output> element that describes the type of document you want to create. The <output> element has a method attribute that can be set to text, html, or xml (the default). Depending on your choice, the XSLT processor will make some minor modifications to the final document. For example, in xml output mode, the XML declaration will automatically be added at the beginning of the document.

For this example, let's assume you don't intend to create a valid XML or HTML document, so you'll use text mode:

```
<?xml version="1.0"?>
<xsl:stylesheet version="1.0" xmlns:xsl="http://www.w3.org/1999/XSL/Transform">
    <xsl:output method="text"/>
</xsl:stylesheet>
```

This XSLT stylesheet contains no templates. You can actually learn a fair bit by applying this simple stylesheet to an XML document. To perform this test, you can use the TransformXML.exe utility included with the companion content for this book. Using this application, you simply need to select an XML file (which will usually have the extension .xml) and a schema file (which will usually have the extension .xsl or .xslt), and click Transform. The application will then display the new, transformed document. As with the other sample applications, this one is written using Visual Basic .NET code, and the source code is provided if you'd like to peer into the inner workings of XML programming.

To perform a simple test, use the QuotationList.xml file first presented in Chapter 2. Because the empty stylesheet doesn't provide any templates, the default template rules come into play. These rules instruct the XSLT processor to move through each element in the XML document, and extract the text of each node. The result is the mess of strung-together text shown in Figure 7-2.

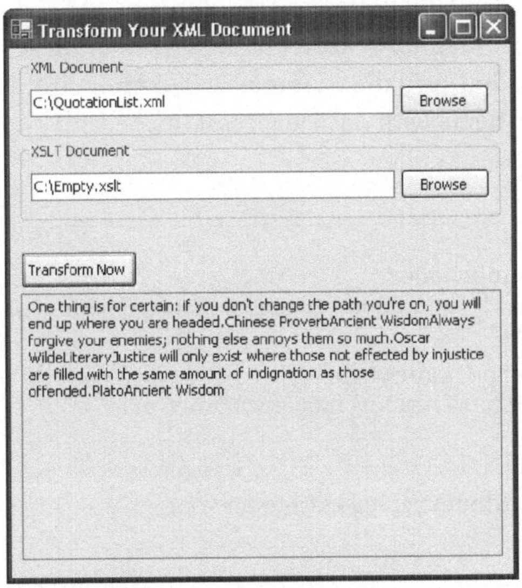

Figure 7-2. Applying the empty stylesheet with the XSLT test application

One of the most important facts you should notice about this example is that the default template rules are applied to every element. This means that the XSLT processor burrows through every level in your XML document as it applies templates.

Building Basic Templates

To craft a more useful stylesheet, you'll need to use templates and a related standard called XML Path Language (XPath). XPath is a syntax for identifying parts of an XML document. Each template in an XSLT document requires an XPath expression. The XSLT processor uses the expression to find the portion of the source document that the template should be applied to. In a sense, XPath is a little like the SELECT command database programmers use to query data from a table. When an XSLT processor applies a stylesheet, it simply moves through the collection of templates, applying them one after the other. Finally, it takes the resulting text and displays it on the screen or saves it to a new file, depending on the task you're performing.

XPath uses a path-like notation, which is similar to directory and filenames in Windows. For example, the path / identifies the root of an XML document, and /quotationList identifies the root <quotationList> elements. The path /quotationList/quotation selects every <quotation> element inside the <quotationList>. Finally, the period (.) always selects the current node. These ingredients are enough to build many basic templates, although the XPath standard also defines syntax for relative paths (which don't begin at the root of the document), and special selection criteria (which can filter out only the nodes you're interested in). Table 7-1 provides an overview of XPath characters. Don't try to absorb all of these at once—the XPath syntax is rich and detailed, and the examples will demonstrate how you can create a wide variety of stylesheets with basic expressions.

Table 7-1. Basic XPath Syntax

Expression	Meaning
/	Starts an absolute path from the root node. /quotationList/quotation selects all <quotation> elements that are children of the root <quotationList> element.
//	Starts a relative path that selects nodes anywhere. //quotation/text selects all the <text> elements that are children of a <quotation> element.
@	Selects an attribute of a node. /quotationList/@id selects the attribute named id from the root <quotationList> element.

(Continued)

Table 7-1. Basic XPath Syntax (Continued)

Expression	Meaning
*	Selects any element in the path. /quotationList/quotation/* selects all the nodes in the <quotation> element (which includes <text>, <source>, and <category> in this example).
|	Combines multiple paths. /quotationList/quotation/text|/quotationList/quotation/source selects both the <source> and <text> element in the <quotation> element.
.	Indicates the current (default) node.
..	Indicates the parent node. If the current node is <text>, then .. refers to the <quotation> node.
[]	Defines selection criteria that can test a contained node or attribute value. /quotationList/quotation[category='Ancient Wisdom'] selects <quotation> elements that contain a <category> element with the indicated value. /quotationList/quotation[@id='496'] selects the <quotation> elements with the indicated attribute value. You can use the and keyword to combine more than one criteria.
starts-with	This function retrieves elements based on what text a contained element starts with. /quotationList/quotation[starts-with(source, 'P')] finds all <quotation> elements that have a <source> element that contains text that starts with the letter P.
position	This function retrieves elements based on position. /quotationList/quotation[position ()=2] selects the second <quotation> element.
count	This function counts the number of elements with the matching name. count(quotation) returns 3, because the sample document has three quotations.

To create a template, you add a <template> element to the <stylesheet> element of your XSLT document. For example, consider the basic XSLT example shown here. It defines a single template, which is highlighted in bold.

```
<?xml version="1.0"?>
<xsl:stylesheet version="1.0" xmlns:xsl="http://www.w3.org/1999/XSL/Transform">
    <xsl:output method="text"/>
    <xsl:template match="/quotationList">
     This is a match!
    </xsl:template>
</xsl:stylesheet>
```

The <template> element requires an attribute named match, which provides the XPath expression that identifies the portion of the source document it should match. The template in this document uses the path /quotationList to match a root element named <quotationList>.

Inside the template, you enter the output that you want placed in the new, transformed document. This content can include text, XML elements, or special XSLT commands that copy text and attribute values from the source document.

When you apply this stylesheet to the quotation list, this is the transformed document you'll see:

```
This is a match!
```

To produce this document, the XSLT processor takes three steps:

1. It loads the XSLT stylesheet and source document into memory.

2. It begins moving through the elements in the source document. It matches the first element, <quotationList>, with the template you provided.

3. It follows the instructions in the template, which are to output a string of predefined text. At this point, its work is complete.

You might be wondering what happens to all the other nodes in the XML document. Shouldn't the default template rules ensure that their content is copied into the target document? In fact, the default template rules never come into play, because the XSLT processor successfully matches the first node it finds, which is the root node. The root node template doesn't indicate that the XSLT processor should consider nested nodes, so the rest of the document is ignored.

The situation would be different if you didn't provide a template for the root node. For example, consider the following XSLT stylesheet, which matches the <text> node:

```
<?xml version="1.0"?>
<xsl:stylesheet version="1.0" xmlns:xsl="http://www.w3.org/1999/XSL/Transform">
    <xsl:output method="text"/>
    <xsl:template match="/quotationList/quotation/text">
    [This is the quotation text.]
    </xsl:template>
</xsl:stylesheet>
```

Now the transformed document contains both the substitution text for the <text> element, and the plain text content for all the other nodes:

```
[This is the quotation text.]
Chinese ProverbAncient Wisdom
 This is the quotation text.
Oscar WildeLiterary
[This is the quotation text.]
PlatoAncient Wisdom
```

To understand why this happens, you need to consider how the XSLT processor works with the document. Here are the steps it takes:

1. It loads the XSLT stylesheet and source document into memory.

2. It begins moving through the elements in the source document. It can't match the root element, <quotationList>, so it uses the default template rules, which are to scan every contained element.

3. The XSLT processor moves to the <text> element, finds the matching template, and then outputs the template content. If there were any elements contained inside the <text> element, it would ignore them.

4. The XSLT processor moves to the <source> element. It doesn't find any matching template, so it uses the default rules, outputting the contained text and processing any contained elements.

5. The XSLT processor repeats the same process for the <category> element.

If you wanted to control the processing of each element, you'd need to create three templates, as shown in the following stylesheet. This example is provided in the companion content as ThreeTemplates.xslt.

```
<?xml version="1.0"?>
<xsl:stylesheet version="1.0" xmlns:xsl="http://www.w3.org/1999/XSL/Transform">
    <xsl:output method="text"/>
    <xsl:template match="text">
    [Text]</xsl:template>
    <xsl:template match="source">
    [Source]</xsl:template>
    <xsl:template match="category">
    [Category]</xsl:template>
</xsl:stylesheet>
```

Note that this stylesheet doesn't use fully qualified paths to match the elements. For example, it uses text instead of /quotationList/quotation/text. This means that the text template will match all <text> elements, no matter where they appear in the source document. Because the <quotationList> doesn't have any elements with the same name in different locations, this shortcut makes sense, although it's entirely optional.

The transformed document looks like this:

```
[Text]
[Source]
[Category]
[Text]
[Source]
[Category]
[Text]
[Source]
[Category]
```

> **TIP** *Whitespace is important in a template. Every space and hard return that you include in the <template> element will be copied to the target document when the template is matched.*

In many cases, you'll want to control the XSLT processing more carefully, preventing some nodes from being used, or influencing the order in which they are read. We'll consider how to solve this problem shortly—but first, it's important to consider how you can create a template that copies the content from your source document, instead of just static text.

Copying Node Values

Usually, templates will contain a mix of text or markup along with the content from the source document. In order to insert a value from the source document, you use the <value-of> element. The <value-of> element includes a select attribute, which contains an XPath expression identifying the node that has the text you want to extract. If you want the value from the current node, you can simply use the period (.) special character, as shown in this stylesheet:

```
<?xml version="1.0"?>
<xsl:stylesheet version="1.0" xmlns:xsl="http://www.w3.org/1999/XSL/Transform">
   <xsl:output method="text"/>
   <xsl:template match="text">
     TEXT: <xsl:value-of select="."/>
   </xsl:template>
   <xsl:template match="source">
     SOURCE: <xsl:value-of select="."/>
   </xsl:template>
   <xsl:template match="category">
     CATEGORY: <xsl:value-of select="."/>
   </xsl:template>
</xsl:stylesheet>
```

This stylesheet is provided with the companion content as ValueOf.xslt. When you use it with the QuotationList.xml file, it produces the following transformed document, which combines headings and the original text from the source document:

```
    TEXT: One thing is for certain: if you don't change the path you're on, you
will end up where you are headed.
    SOURCE: Chinese Proverb
    CATEGORY: Ancient Wisdom
    TEXT: Always forgive your enemies; nothing else annoys them so much.
    SOURCE: Oscar Wilde
    CATEGORY: Literary
    TEXT: Justice will only exist where those not affected by injustice are filled
with the same amount of indignation as those offended.
    SOURCE: Plato
    CATEGORY: Ancient Wisdom
```

As with most things in XML, there is more than one way to copy values from the source document. Instead of individually matching the <text>, <source>, and <category> elements, you can simply match the <quotation> element that contains them. You can then copy the values from the nested elements in any order you choose. The following stylesheet uses this technique to create a list of quotations with just the source and category information:

```
<?xml version="1.0"?>
<xsl:stylesheet version="1.0" xmlns:xsl="http://www.w3.org/1999/XSL/Transform">
   <xsl:output method="text"/>
   <xsl:template match="quotation">
     Matched 1 <xsl:value-of select="category"/> quotation from category
<xsl:value-of select="source"/>
   </xsl:template>
</xsl:stylesheet>
```

Here's the transformed document:

```
Matched 1 Ancient Wisdom quotation from category Chinese Proverb
Matched 1 Literary quotation from category Oscar Wilde
Matched 1 Ancient Wisdom quotation from category Plato
```

> **NOTE** *<value-of> is only one of many elements that are defined in the XSLT language and can be used in templates. Other elements allow you to perform conditional logic, execute loops, apply sorting and grouping, and much more. We won't consider advanced XSLT in this book, although if you're interested you can refer to a comprehensive book like* XSLT *by Doug Tidwell (O'Reilly & Associates, 2001).*

Applying Templates

By default, the XSLT processor reads the source XML document from top to bottom, starting with the root node. Templates are applied as matching nodes are found. But what happens if you want to change the order that a document is processed? Perhaps you want to place some information from the end of the source document at the start of the new document, or maybe you want to prevent certain elements from being processed at all.

In XSLT, the <apply-templates> element lets you control processing order. It takes a select attribute with an XPath expression that identifies the portion of the document that should be processed next. As an example, consider the ValueOf.xlst stylesheet shown earlier. It provided separate templates that matched the <text>, <source>, and <category> elements. If you wanted to alter the order in which these elements are processed, you could create a template that matched the <quotation> element. This template could then use <apply-template> to control how the contained elements are processed. In the following rewritten example, the order is <source>, <category>, <text>. This stylesheet is provided with the companion content as ApplyTemplates.xslt.

```
<?xml version="1.0"?>
<xsl:stylesheet version="1.0" xmlns:xsl="http://www.w3.org/1999/XSL/Transform">
    <xsl:output method="text"/>

    <xsl:template match="quotationList/quotation">
        <xsl:apply-templates select="source"/>
        <xsl:apply-templates select="category"/>
        <xsl:apply-templates select="text"/>
    </xsl:template>
```

```
  <xsl:template match="text">
    TEXT: <xsl:value-of select="."/>
  </xsl:template>
  <xsl:template match="source">
    SOURCE: <xsl:value-of select="."/>
  </xsl:template>
  <xsl:template match="category">
    CATEGORY: <xsl:value-of select="."/>
  </xsl:template>
</xsl:stylesheet>
```

In this case, the output looks the same as before, only now the order of content in the output document doesn't match the order of content in the source document. Interestingly, if you want to leave out one of these elements, just remove the corresponding <apply-templates> statement. Remember, once the XSLT processor matches an element, it won't process any child elements unless you explicitly instruct it to with an <apply-templates> command.

> **TIP** *You could perform a similar reordering just by writing a <quotation> template that includes several embedded <value-of> tags, as shown earlier. As with XML schemas, it's completely up to you whether you want to break down your XSLT stylesheet into several smaller templates and use <apply-templates> to control the processing order, or write larger templates that incorporate multiple values using <value-of>.*

With a few slight changes, you can completely alter the way the stylesheet works. Consider the next example, which matches the root node, and then applies the template to the contained <source> and <category> nodes. It also uses the XPath count() function to count the number of <quotation> elements in the document.

```
<?xml version="1.0"?>
<xsl:stylesheet version="1.0" xmlns:xsl="http://www.w3.org/1999/XSL/Transform">
  <xsl:output method="text"/>

  <xsl:template match="quotationList">
    There are <xsl:value-of select="count(quotation)"/> quotations.

    Sources include: <xsl:apply-templates select="quotation/source"/>

    Categories include: <xsl:apply-templates select="quotation/category"/>
  </xsl:template>
```

```
<xsl:template match="source">
    * <xsl:value-of select="."/></xsl:template>
<xsl:template match="category">
    * <xsl:value-of select="."/></xsl:template>
</xsl:stylesheet>
```

> **TIP** *XPath includes a number of useful functions that you can use to perform various types of calculations. You can find a quick reference that lists these built-in functions at http://www.w3schools.com/xpath/xpath_functions.asp.*

In this example, the source from every quotation is extracted first, and then the category of every quotation is extracted. The reordered document is shown here:

```
There are 3 quotations.

Sources include:
    * Chinese Proverb
    * Oscar Wilde
    * Plato

Categories include:
    * Ancient Wisdom
    * Literary
    * Ancient Wisdom
```

Now that you understand how node processing works, you can better understand the default processing rules. Every time an element is found that doesn't have a matching template, the XSLT processor uses the following template:

```
<xsl:template match="*|/">
    <xsl:apply-templates/>
</xsl:template>
```

This template specifically matches the root node (with the /) or any other node (with the * wildcard). These two conditions are combined using the special pipe (|) character, which means "or." This template simply uses <apply-templates> to process all the contained elements.

If the XSLT processor encounters a node with text content or attributes, it uses the following template, which uses <value-of> to copy any text or attribute values (but not names) to the transformed document.

```
<xsl:template match="text( )|@*">
    <xsl:value-of select="."/>
</xsl:template>
```

When you create templates for elements, you override these rules by substituting your own.

Conditional Templates

Using the <apply-templates> tag also allows you to selectively filter the content you want to use. You do this by using the square brackets, [ ], to define selection criteria. For example, the following <apply-templates> tag instructs XSLT to process the <quotation> element, provided the nested <category> element contains the text "Ancient Wisdom".

```
<xsl:apply-templates select="quotation[category='Ancient Wisdom']"/>
```

You could use this template in a stylesheet that only displays the quotations in this category:

```
<?xml version="1.0"?>
<xsl:stylesheet version="1.0" xmlns:xsl="http://www.w3.org/1999/XSL/Transform">
    <xsl:output method="text"/>
    <xsl:template match="quotationList">
        <xsl:apply-templates select="quotation[category='Ancient Wisdom']"/>
    </xsl:template>
    <xsl:template match="quotation">
      "<xsl:value-of select="text"/>" (<xsl:value-of select="source"/>)
    </xsl:template>
</xsl:stylesheet>
```

The transformed document would contain the text of only two quotations, instead of the full three:

```
    "One thing is for certain: if you don't change the path you're on, you will
end up where you are headed." (Chinese Proverb)

    "Justice will only exist where those not affected by injustice are filled with
the same amount of indignation as those offended." (Plato)
```

229

XSLT and Namespaces

It's almost as easy to use XSLT with namespaces as without. The only difference is that when you want to use XML documents that use namespaces, you must define the namespace in your stylesheet, and you must make sure your templates use the namespace prefix when selecting or matching nodes. For example, if the QuotationList.xml file uses the namespace http://www.prosetech.com/Quotations, you would first define this namespace at the beginning of the XSLT document and assign a prefix:

```
<xsl:stylesheet version="1.0" xmlns:xsl="http://www.w3.org/1999/XSL/Transform"
 xmlns:quote=" http://www.prosetech.com/Quotations">
```

You would then use it whenever you include an XPath expression:

```
<xsl:template match="quote:quotation">
    "<xsl:value-of select="quote:text"/>" (<xsl:value-of select="quote:source"/>)
</xsl:template>
```

As is always the case with XML, elements are treated as though they are completely different if they are in separate namespaces, even if they share the same element name.

This rounds out this chapter's discussion of XSLT basics. In the following sections, you'll learn about a few practical ways to use stylesheets.

Converting XML to HTML

So far, all the examples have created simple text documents. A more common use of XSLT is to generate a new XML document, or an HTML document for a web page. In this case, the basic concepts are the same—the only difference is the content you place in each of your templates.

For example, every HTML document starts with the tag <html> and ends with </html>. Formatting is described using additional tags, like <p> for paragraph, <br> for a line break, and <h1>, <h2>, and <h3> for various heading styles.

The first step when creating an XSLT for transforming XML into HTML is to change the <output> element to html mode, as shown here:

```
<xsl:output method="html"/>
```

Next, you should create a template that matches the root element. This template will contain all the HTML markup for starting the document, followed by one or more <apply-template> instructions, and finally the HTML markup for ending the document.

```
<xsl:template match="quotationList">
    <html>
    <head><title>Quotation List</title></head>
    <body>
        <ul>
            <xsl:apply-templates select="quotation"/>
        </ul>
    </body>
    </html>
</xsl:template>
```

This template matches the root element, starts the document, defines the title (which will appear in the caption of the Internet Explorer window), starts a new bulleted list with the <ul> tag, and then applies templates to all nested <quotation> elements. Each <quotation> is converted to a separate HTML bulleted item with this template:

```
<xsl:template match="quotation">
    <li>"<xsl:value-of select="text"/>" <i>
(<xsl:value-of select="source"/>)</i></li>
</xsl:template>
```

The transformed HTML document is shown here:

```
<html>
  <head>
    <title>Quotation List</title>
  </head>
  <body>
    <ul>
      <li>"One thing is for certain: if you don't change the path you're on, you
will end up where you are headed." <i>(Chinese Proverb)</i></li>
      <li>"Always forgive your enemies; nothing else annoys them so much."
<i>(Oscar Wilde)</i></li>
      <li>"Justice will only exist where those not affected by injustice are filled
with the same amount of indignation as those offended." <i>(Plato)</i></li>
    </ul>
  </body>
</html>
```

To get a better idea of what this amounts to, it helps to view this HTML in an Internet browser. If you are using version 6 or later of Internet Explorer or Netscape, you can perform this transformation using a linked XSLT file. Simply add the following processing instruction to the QuoteList.xml document, immediately after the XML declaration:

```
<?xml-stylesheet type="text/xsl" href="HTMLQuotationList.xslt"?>
```

This tag identifies the XSLT document that should be used to display the XML document. As long as it's in the same directory, Internet Explorer will find and apply it automatically when you open the XML document. The result is shown in Figure 7-3. To try out this example, look for the HTMLQuotationList.xml file with the companion content for this chapter.

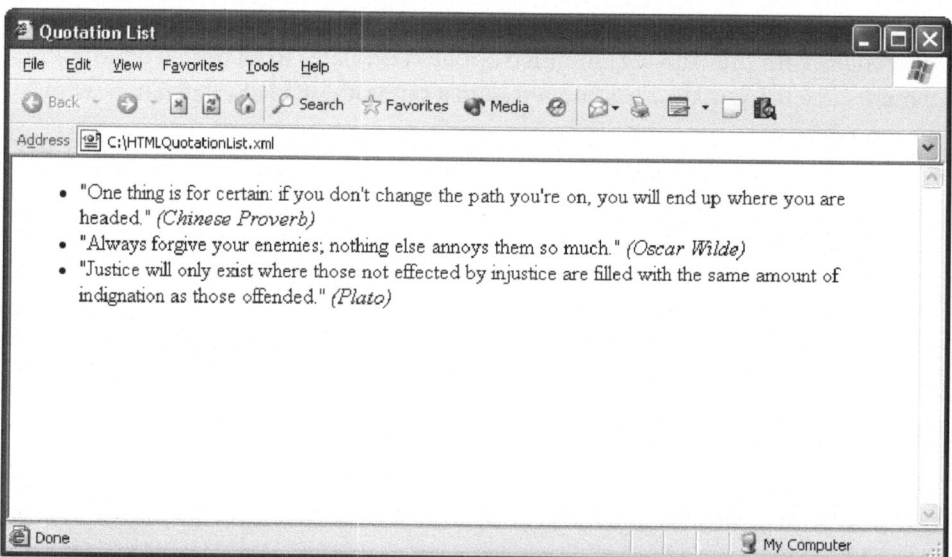

Figure 7-3. Applying a transformation to HTML in the browser

Templates for generating XML can sometimes be difficult to follow, because they blend elements from the XSLT language with HTML tags. This is allowed because the XSLT processor ignores any tags that aren't in the XSLT namespace. It simply copies these tags from the template into the new document. However, your XSLT document can't contain any combination of tags that would be considered invalid. For example, you can't open an HTML tag in one template and expect to close it in another template—this would leave you with incorrectly nested tags, and the XSLT processor would refuse to read your stylesheet. Similarly, you can't include a start tag that doesn't have a matching end tag. This even applies to

HTML tags like <br> and <img>, which are commonly used without closing tags. In an XSLT template, these tags must be written in true XML style as empty tags, such as <br /> and <img />, or
</br> and <img></img>. Interestingly enough, the XSLT processor will actually convert these XML tags back into their HTML versions, provided you have set the output method to html.

```
<xsl:output method="html"/>
```

Thus, this template:

```
<xsl:template match="quotation">
    "<xsl:value-of select="text"/>" <br/>
</xsl:template>
```

generates this output:

```
"One thing is for certain ..." <br>
```

This ensures compatibility with browsers that may not accept the empty element syntax.

Transforming XML to HTML raises some interesting possibilities. For example, you can use Word or Excel to map a rich Office document, take the exported XML, and then display it on a web page without needing to write a specialized application. Best of all, you only need to write one XSLT stylesheet for each document type. For example, if you wanted to display Word memo documents, you could create a memo XSLT, and use it with the exported XML from any Word memo. You'll see XSLT used in a situation like this in the next chapter.

HTML and Tables

When converting XML to HTML, it's often important to present the document content in an HTML table. This isn't particularly difficult—in fact, you simply need to follow the principles explained earlier.

In this example, you'll work with the product catalog shown here:

```
<?xml version="1.0" ?>
<?xml-stylesheet type="text/xsl" href="HTMLProductCatalog.xslt"?>
<productCatalog>
    <catalogName>Acme Fall 2003 Catalog</catalogName>
    <expiryDate>2004-01-01</expiryDate>
```

```
    <products>
        <product id="1001">
            <productName>Magic Ring</productName>
            <productPrice>342.10</productPrice>
            <inStock>true</inStock>
        </product>
        <product id="1002">
            <productName>Flying Carpet</productName>
            <productPrice>982.99</productPrice>
            <inStock>true</inStock>
        </product>
        <product id="1003">
            <productName>Genie Lamp</productName>
            <productPrice>82.99</productPrice>
            <inStock>false</inStock>
        </product>
    </products>
</productCatalog>
```

This XML document contains three products, and references a stylesheet named HTMLProductCatalog.xslt. This stylesheet uses the catalog name as the title, and formats the products into a table using the table tags <table>, <tr> (table row), and <td> (table cell). In addition, this stylesheet demonstrates how to rearrange the order in which elements are processed (by tacking the expiry date onto the end of the page), and even includes a tiny piece of conditional logic with the help of the XSLT <if> element. To help you see the structure, the XSLT elements are highlighted, while the HTML elements that are a part of each template are not.

```
<?xml version="1.0"?>
<xsl:stylesheet version="1.0" xmlns:xsl="http://www.w3.org/1999/XSL/Transform">
    <xsl:output method="html"/>
    <xsl:template match="productCatalog">
        <html>
        <head><title>ProductCatalog</title></head>
        <body>
            <xsl:apply-templates select="catalogName"/>
            <table border="1" cellpadding="2" width="100%">
                <xsl:apply-templates select="products/product"/>
            </table>
            <xsl:apply-templates select="expiryDate"/>
        </body>
        </html>
    </xsl:template>
```

```
<xsl:template match="catalogName">
  <h2><xsl:value-of select="."/></h2>
</xsl:template>

<xsl:template match="product">
    <tr>
        <td><xsl:value-of select="@id"/></td>
        <td><xsl:value-of select="productName"/></td>
        <td>$<xsl:value-of select="productPrice"/></td>
        <td> <xsl:if test="inStock='false'">
            <font color="#FF0000">Sold out!</font>
        </xsl:if></td>
    </tr>
</xsl:template>

<xsl:template match="expiryDate">
  <br/><h5><i>expires <xsl:value-of select="."/></i></h5>
</xsl:template>
</xsl:stylesheet>
```

Figure 7-4 shows the transformed price list.

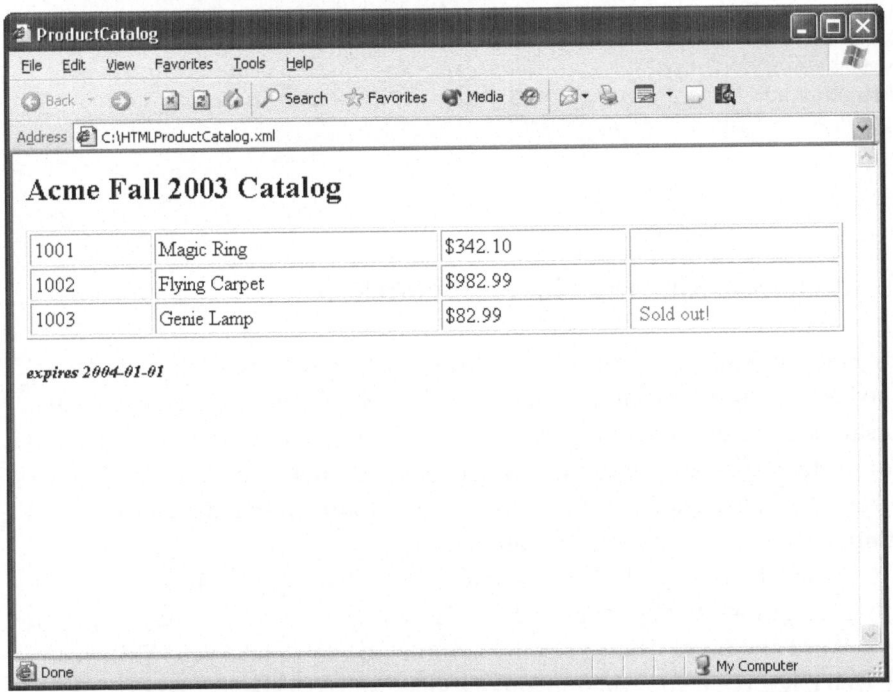

Figure 7-4. Transforming XML into an HTML table

To try out this example, look for the HTMLProductCatalog.xml file with the companion content for this chapter. Because this file includes the <?xml-stylesheet?> processing instruction, you can open it directly with Internet Explorer 6.

Changing the Structure of XML

Another common use of XSLT is to convert the structure of an XML document. Often, this modification is used to change a document in one markup into the markup required by a different application or business. This process of transformation is handled in exactly the same way as the XML-to-HTML conversion, except instead of using HTML elements, you use the elements from the new markup. In addition, you should specify XML mode using the <output> element, which ensures that the XML declaration will be added at the beginning of the generated document.

This kind of transformation can get tricky, particularly if you need to group elements, change nested relationships, combine more than one document, or alter the actual element content. However, once the XSLT is perfected, it can be reused in countless situations.

> **TIP** *You can use XSLT to overcome some of the XML limitations in programs like Excel, Word, and Access. For example, consider Access, which always forces you to use its default document structure when exporting XML. You could convert the XML generated by Access into the XML you really want using a custom XSLT stylesheet.*

XSLT with WordML and SpreadsheetML

Unless you're an XML guru, you've probably had enough of creating your own XSLT stylesheets by this point. The richness of the XSLT markup language means that creating a complex document can feel like writing a computer program, and it isn't for the faint of heart. Now that you've embraced Microsoft Office 2003 and its support for XML, you expect to have easy access to some premade XSLT files that will simplify your life. So does Microsoft deliver?

The answer is yes—partly. Unfortunately, Office 2003 doesn't have any fancy tools that can automatically generate XSLT files based on the XML mappings you create in Word and Excel. There's also no automated way to take your XML to an HTML web page. What you will find are prebuilt XSLT stylesheets that can extract

Word-specific and Excel-specific information from WordML and SpreadsheetML documents. But in order to get these stylesheets, you'll need to do a little extra work. They aren't included with the core Office 2003 CDs (or DVD)—instead, they must be downloaded from Microsoft's web site at http://msdn.microsoft.com/ downloads/list/office2k3.asp. Search for the Microsoft Word XML Content Development Kit (CDK), which includes application samples, the WordML schema, and XSLT files that can be used for both Word and Excel. Or, if you don't want to go to all this trouble, you'll find some of the same XSLT files in the companion content for this chapter, in the directory OfficeXSLT. You'll also find the all-purpose Word2HTML.xslt stylesheet, which can convert most basic WordML documents into read-only HTML web pages for online viewing.

> **TIP** *If you're brave, try examining the XSLT code in these Office stylesheets. Some are extremely complex, making use of not only advanced HTML, but also intricate conditional XSLT tags.*

Office and XSLT

Each Office XSLT stylesheet outputs a HTML document. The difference is what that document contains. Most stylesheets will display meta information about the document, such as when it was created, what formatting was used, and what comments are marked. Other stylesheets can extract the actual document content.

Table 7-2 lists some of the most useful Office XSLT stylesheets, and describes what they do.

Table 7-2. Prebuilt Office XSLT Stylesheets

XSLT	Document Type	Description
Word2HTML.xslt	Word	Displays an entire Word document as a rich web page
wdBookmarks.xslt	Word	Displays a table that lists the bookmarks you've placed in the document
wdBuiltInDocProps.xslt/ xlBuiltInDocProps.xslt	Word/Excel	Displays a table that lists some basic document metadata, including the title and author, and the subject, manager, company, and category (if these are defined)
wdComments.xslt/ xlComments.xslt	Word/Excel	Displays a table that lists all the comments in the document, along with their creation date and author (The text on which the comment is applied isn't indicated.)

(Continued)

Table 7-2. Prebuilt Office XSLT Stylesheets (Continued)

XSLT	Document Type	Description
wdCustomDocProps.xslt/ xlCustomDocProps.xslt	Word/Excel	Displays a table that lists any custom document properties that have been defined for the document
wdStatistics.xslt	Word	Displays a table that lists the core document statistics, like page, word, paragraph, line, and character counts, and basic information about the author, template, and total editing time
wdStyles.xslt	Word	Displays a table that lists all the styles defined in the document, and indicates the font used by each one
xlNames.xslt	Excel	Displays a table that lists the named ranges defined in the spreadsheet

If you are programming a custom application, you'll probably use a built-in XSLT processor to apply these stylesheets. This technique is shown with a dynamic web page in the next chapter. If you aren't creating an application, the easiest way to test these stylesheets is to add the <?xml-stylesheet?> processing instruction that was described earlier. For example, to link a document to the Word2HTML.xslt transform, place the file in the same directory as the document, and add the following processing instruction to your WordML file:

```
<?xml-stylesheet type="text/xsl" href="Word2Html.xslt"?>
```

And then delete or comment out the <?mso-application?> processing instruction that tells Word or Excel to load the document:

```
<!-- <?mso-application progid="Word.Document"?> -->
```

You can now double-click to load the document into Internet Explorer. As an example, consider the simple Word document shown in Figure 7-5.

Using the WordML to HTML stylesheet (Word2HTML.xslt), you can convert this document to the impressive graphical web page shown in Figure 7-6. Internet Explorer even displays the comment text in a pop-up, floating window.

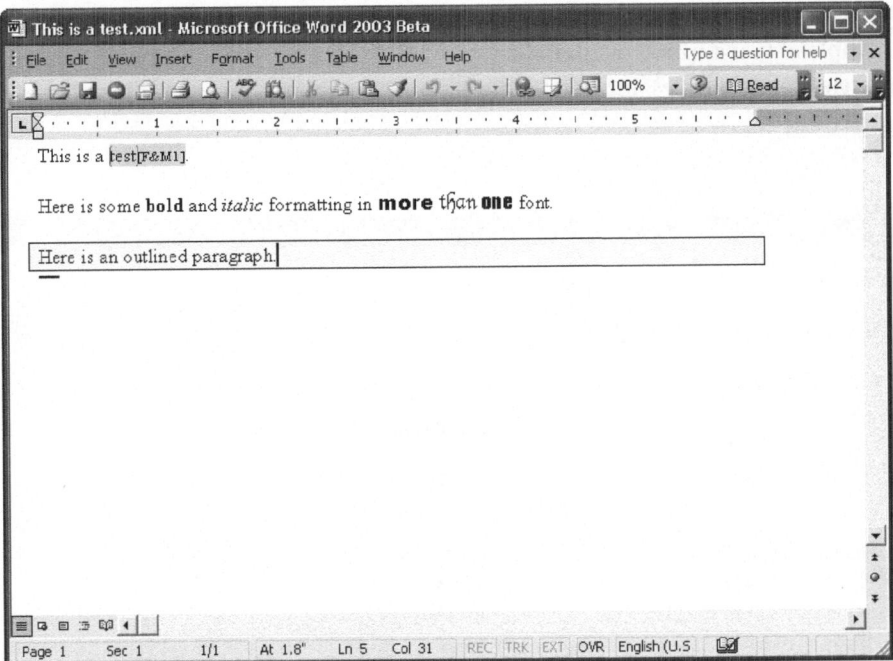

Figure 7-5. A basic Word document

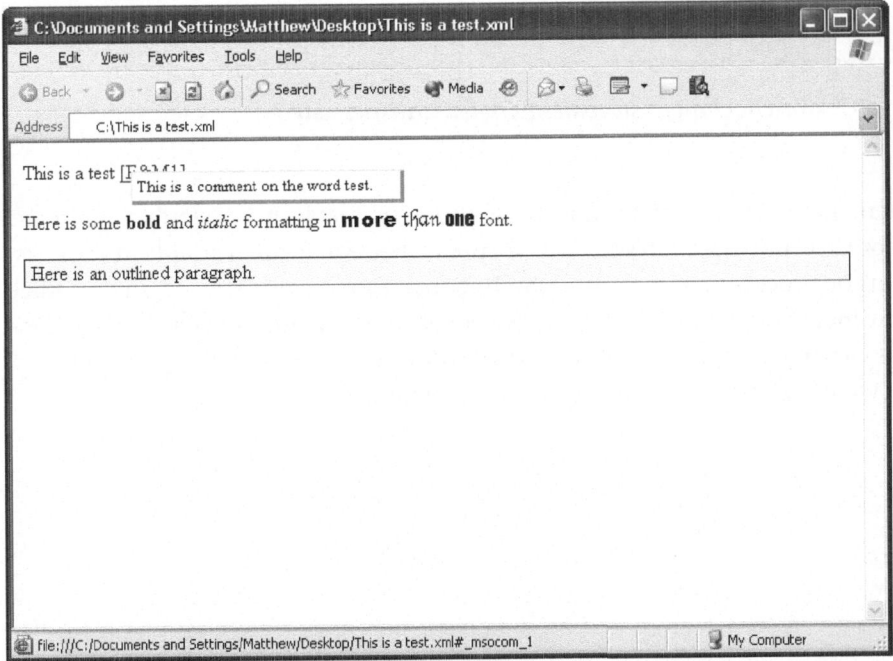

Figure 7-6. The basic Word document transformed by Word2HTML

To extract document metadata, you would use one of the other XSLT files. For example, if you applied wdStatistics.xslt to the same file (by modifying the <?xml-stylesheet?> processing instruction), you'd see the formatted table shown in Figure 7-7.

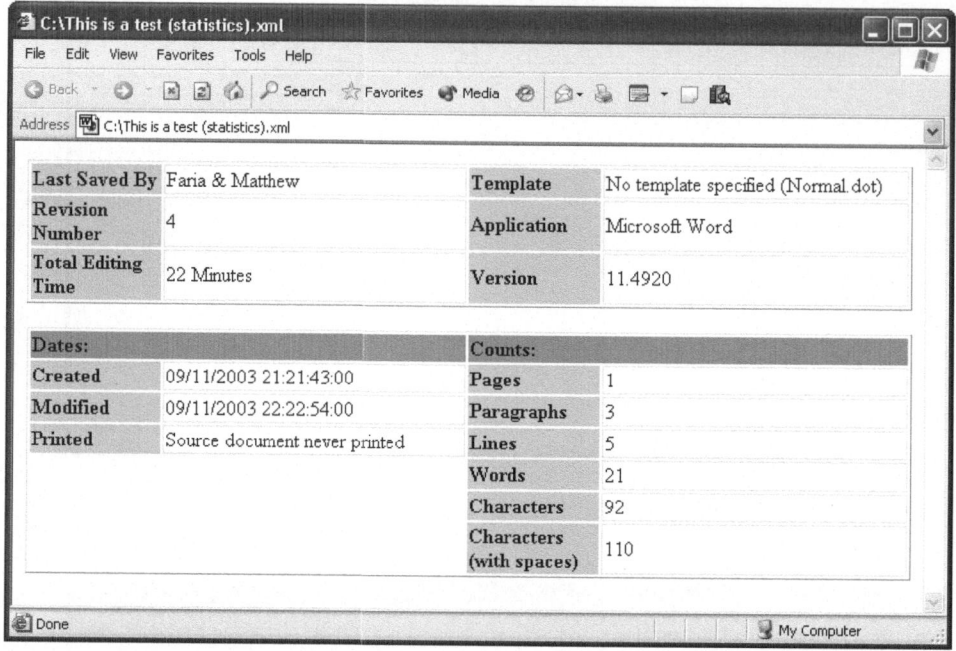

Figure 7-7. Word document statistics with wdStatistics.xslt

Remember, in order to be able to use these XSLT stylesheets, you'll require the Word or Excel document in WordML or SpreadsheetML form. A simple .doc or .xls file can't be processed in the same way. But once you've standardized on the Office XML formats, you'll find many XSLT stylesheets that can automate all sorts of document viewing tasks. In fact, third-party vendors are likely to develop and sell their own transformations for specific document tasks.

XSLT in Word

The XSLT experiments performed so far in this chapter have taken place outside of the Office applications. Even though Microsoft pledges a strong support for XSLT, it isn't closely integrated into the front end of most of the Office applications. The exception is Word, which provides the ability to apply an XSLT stylesheet when opening, saving, or previewing a document.

To apply a stylesheet when opening a document, highlight the document in the Open dialog box, and then click the arrow on the right-side of the Open button. This shows a drop-down menu that includes as one of its options "Open with Transform" (see Figure 7-8).

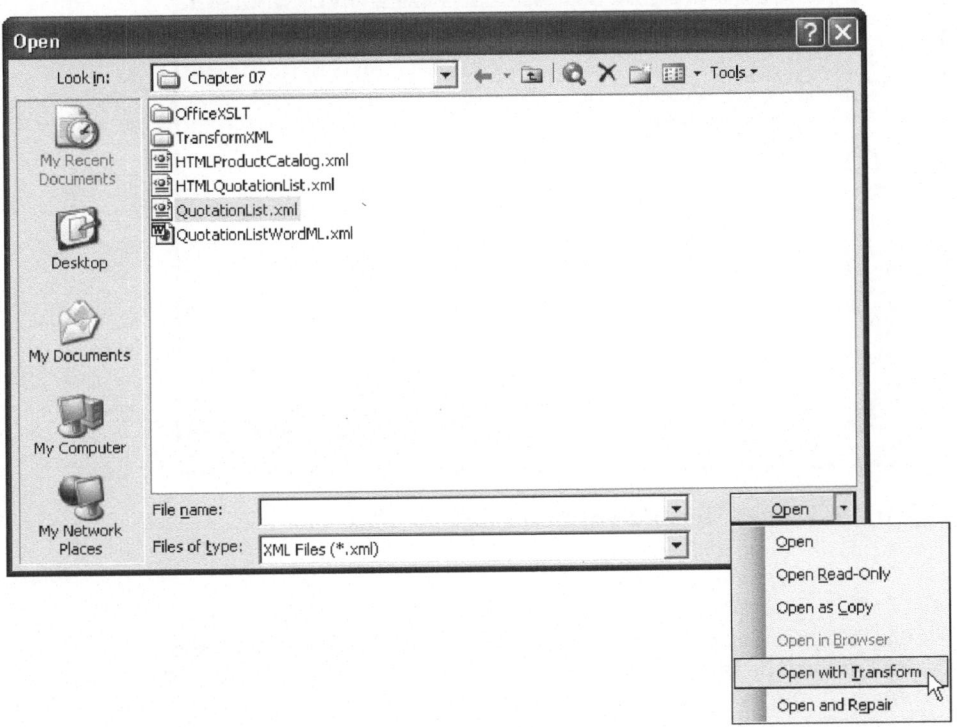

Figure 7-8. Opening a Word document through an XSLT

If you select this item, a second Open dialog box will appear through which you can select the XSLT you want to use. Word will then apply the stylesheet, and attempt to open the resulting document. For example, if the resulting document is another XML document, it will be opened in text mode. If the resulting document is an HTML page, Word will open it in web layout view.

When saving an XML document, you have the ability to apply a transformation before the document is written. Simply ensure that the "Apply transform" checkbox is selected in the Save As dialog box, as shown in Figure 7-9, and then click the Transform button to select the XSLT file. You can apply the transform to the WordML file or the data-only view.

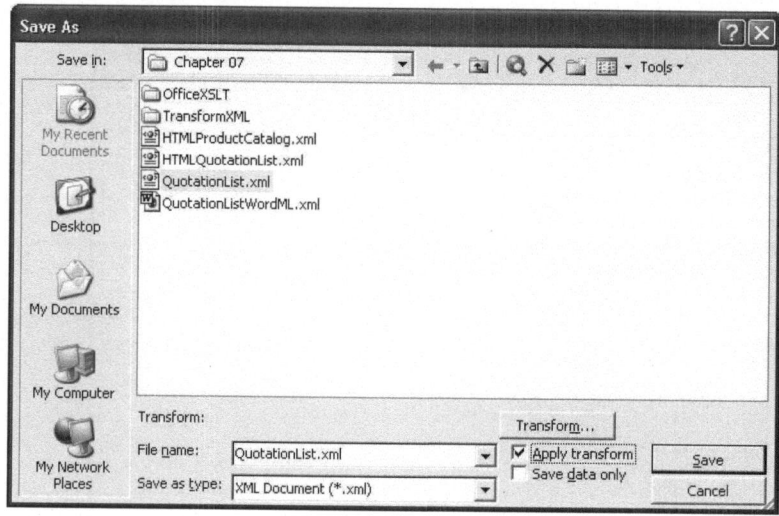

Figure 7-9. Saving a Word document through an XSLT

CAUTION *Remember, when you apply an XSLT you're changing the document, and potentially losing some of its original information. If you save or open a document through a transformation, be careful not to overwrite the original, as you'll probably lose some important information.*

More interestingly, you can use XSLT stylesheets as a special type of Word template. The idea is that an organization might create one or more XSLT stylesheets that can transform your custom XML markup into different types of formatted WordML. You can attach these stylesheets to your document by adding them to

Word's schema library, and then use them to preview how your custom XML can be formatted. This approach requires someone to develop the custom XSLT stylesheets for generating the WordML, which may be quite tedious. However, once the investment is made, you're able to further close the gap between your custom XML and WordML.

To try out this technique, you can use the data-only Memo.xml file created in Chapter 4. The Word XML Content Development Kit provides three XSLT stylesheets that can format the mapped memo using the WordML tags explored in Chapter 6. These stylesheets, named contemporary.xslt, elegant.xslt, and professional.xslt, are included with the companion content for this chapter in the Memo directory. To use them, follow these steps:

1. Choose Tools ➤ Templates and Add-Ins from the menu, and select the XML Schema tab.

2. On the XML Schema tab, click the Schema Library button.

3. Select the Memo schema in the library (urn:schemas-microsoft-com.office.demos.memo).

4. Make sure that Word is selected in the "Use solution with" drop-down box. Click the Add Solution button.

5. Browse to the location where the stylesheets are stored. You can find them in the Chapter 07\Memo directory with the companion content. Select the first file (contemporary.xslt), and click Open.

6. When prompted, enter a descriptive name for the stylesheet you're adding (see Figure 7-10). For example, use the word "Contemporary".

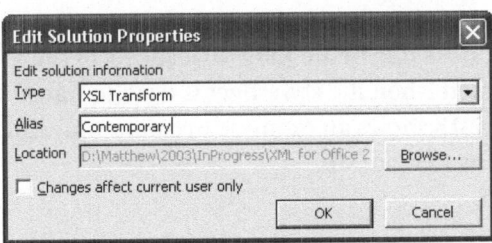

Figure 7-10. Adding an XSLT to the schema library

7. Repeat steps 4, 5, and 6 to add the elegant.xslt and professional.xslt stylesheets. You should now see all the transformations listed in the solution list box, as shown in Figure 7-11. You can also specify the default stylesheet that should be used with this XML markup.

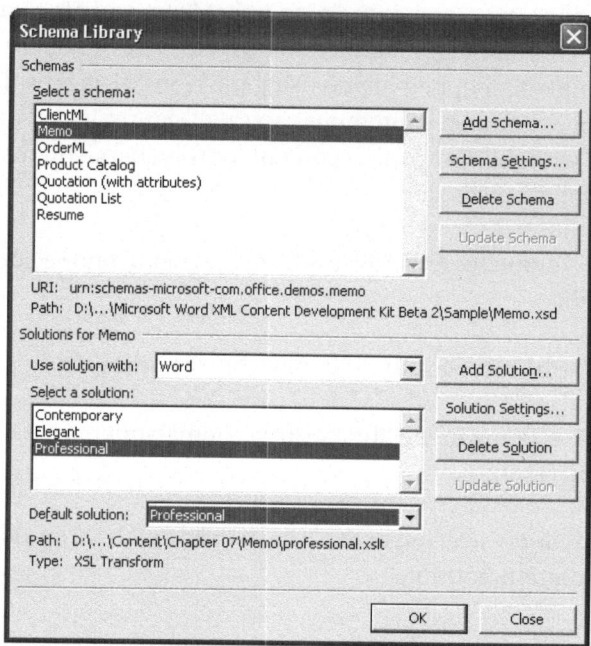

Figure 7-11. The schema library with three linked stylesheets

These stylesheets will be available the next time you open a document that uses the custom memo markup language. This must be a data-only memo file, not a full WordML file. When you open a data-only memo document, the XML Document pane will show a list of views. Select data-only to see the bare XML markup (as shown in Figure 7-12), and choose one of the XSLT stylesheets to see the WordML document that's generated when the stylesheet is used to transform the data-only document. Figure 7-13 shows an example of a data-only XML document that's been transformed to WordML.

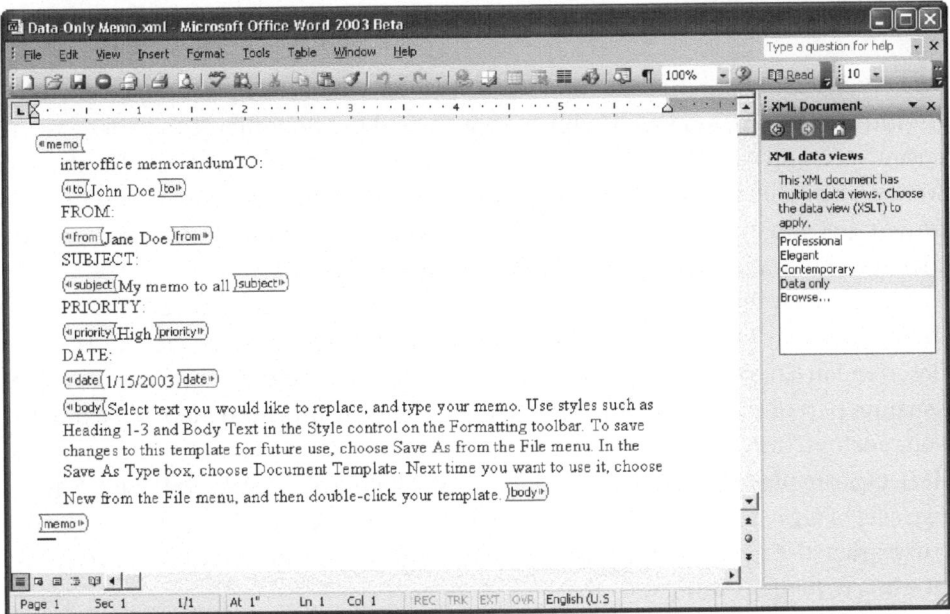

Figure 7-12. The data-only view of the memo XML

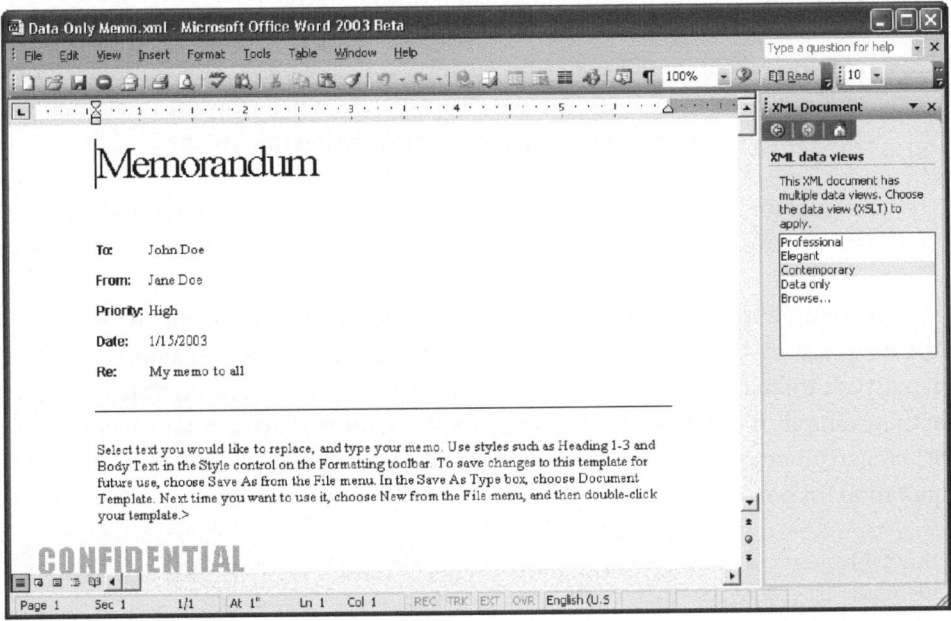

Figure 7-13. The memo XML transformed with elegant.xslt

Changing WordML to Your Custom XML

What if you could use the rich Office XML formats when saving a mapped Excel or Word document, but still be able to transform these documents to your own custom markup with a moment's notice? This would give you the best of both worlds—not only would you retain the rich formatting information in the Office format, but you would also be able to plug your document into business processes that don't know anything about WordML or SpreadsheetML.

It turns out that this magic *is* possible—but only for Word. The reason is the difference in the way WordML and SpreadsheetML documents are stored, as described in Chapter 6. In SpreadsheetML, the mapping information is stored in a separate part of the document. There's no easy way to apply the map and extract your custom XML without running Excel. With WordML, however, your custom XML tags are placed directly in the document, along with the WordML tags. The two sets of tags are distinguished based on their namespace. Using an XSLT, you can extract just the elements that are a part of your namespace, without even needing to load up Word.

The XSLT you'll need is a little more complicated than the examples you've seen in this chapter. It consists of three templates:

- A template that matches all nodes, but does nothing.

- A template that matches all your custom XML elements. This template looks for any elements in the namespace you specify. It uses the XSLT <element> tag to copy each element it finds to the destination document.

- A template that matches all Word text tags. This template copies the contained text inside the text tag.

An example stylesheet is shown next. Note that this stylesheet can be used for just about any mapped WordML document. However, you'll need to adjust the namespace it's searching for to match the namespace of your custom XML markup. In this example, the stylesheet copies tags from the http://www.prosetech.com/Schemas/QuotationList namespace, which is the namespace used for the mapped quotation list document.

```
<xsl:stylesheet xmlns:xsl="http://www.w3.org/1999/XSL/Transform" version="1.0"
 xmlns:w="http://schemas.microsoft.com/office/word/2003/2/wordml"
 xmlns:nso="http://www.prosetech.com/Schemas/QuotationList">

  <xsl:output method="xml" indent="yes"/>
```

```
<!-- This catches all nodes, and ignores them, unless
     one of the following two templates is matched. -->
<xsl:template match="@* | node()">
    <xsl:apply-templates/>
</xsl:template>

<!-- Every time an element is matched in the target namespace,
     output the element tag, and then process all children. -->
<xsl:template match="ns0:*" >
    <xsl:element name="{name()}">
        <xsl:apply-templates/>
    </xsl:element>
</xsl:template>

<!-- Copy the value of any text elements. -->
<xsl:template match="w:t">
    <xsl:value-of select="."/>
</xsl:template>
```

```
</xsl:stylesheet>
```

If you use this stylesheet with the full QuotationList.xml WordML document (first presented in Chapter 6), you'll end up with the following data-only XML:

```
<?xml version="1.0" encoding="utf-8"?>
<ns0:quotationList xmlns:ns0="http://www.prosetech.com/Schemas/QuotationList">
  <ns0:quotation>
    <ns0:text>One thing is for certain: if you don't change the path you're on, you
will end up where you are headed.</ns0:text>
    <ns0:source>Chinese Proverb</ns0:source>
    <ns0:category>Ancient Wisdom</ns0:category>
  </ns0:quotation>
  <ns0:quotation>
    <ns0:text>Always forgive your enemies; nothing else annoys them
so much.</ns0:text>
    <ns0:source>Oscar Wilde</ns0:source>
    <ns0:category>Literary</ns0:category>
  </ns0:quotation>
  <ns0:quotation>
    <ns0:text>Justice will only exist where those not affected by injustice are
filled with the same amount of indignation as those offended.</ns0:text>
    <ns0:source>Plato</ns0:source>
    <ns0:category>Ancient Wisdom</ns0:category>
  </ns0:quotation>
</ns0:quotationList>
```

You can try this example using the TransformXML utility included with the companion content.

The Last Word

This chapter explored XSLT, the last ingredient in the Office XML story. With a carefully crafted XSLT document, you can convert one type of XML markup into another, or make the jump from XML to HTML, or even to WordML and back. For an excellent tutorial on XSLT that introduces some of the features that weren't covered in this chapter, you can refer to http://www.w3schools.com/xsl.

XSLT plays a key role in bringing together businesses and processes that use different XML standards, and it's an important player in Office 2003. In the next chapter, you'll see a complete solution that incorporates XSLT.

CHAPTER 8

Managing Workflow with XML Web Services

OVER THE LAST seven chapters, you've learned the basics of XML, XML Schema, and XSLT. You've also learned the ways that the Office 2003 applications can use these XML standards to import, export, and transform data. On their own, these techniques are useful, but often awkward. They force the Office user to carry out certain repetitive tasks, like exporting and importing data. They also won't solve the problem of how to seamlessly route data between Office applications and business processes.

In order to answer this challenge, you need to build a custom solution using the Office XML features as building blocks. This solution will almost always require some custom code that automates the process. For example, a developer might create a stand-alone application that generates prefilled Word templates using WordML. Or, an organization might use VBA code in an Excel macro to submit completed worksheets to another application over the Internet. In both cases, the principle is the same—you use XML to exchange data between an Office application and a custom business application.

In this chapter, I'll walk you through a complete end-to-end example that demonstrates how a little custom code and XML markup can automate a business process. With this example, Excel users will be able to send expense reports directly to a centralized database, without needing to manually export an XML file. Other users will be able to review expense report summaries using a web page on the local Intranet.

There are many different ways that this solution can be built, depending on the programming language, level of detail, and feature set you need. In the example shown in this chapter, three assumptions are made:

- The application is designed as a straightforward proof-of-concept example. That means it includes all the pieces to show the end-to-end process, but it doesn't include many niceties, or additional logic for handling errors. Professional developers would almost certainly add this extra code.

- The application presents the shortest possible code to demonstrate the concept. However, unless you're a developer, at least some of it will be new and foreign. Rather than become sidetracked with a detailed introduction to .NET, I'll refer you to other introductory books if you'd like to explore these aspects in more detail.[1]

- The application will use freely downloadable software components. In other words, you'll use Web Matrix instead of Visual Studio .NET to write the server-side logic, and use an Access database instead of SQL Server. This allows you to test the application on your local computer without needing to purchase any other development tools. The actual approach and concepts are almost identical to those that would be used with the full-priced products.

> **NOTE** *This chapter delves into some programming concepts. While you don't need to be a programmer to follow through the steps I'll give, you won't get the most out of all the details unless you know a little bit about .NET and object-oriented programming. Don't let this scare you away if you don't, though—it's still an excellent example to show you how different components can interact in a business system using XML and Web services.*

An Overview of the Expense Report Workflow

A common problem with Office documents is that valuable data becomes locked into individual spreadsheet and word processor files, most of which are stored on individual user computers. This makes it impossible to analyze all the information at once, track it properly, or share it between different users and business processes.

The simple solution is to *centralize* the storage of information. In most businesses, this means storing the business data in a database on a company server. Databases allow multiple users to search and manipulate vast amounts of information at the same time. They also guarantee the integrity of that information, making it almost impossible for conflicting changes to result in corrupted data.

---

1. You might wonder whether it's possible to create this application without using .NET. Unfortunately, that task would be extremely difficult because this example requires a Web service. Web services can be built quite easily with .NET (and much more awkwardly with Visual Basic 6, which requires the help of a separately downloadable tool and introduces some significant headaches). You can't build a Web service with VBA, the macro language that's a part of Office 2003.

Database solutions are easy to imagine, but difficult to implement with Office. The problem is that Office applications are designed to be stand-alone software tools. They don't offer many built-in tools for centralizing information. To implement a database solution with Office, developers usually need to code extremely complex logic. For example, what if a user wants to submit the information from a Word-based news article while working at home? Somehow, a developer needs to code logic to extract the relevant information from the document, and then send it over the Internet to another application, which must then connect to the database and insert the details. Coding this type of logic with the previous generation of Office applications is difficult at best. Your code needs to make assumptions about data content based on extraneous details like formatting, positioning, or styles. That makes it quite easy to introduce an error—for example, if the source document is reformatted, the macro code might grab the wrong information. With XML, this potential for ambiguity is greatly diminished, because the XML mapping clearly indicates where each piece of data is.

With the XML features in Office 2003 and Microsoft's new .NET platform, these types of solutions are finally practical—if not easy. The expense report solution uses exactly this approach to allow employees to submit their expense reports to a centralized database, without requiring pages of low-level code.

The expense report workflow works like this:

1. An employee fills out an expense report spreadsheet, using the XML mapped expense report template.

2. The employee clicks a button to submit the report. This button runs a VBA macro, which exports the XML and sends it to an ASP.NET Web service running on another computer. This Web service could be running on a local company intranet, in which case the macro code will only work while the user is in the office. Alternatively, it could be hosted on a full-blown web server, allowing users to submit data over the Internet no matter where they are.

> **NOTE** *VBA stands for Visual Basic for Applications. VBA is a scaled-down version of the Visual Basic language that's built into other products, like Office.*

3. The Web service takes the XML, converts it into the expected data format, and inserts it into an Access database. (For better scalability, a full-fledged SQL Server database could be used.)

NOTE *This example uses Access as the back-end database, because it's a part of the Microsoft Office 2003 software suite. However, Microsoft Access is intended to serve small businesses by acting as a desktop database engine. Before deploying this test application in the real world, you would probably replace Access with an industrial-strength database product like SQL Server or Oracle. The code you would use remains very similar.*

4. A separate web page allows users to view information about all the expense reports that have been submitted. It extracts the data from the database, converts it to XML, and then uses XSLT to display as formatted HTML.

What Is a Web Service?

You can think of a Web service as a self-contained code routine that runs on a web server. Another application, hosted on a client computer, can communicate with the Web service using XML messages.

A Web service is similar to a web page in the way that it's used over the Internet. The difference is that a user interacts directly with a web page, while another software application is required to interact with a Web service. For example, when you go to your bank's web site to check your account history, you use one or more web pages. On the other hand, when you use a third-party financial program to download your bank transactions, the financial program uses a Web service provided by your bank to retrieve the information it needs.

Web services are sometimes called XML Web services to emphasize the fact that they use XML-based languages to exchange data with other applications. This allows them to be used by applications running on just about any computer platform, operating system, and programming language, so long as it provides an XML parser. Most Web services use the SOAP and WSDL standards. WSDL is an XML-based language for describing Web services. An automated tool can scan a Web service's WSDL document, and then generate the code needed to interact with the Web service. SOAP is an XML-based language used to format the messages that are sent to and from a Web service. For example, if you want to request a list of transactions from your bank's Web service, you might send a SOAP request document with information like your client number, password, and the date range that you're interested in. The bank would send a SOAP response document with the list of transactions. All of this communication happens over an HTTP channel, which is the communication protocol of the Internet.

This workflow has lots of opportunity for expansion. The key step is transferring the Excel information to a central database. Once this is accomplished, you can build other web pages that allow users to manipulate this information (for example, marking some expense reports as approved, while denying others). Or, you can build a VBA macro to import this data into another Excel spreadsheet or Word document. Toward the end of this chapter, you'll see a few other scenarios that allow you to automate workflows with different types of documents using XML and a little custom code.

Technically, you can perform these tasks without using XML at all. In fact, if you've programmed with Office before, you may have created scripts and macros that extract data using styles, cell numbers, or some other criteria, and stored it in some non-XML format. Part of the problem with this approach is that it often forces you to reinvent the wheel. For example, if you need to validate and transform your information, or if you need to use complex data structures, you'll be forced to create your own ad hoc solutions. These are problems that XML already deals with natively. Finally, ad hoc solutions tend to be very brittle, which means that minor changes in the Office document can cause serious problems and even stop the custom code from working. This problem results because ad hoc code is typically very long, and usually needs to rely on positional information (like hard-coded paragraph and row numbers). If the structure of the document changes, the solution code also needs to be modified. With the XML mapping features in Office, you won't need to hard code any of these details.

The expense report solution requires four components:

- An expense report template, with the defined XML mappings

- A VBA macro to export the XML and send it to the Web service

- An ASP.NET Web service to retrieve the XML, and store it in the database

- An ASP.NET web page that retrieves summary information from the database, and allows users to view it

Figure 8-1 diagrams the workflow used in this example. The diagram is split up to show the difference between the client computer and the server computer where all the information is stored. However, you can test this solution on a single computer, which will contain all the components of this solution.

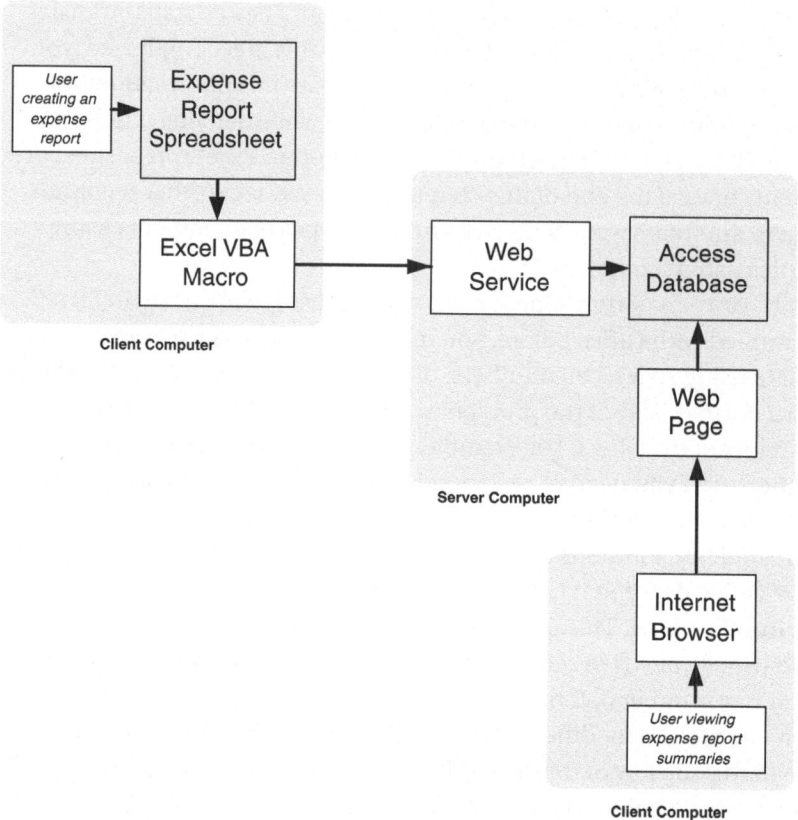

Figure 8-1. The expense report workflow

Installing the Prerequisites

In order to use the example, you need to ensure your computer has the following installed software:

- *Office 2003:* In this example, you'll use Excel to create documents and Access as the server-side database.

- *IIS (Internet Information Services):* IIS is an optional component included with the Windows XP Professional and Windows 2000 Professional operating systems. It allows you to host Web services and web pages, so that other computers can use them.

- *.NET Framework:* This is the engine that powers all .NET applications, including Web services.

- *Web Matrix:* This is the development tool you use to create .NET web applications, like web pages and Web services.

- *The SOAP Toolkit:* This component allows applications to send XML messages to Web services. The spreadsheet macro will rely on this component to send the expense report details to the Web service.

Remember, the easiest way to test this solution is to install everything on the same computer. However, in a real-world scenario, you would split the system between one or more clients and a central server. The client would require the following software:

- Excel 2003

- The SOAP Toolkit

The server would require these components:

- Access 2003 (or SQL Server)

- .NET Framework

- IIS

In addition, Web Matrix and the .NET Framework would need to be installed on the computer where you want to develop and test the Web service.

The following sections describe how to install these ingredients.

Internet Information Services

Web servers run special software to support mail exchange, FTP, and HTTP access, and everything else clients need in order to access web content. On the Microsoft Windows operating system, the built-in Internet Information Services (IIS) component plays this role.

Installing IIS is easy. Here are the steps you follow on a Windows 2000 or Windows XP computer:

1. Click Start, and select Settings ➤ Control Panel.

2. Choose Add or Remove Programs.

3. Click Add/Remove Windows Components.

4. If Internet Information Services is checked, you already have this component installed. Otherwise, click it and click Next to install the required IIS files. You'll probably need to have your Windows setup CD handy.

When IIS is installed, it automatically creates a directory that represents your web site. This is the directory c:\Inetpub\wwwroot. Any files in this directory will appear as though they are in the root of your web server. To test that IIS is installed correctly, browse to the c:\Inetpub\wwwroot directory, and verify that it contains a file called localstart.asp. This is a simple ASP file that is automatically installed with IIS. To verify that IIS is working correctly, you can request the localstart.asp file in a web browser. Just open an application like Internet Explorer, and type in the request **http://localhost/localstart.asp**. IIS will receive your request, and you'll receive a generic introductory page in your browser.

NOTE *Localhost is a special "loopback" alias that always refers to the local computer, whatever its name. That means you can try http://localhost/localstart.asp on any computer to test whether IIS is installed. To try and test whether you can access IIS on one computer from another computer, you can use a request like http://[ComputerName]/localstart.asp, where [ComputerName] is the name of the computer that has IIS installed on it.*

.NET Framework and Web Matrix

The .NET Framework is the engine that allows .NET applications to run. It's installed with the latest Microsoft operating systems (in this case, Windows 2003 Server), bundled with many .NET applications, and available through the Windows Update feature. Web Matrix is a free development tool for creating .NET-powered web sites. It's an alternative to the full Visual Studio .NET environment, which retails for a considerable cost. Using Web Matrix, you have access to the same .NET Framework and library of features. The only difference is that the development environment where you create your programs lacks a few niceties.

To install both the .NET Framework and Web Matrix, surf to http://www.asp.net/webmatrix, and choose the Download Now link. You'll be led through three steps. First, you must install the .NET Framework SDK (Software Development Kit), which requires the utilities needed to create and compile .NET code. Next, you must download and install Web Matrix. Finally, you can download any optional add-ons that you'd like to use. The web page and setup wizard shown in Figure 8-2 will walk you through all the necessary steps.

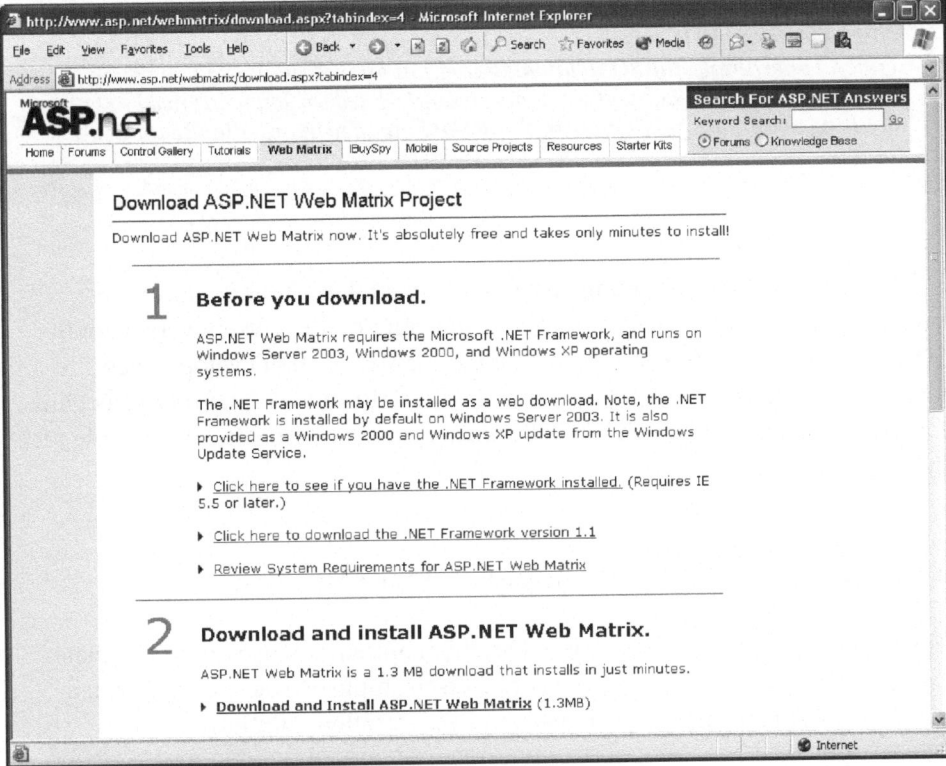

Figure 8-2. Installing the .NET Framework and Web Matrix

> **TIP** *For a general primer to Web Matrix, refer to the user guide on the http://www.asp.net/webmatrix site, or read a dedicated book like the* Web Matrix Developer's Guide *by John Paul Mueller (Apress, 2002). For an introduction to the full ASP.NET platform with Visual Studio .NET, you can read my own* Beginning ASP.NET in VB .NET: From Novice to Pro *(Apress, 2004).*

The SOAP Toolkit

The SOAP Toolkit allows you to call Web services from other applications. You can use the SOAP Toolkit in a Visual Basic 6 application, or in a VBA macro, as you'll see in this example.

> **NOTE** *SOAP is an XML-based language that's used to send messages to a Web service. For example, the SOAP language defines an <envelope> tag, in which you place the XML document you want to send. However, you won't need to know anything about the tags defined in the SOAP language in order to use the SOAP Toolkit.*

Downloading and installing the SOAP Toolkit takes a matter of minutes, unlike the much larger .NET Framework. You can find the current version of the SOAP Toolkit by searching for "SOAP Toolkit" at Microsoft's developer web site, http://msdn.microsoft.com. At the time of this writing, you can find a direct link for downloading the SOAP Toolkit 3.0 at http://msdn.microsoft.com/downloads/list/websrv.asp.

Building the Expense Report Workflow

The expense report workflow is based on the mapped expense report template designed in Chapter 3. Using some code, this example will be changed from a stand-alone spreadsheet to part of a complete workflow solution.

Creating the Database

The first step is to generate the database where the expense report information will be stored. In this example, you'll use Access, because it's included with Office. (SQL Server would be a better choice, however, because it's designed for server-side use, in which multiple users will need to access the database at the same time. The desktop Access engine can't compete in performance, safety, or scalability.)

You'll require two tables in the Access database. The first table, ExpenseReport, tracks each submitted expense report. The second table, ExpenseItem, tracks an individual item in an expense report. Thus, each record in the ExpenseReport table will be related to one or more child records in the ExpenseItem table. This two-part structure (shown in Figure 8-3) is the most efficient way to store the data, and it allows an expense report to contain an unlimited number of items.

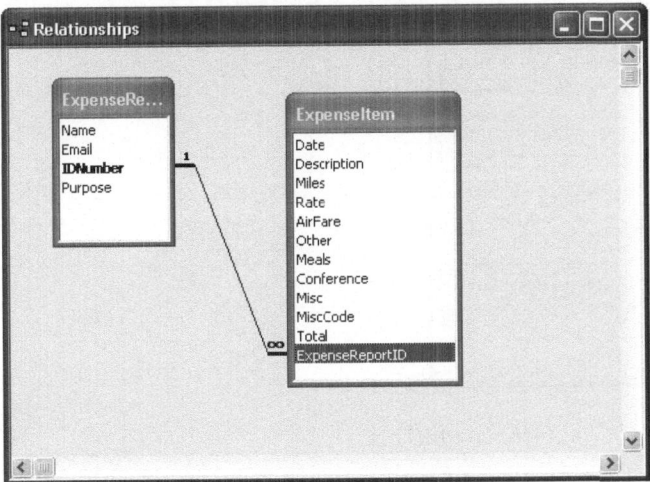

Figure 8-3. The expense report database

To quickly create these tables, you can use the XML import features of Access, and the ExpenseSchema.xsd file from the Chapter 3 examples. The XML import capability in Access is actually more useful than the XML export feature. Remember, when exporting XML you'll face the following limitations:

- You won't be able to specify a custom namespace.

- You won't be able to change tag names. The elements will always be named according to the table and column names, and the root element will always be called <dataroot>.

- You won't be able to export more than one table to the same schema without creating a relationship.

These rules are loosened when importing a schema. To create database tables based on ExpenseSchema.xsd, begin by creating a new empty database file named Expenses.mdb. Next, select File ➤ Get External Data ➤ Import from the menu.

Choose XML in the file type list at the bottom of the Import window, select the ExpenseSchema.xsd file, and click Import. In the Import XML window, click OK to accept both the Meta and ExpenseItem tables (see Figure 8-4).

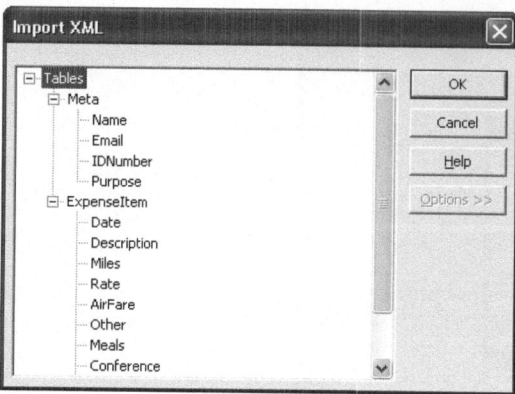

Figure 8-4. Importing tables in an XML schema

This will add two tables to your database, as shown in Figure 8-5. You can now customize these tables to more accurately reflect the information you want to store. First of all, rename Meta to ExpenseReport by right-clicking the table name and choosing Rename.

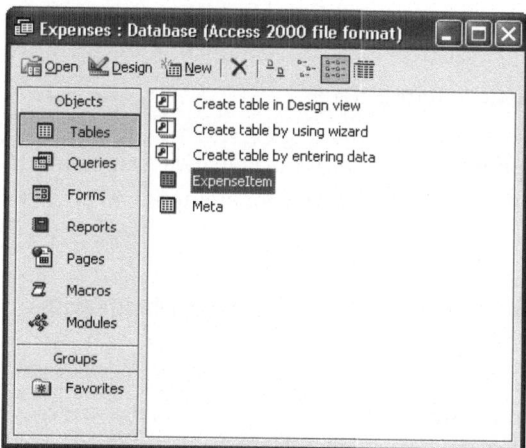

Figure 8-5. The imported tables

Next, you'll need to link the ExpenseReport and ExpenseItem tables. Begin by right-clicking the ExpenseReport table, and choosing Design View. Right-click the IDNumber column, and choose Primary Key. Then close the design view.

Next, right-click the ExpenseItem table, and choose Design View. At the bottom of the column list, add a text column named ExpenseReportID. The value in this column will bind the ExpenseItem record to a corresponding ExpenseReport record. If you'd like, you can explicitly define this relationship. Just select Tools ➤ Relationships from the menu and create the one-to-many relationship shown in Figure 8-6 by dragging the IDNumber column in the ExpenseReport table to the ExpenseReportID column in the ExpenseItem table. You can find the completed database with the online examples.

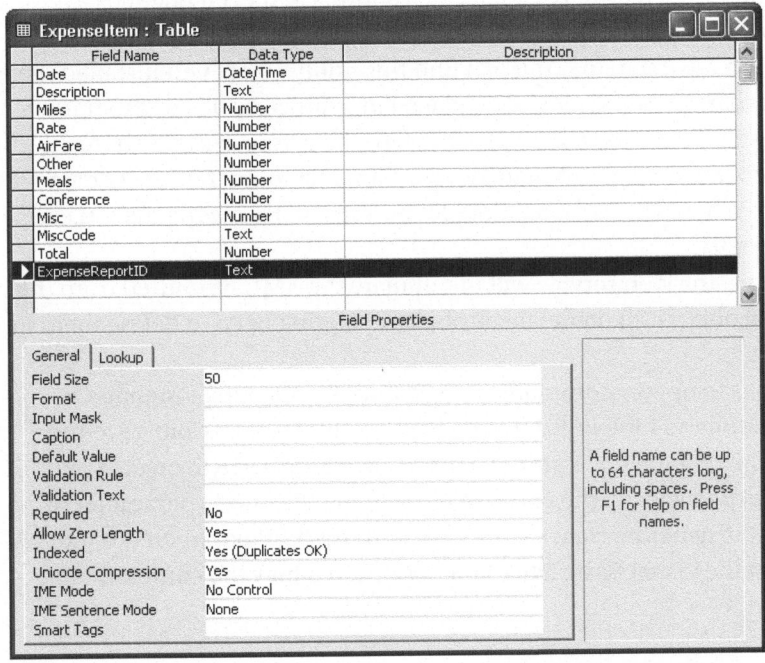

Figure 8-6. Linking the ExpenseReport and ExpenseItem tables

> **TIP** *In this example, you can assume that the ID number taken from the spreadsheet is unique and can be used as a primary key. In many cases you would want to make this process a little bit more sophisticated, and use an auto-increment number, which is a unique number generated automatically by the database. You could then send this number back to the spreadsheet when the record is created, and the spreadsheet would display the generated number.*

Creating the Web Service Objects

In the next stage, the code becomes a little more intricate. The problem is that most programming languages don't deal directly with XML. In fact, manipulating XML can be tedious and error-prone. It's more common to find that programming languages use *objects,* elements that store a set of related data and allow you to perform well-defined tasks. In fact, many languages expect you to work with objects, but convert the objects into an XML representation whenever they need to be transmitted to another piece of software or stored in a permanent location.

The .NET Framework allows you to use this approach. It even includes a special command-line utility called xsd.exe, which can create the code for your objects based on an XML schema. You can find this utility where you installed the .NET Framework SDK—typically it will be placed in a directory like c:\Program Files\Microsoft.NET\FrameworkSDK\Bin. To make life a little easier, you might want to create a single directory to hold all your files, including the Access database and ExpenseSchema.xsd schema document. You can then copy the xsd.exe utility to this directory.

In this example, the Web service will manipulate the XML submitted from the spreadsheet using objects. To create these objects, you first need to define them in code using xsd.exe.

The first step is to open a command-line prompt by selecting Programs ➤ Accessories ➤ Command Line Prompt from the Windows menu. Change to the directory where the schema file is stored. Finally, use the xsd.exe to create your code file. You'll need to specify the name of the schema file, the /c parameter to indicate you want to generate class definitions, and the /l:VB parameter to indicate you are using the Visual Basic .NET language. Here's how the command line will look:

```
xsd ExpenseSchema.xsd /c /l:VB
```

The xsd.exe utility will generate the code file, and you'll see the output shown in Figure 8-7.

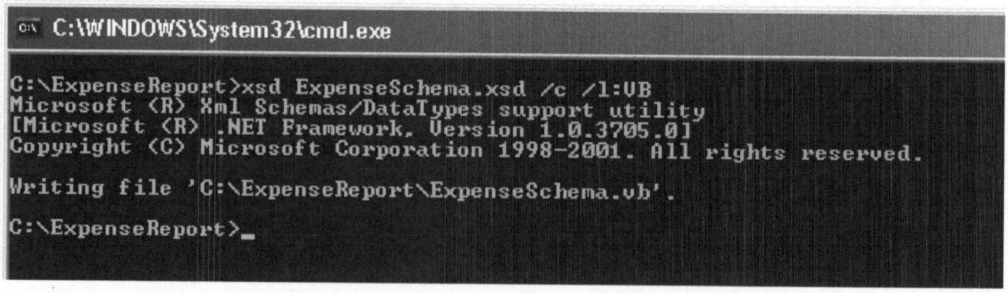

Figure 8-7. Creating objects based on XML

You can open the code file in any text editor, including Notepad. You'll find three classes. (Each class is a definition that can be used to create live objects in an application.) The classes represent an expense item, the metadata for an expense report, and the complete expense report. For example, here's the (slightly simplified) code that defines the structure of an expense item:

```
Public Class RootExpenseItem
    Public [Date] As Date
    Public Description As String
    Public Miles As Integer
    Public Rate As Decimal
    Public AirFare As Decimal
    Public Other As Decimal
    Public Meals As Decimal
    Public Conference As Decimal
    Public Misc As Decimal
    Public MiscCode As String
    Public Total As Decimal
End Class
```

This code indicates that every expense item is made up of a date, description, number of miles, rate, airfare, and so on. These details are drawn directly from the schema.

Similarly, the metadata stores the name, e-mail, ID number, and purpose:

```
Public Class RootMeta
    Public Name As String
    Public Email As String
    Public IDNumber As String
    Public Purpose As String
End Class
```

When you look at the class for the expense report, you'll notice that it contains one or more expense items (technically known as an *array*), and a single instance of the expense report metadata.

```
Public Class Root
    Public Meta As RootMeta
    Public ExpenseItem() As RootExpenseItem
End Class
```

You'll use this code in the Web service created in the next section.

Creating the Web Service

The Web service is the key piece of code in this solution. It takes the submitted information from the spreadsheet, and creates the required records in the database. It's also the most complex piece of the equation, although it requires less than 30 lines of code.

Remember, a Web service has no visual interface. It's a piece of code that runs on the server computer, in the background, whenever it receives a message from an Excel user. The Web service is written more or less like an ordinary function in the Visual Basic programming language. The .NET Framework takes care of changing the received SOAP message into the appropriate Visual Basic .NET data types (like numbers, strings, dates, and so on). The Web service code never manipulates XML directly.

To create the Web service, start Web Matrix by selecting Programs ➤ Microsoft ASP.NET Web Matrix ➤ ASP.NET Web Matrix from the Start menu. In the Add New File window, make the following selections:

- Choose the XML Web Service icon.

- Specify the appropriate directory.

- Use the filename ExpenseReportService.asmx.

- Use the class name ReportService.

- Use the namespace name Expenses.

These names do not affect the functioning of your service, just how it's organized and described. Once you have made your selections, click OK to create the Web service file (see Figure 8-8).

The basic structure of any Web service is a class that contains one or more web methods. Web methods are simply functions (distinct blocks of code that perform a programming task) that can be invoked from another computer or even over the Internet. In this case, you only need a single web method. This web method will accept an expense report, and insert it into the Access database on the server.

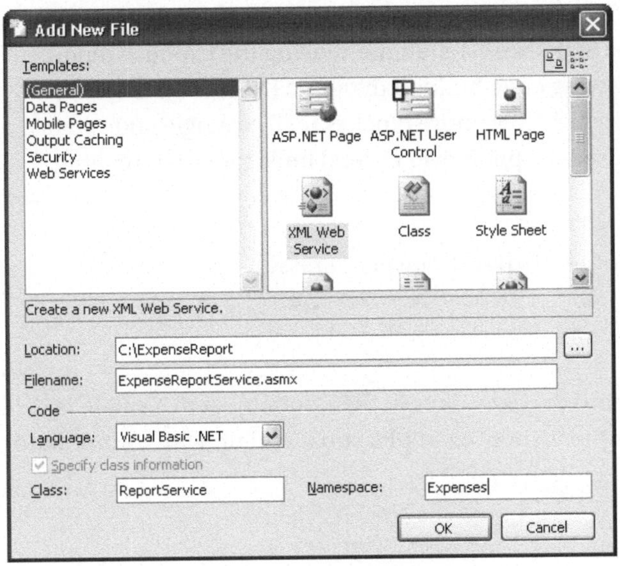

Figure 8-8. Creating a new Web service

Before continuing, you must copy the code from the generated ExpenseSchema.vb file into the Web service. Begin copying at the line "This source code was auto-generated by xsd" and include the remainder of the file. Paste it just after the code in the Web service file. (If you are at all uncertain of how to insert this code, refer to the completed ExpenseReportService.asmx file with the companion content.)

Now you need to create the web method itself. The basic skeleton you'll need is as follows:

```
Public Class ReportService

    <WebMethod> Public Function SubmitReport(Root as Root) As String
        ' [Code goes here.]
    End Function

End Class
```

In this example, there is a ReportService Web service class that contains a single web method called SubmitReport(). SubmitReport() accepts a Root object, which represents a complete expense report, and returns a string of text with a confirmation message.

The code you need uses SQL to insert records into the appropriate tables. The basic principle is to build up a SQL INSERT statement using the expense report objects. For example, the following code builds a dynamic INSERT statement for creating the ExpenseReport record. This entire block is really a single code statement—the underscore (_) is used to split it over several lines for easier reading.

```
Dim SQL As String = _
  "INSERT INTO ExpenseReport (Name, Email, IDNumber, Purpose) " & _
  "VALUES ('" & Root.Meta.Name & "','" & Root.Meta.Email & "','" & _
  Root.Meta.IDNumber & "','" & Root.Meta.Purpose & "')"
```

When this code runs, it converts the values in the Root object to a single text command. Using the default spreadsheet example, you'll end up with a command like this:

```
INSERT INTO ExpenseReport (Name, Email, IDNumber, Purpose)
VALUES ('Karen Archer', 'karena','123987', 'Business trip to chicago')
```

This inserts the list of values into the appropriate columns in an ExpenseReport record. Similar logic is used to insert each expense item. In this case, the code loops through the array of expense item objects. For each object, it generates a new INSERT statement.

To actually execute the INSERT statements, you need to use ADO.NET, which is the name of the data access technology included with .NET. ADO.NET defines command and connection objects that allow you to communicate with any database, whether it's Access, SQL Server, Oracle, or something entirely different. A discussion of ADO.NET is beyond the scope of this book, but you'll glean a fair bit of information by looking at the completed web method code, which shows it in action:

```
<WebMethod> Public Function SubmitReport(Root as Root) As String

  ' Create a connection to the database.
  Dim ConnectionString As String = _
   "Provider=Microsoft.Jet.OLEDB.4.0;Data Source=c:\ExpenseReport\Expenses.mdb"
  Dim Connection As New OleDbConnection(ConnectionString)
  Connection.Open()
```

```
' Create the ExpenseReport record.
Dim SQL As String = _
    "INSERT INTO ExpenseReport (Name, Email, IDNumber, Purpose) " & _
    "VALUES ('" & Root.Meta.Name & "','" & Root.Meta.Email & "','" & _
    Root.Meta.IDNumber & "','" & Root.Meta.Purpose & "')"
Dim Command As New OleDbCommand(SQL, Connection)
Command.ExecuteNonQuery()


' Create all the linked ExpenseItem records.
Dim Item As RootExpenseItem
For Each Item In Root.ExpenseItem
    SQL = "INSERT INTO ExpenseItem " & _
        "(Date, Description, Miles, Rate, AirFare, Other, Meals, " & _
        "Conference, Misc, MiscCode, Total, ExpenseReportID)" & _
        "VALUES ('" & Item.Date & "','" & Item.Description & "'," & _
        Item.Miles & "," & Item.Rate & "," & Item.AirFare & "," & _
        Item.Other & "," & Item.Meals & "," & Item.Conference & "," & _
        Item.Misc & ",'" & Item.MiscCode & "'," & Item.Total & ",'" & _
        Root.Meta.IDNumber & "')"

    Command.CommandText = SQL
    Command.ExecuteNonQuery()
Next


' Close the connection.
Connection.Close()


Return Root.Meta.Name & " was successfully added to the database."
End Function
```

The very last line of code returns a confirmation message indicating that all the steps completed successfully. In a typical Web service, you would enhance this code with error handling, and use a transaction to make sure that if an error occurs, the database isn't left with only some of the expense report data.

An Alternate Approach to XML in a Web Service

The current SubmitReport() Web service makes use of .NET's ability to convert XML to objects. Even though the Web service receives an XML document, it's able to seamlessly convert it into the desired group of objects. This magic isn't always possible, because the type of XML you need to process might not be directly translatable into an object. In this situation, you can use another equally valid approach. Instead of accepting a specific object, create a Web service that accepts XML data, like this:

```
<WebMethod> Public Function SubmitReport(Data as XmlNode) As String
    ' (Code omitted.)
End Function
```

Now you can read the elements and data contained in the submitted XML using the properties and methods of the XmlNode object. The XmlNode object can contain any type of information (as long as it's valid XML data). For example, an XmlNode might represent an element that contains more elements (represented as additional XmlNode objects). You can learn more about using XML in .NET with a number of introductory .NET books, or through the tutorials provided by Microsoft at http://samples.gotdotnet.com/quickstart/howto/doc/xml/overviewofxml.aspx.

Exposing the Web Service

Once you've created the Web service, you need to make sure it's available to remote clients. You do this by exposing the directory that contains the Web service as a *virtual directory*.

You can create virtual directories in several ways, including by using the IIS administrative utility. However, the quickest route is using Windows Explorer. Simply right-click the directory and select Properties. Next, select the Web Sharing tab. On the Web Sharing tab (shown in Figure 8-9), select "Share this folder".

The Edit Alias window will appear where you can configure other options for the directory. In order to make sure the Web service in the directory is available to other users, you must enable Read access, and make sure that the Execute (includes scripts) option is selected, as shown in Figure 8-10.

Finally, make note of the directory alias. Remote computers will need to know the computer name, the directory alias, and the Web service filename in order to access the Web service.

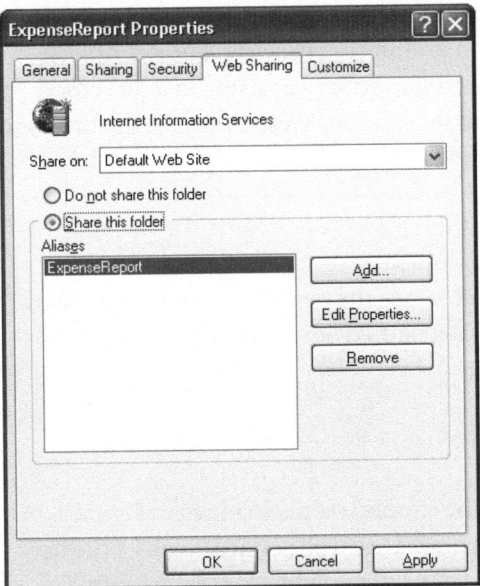

Figure 8-9. Sharing a directory on the web

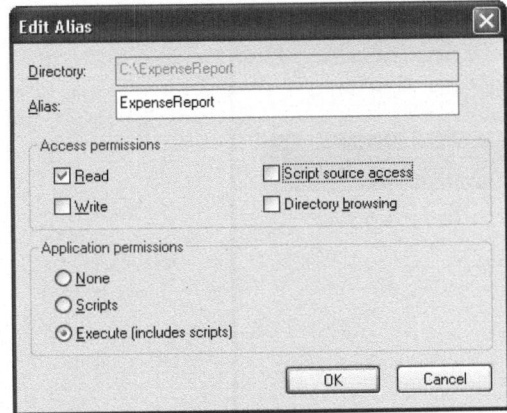

Figure 8-10. Web directory permissions

TIP *Remember, your shared directory will only be available to users who can access your computer remotely. If your computer is a web server, the directory will indeed be exposed over the entire Internet. But if your computer isn't a web server, the only users who'll be able to access it are those on the same local network as you.*

To test whether the Web service is available over the Internet, you should be able to request the Web service test page in an Internet browser. For example, if you placed a Web service file named ExpenseReportService.asmx in a directory with the web alias ExpenseReport, you can request this Web service in the browser using the following path:

```
http://localhost/ExposeReport/ExpenseReportService.asmx
```

On another computer, you would need to use the computer name. For example, if the computer with the Web service was named ServerA, you would use this path in your browser:

```
http://ServerA/ExposeReport/ExpenseReportService.asmx
```

When you perform this test, you'll see the simple test page shown in Figure 8-11, which allows you to see basic information about the Web service, such as the list of available web methods. This is intended as a convenience for testing only. Remember, Web services are not intended to be used directly by a user in a web browser. Instead, Web services are used by other applications.

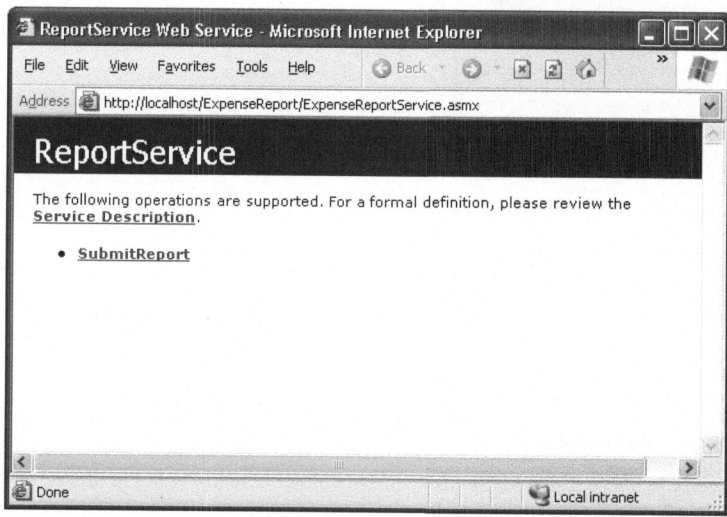

Figure 8-11. The Web service test page

The first time you request the Web service or its test page, there will be a slight delay while your code is compiled in the background by the ASP.NET engine.

Creating the Excel VBA Macro

The final ingredient is to create an Excel macro that will export the XML for the spreadsheet, and submit it to the Web service. This step won't be too complicated because of the design choices made earlier. Because the Web service is based on the report objects, which are themselves based on the ExpenseSchema.xsd, you'll be able to submit the expense report XML directly to the Web service. The Web service will convert this XML into the expense report objects, and then run the web method code.

To create the VBA macro, begin by opening the Excel expense report spreadsheet. Then, select Tools ➤ Macro ➤ Visual Basic Editor. This loads the Visual Basic editor where you can write code "behind" your Excel spreadsheet. In the project window on the left of the Visual Basic editor, double-click Sheet1 under the Microsoft Excel Objects folder. Next, define a basic subroutine named Submit, as shown in Figure 8-12.

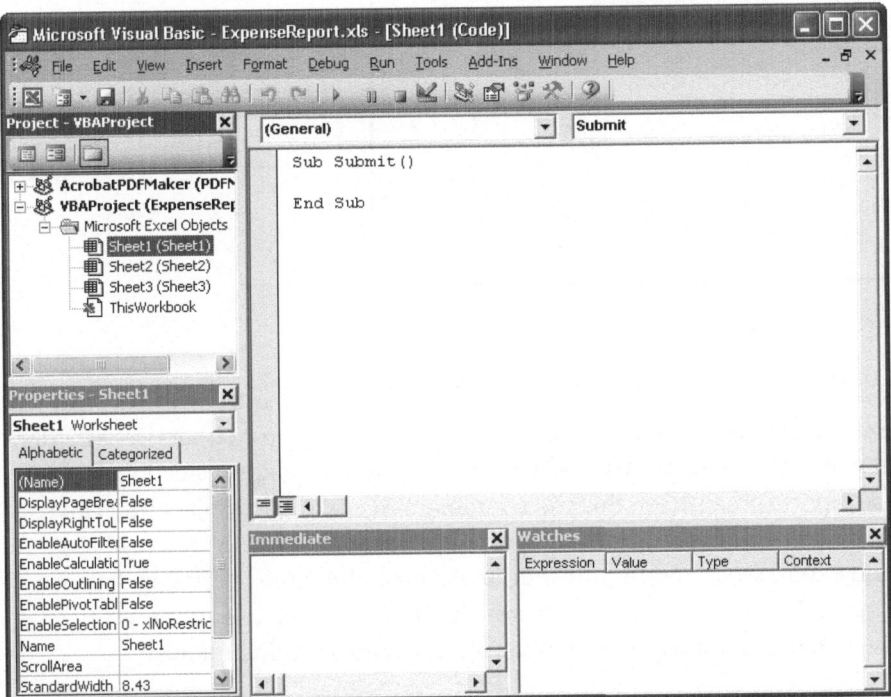

Figure 8-12. The VBA subroutine

Before writing the code, you need to add references to the SOAP Toolkit. This will allow your code to work with XML and send SOAP messages. Select Tools ➤ References from the Visual Basic menu. Scroll through the list to find the following two items, and place a checkmark next to each one:

- Microsoft SOAP Type Library v3.0

- Microsoft XML, v5.0

Click OK to accept these references as shown in Figure 8-13.

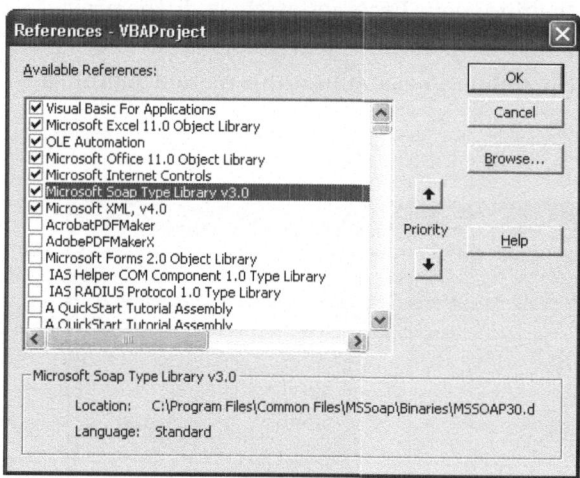

Figure 8-13. Adding references

Now all that's left is to export the XML and send it to the Web service. In order to extract the XML, you can use the ActiveWorkbook.XmlMaps collection. In the expense report spreadsheet, this will contain a single XmlMap object. You can use the methods of this object such as Export() and Import() to write and read XML files, and ExportXml() and ImportXml() to perform the same task using data in a string instead of in an external file. Here's the code that will take the current expense report and transform it into the appropriate XML document:

```
Dim XMLString As String
ActiveWorkbook.XmlMaps(1).ExportXml XMLString
```

In order to send this data to a Web service, you need to package it up into a SOAP message. That means you need to extract the inner XML content, and place it inside the SOAP envelope tag. Fortunately, this is an easy task if you use the DOMDocument40 object, which represents an in-memory XML document. First, you need to load the XML string into a new DOMDocument object.

```
Dim Doc As New DOMDocument
Doc.LoadXml XMLString
```

Then, you need to extract the inner part of the XML document.

```
Dim ReportData As IXMLDOMNodeList
Set ReportData = Doc.childNodes(0).childNodes
```

At this point, the ReportData object contains the <Meta> and <ExpenseItem> tags. It doesn't contain the <Root> element. This XML can now be inserted directly in a SOAP package and sent to the SubmitReport() web method.

To send the report data to a Web service, you can use the SoapClient30 object. Before using this object, you must configure it by specifying a Web Services Description Language (WSDL) document. The WSDL document describes the interface of the Web service, including a list of its web methods, and the parameters and data types required by each web method. You can generate a WSDL document from any ASP.NET Web service just by adding ?WSDL to the end of the URL. Thus, the WSDL document for the report service is something like this (assuming you used the directory alias ExpenseReport):

```
http://localhost/ExpenseReport/ExpenseReportService.asmx?WSDL
```

To create and configure the SoapClient30 object, you would use this code:

```
Dim Soap As New MSSOAPLib30.SoapClient30
Soap.MSSoapInit "http://localhost/ExpenseReport/ExpenseReportService.asmx?WSDL"
```

TIP *You can request the WSDL document in a web browser to take a look at the WSDL description for yourself.*

Now you can call the methods of the report service *through* the SoapClient30 object. In this case, you'll use the SubmitReport() web method, and send the XML data.

```
Soap.SubmitReport ReportData
```

The structure of the SOAP message you're sending is shown in the following code. Note that it's made up of two parts. The root <Envelope> and <Body> tags are in the namespace, and they make up the standard package for the XML data you're sending. Inside this package, in the namespace designated for the expense schema Web service, is a <SubmitReport> tag, identifying the method in the Web service that you are communicating with. Finally, the remainder of the message contains the <Root>, <Meta>, and <ExpenseItem> tags for the expense schema report.

```
<?xml version="1.0" encoding="utf-8"?>
<soap:Envelope xmlns:xsi="http://www.w3.org/2001/XMLSchema-instance"
 xmlns:xsd="http://www.w3.org/2001/XMLSchema"
 xmlns:soap="http://schemas.xmlsoap.org/soap/envelope/">
  <soap:Body>
    <SubmitReport xmlns="http://www.prosetech.com/Schemas/ExpenseReport">
      <Root>
        <Meta>
          <Name>...</Name>
          <Email>...</Email>
          <IDNumber>...</IDNumber>
          <Purpose>...</Purpose>
        </Meta>
        <ExpenseItem>
          <Date>...</Date>
          <Description>...</Description>
          <Miles>...</Miles>
          <Rate>...</Rate>
          <AirFare>...</AirFare>
          <Other>...</Other>
          <Meals>...</Meals>
          <Conference>...</Conference>
          <Misc>...</Misc>
          <MiscCode>...</MiscCode>
          <Total>...</Total>
        </ExpenseItem>
      </Root>
    </SubmitReport>
  </soap:Body>
</soap:Envelope>
```

The complete macro code is shown here:

```
Sub Submit()
    On Error GoTo submitErr

    If ActiveWorkbook.XmlMaps.Count > 0 Then
        ' Load the XML data from the spreadsheet into a string.
        Dim XMLString As String
        ActiveWorkbook.XmlMaps(1).ExportXml XMLString

        ' Drill down one level into the XML.
        ' (In other words, select everything except the root node.)
        Dim Doc As New DOMDocument40
        Doc.LoadXml XMLString
        Dim ReportData As IXMLDOMNodeList
        Set ReportData = Doc.childNodes(0).childNodes

        ' Prepare to use the Web service.
        Dim Soap As New MSSOAPLib30.SoapClient30
        Soap.MSSoapInit _
          "http://localhost/ExpenseReport/ExpenseReportService.asmx?WSDL"

        ' Submit the XML to the Web service.
        Dim Response As String
        Response = Soap.SubmitReport(ReportData)

        MsgBox Response
    End If

    Exit Sub

submitErr:
MsgBox Err.Description
End Sub
```

To allow the user to submit the spreadsheet data easily, you need to connect this code to the spreadsheet. Typically, you'll insert a button that the user can click to run the macro. To do this, select View ➤ Toolbars ➤ Forms. A floating toolbar will appear with various controls. Using this toolbar, select the button icon as shown in Figure 8-14.

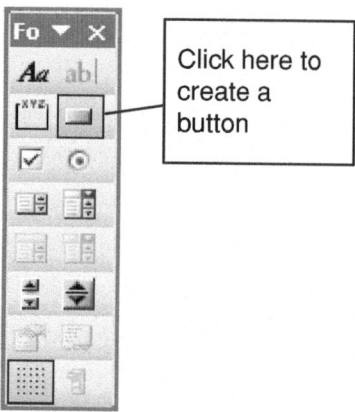

Figure 8-14. The forms toolbar for adding a button to a spreadsheet

Next, draw the button onto your spreadsheet. When the Assign Macro window shown in Figure 8-15 appears, choose the macro function you created, and click OK.

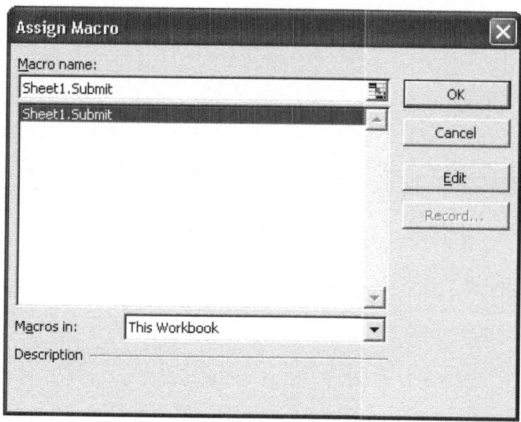

Figure 8-15. Attaching a subroutine to a button

Finally, change the text in the button to be "Submit". An example of how your completed spreadsheet might look is shown in Figure 8-16.

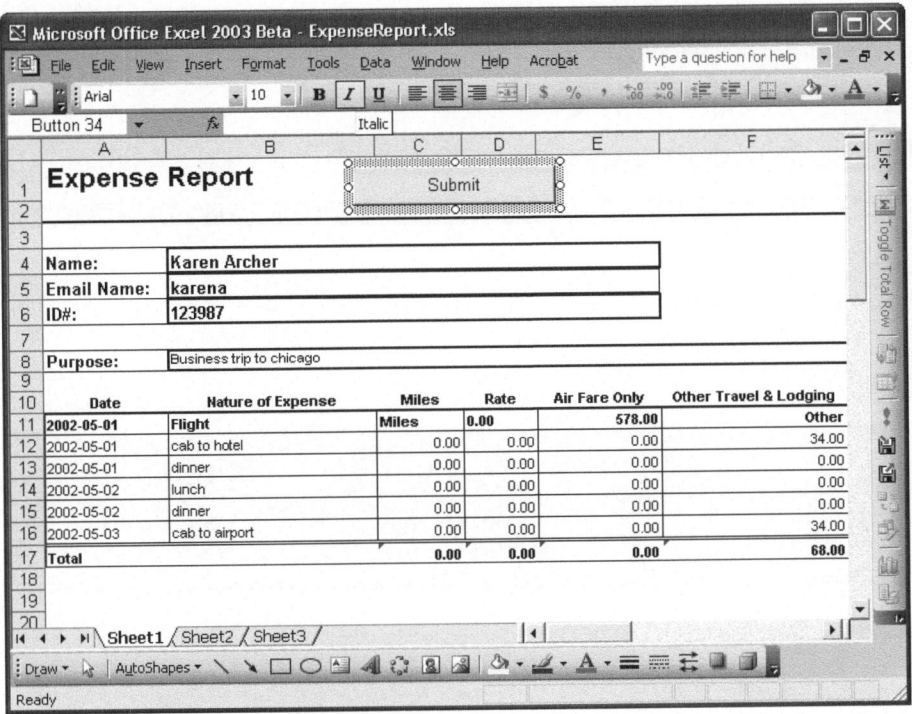

Figure 8-16. A spreadsheet that's connected to a Web service

Running a Test

Now that the code is complete, you can test it out by following these steps:

1. Fill out the expense table in the spreadsheet.

2. Click the Submit button. You should see a confirmation message informing you that the records have been added to the database. If an error occurs, you will see a message box informing you about the error.

3. Check the Access database to see whether the expense report records have been added.

For example, if you submit the spreadsheet shown in Figure 8-16, you should see the records shown in Figure 8-17.

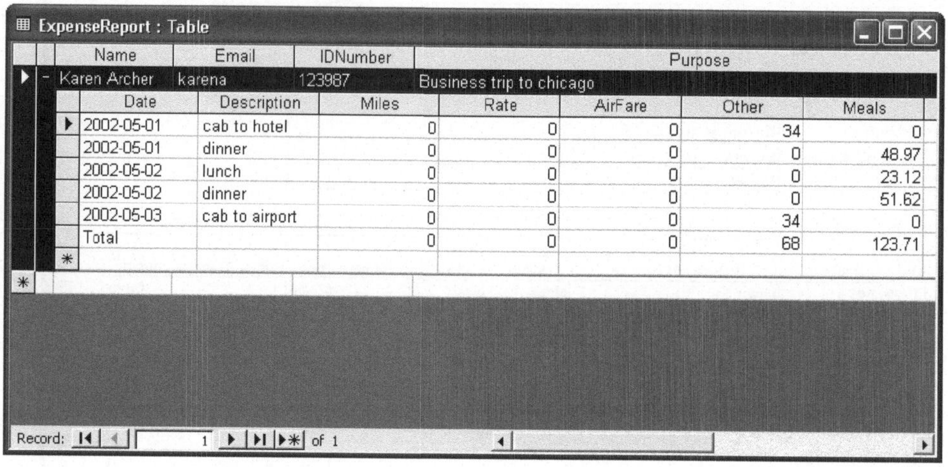
ExpenseReport : Table

Name	Email	IDNumber	Purpose
Karen Archer	karena	123987	Business trip to chicago

Date	Description	Miles	Rate	AirFare	Other	Meals
2002-05-01	cab to hotel	0	0	0	34	0
2002-05-01	dinner	0	0	0	0	48.97
2002-05-02	lunch	0	0	0	0	23.12
2002-05-02	dinner	0	0	0	0	51.62
2002-05-03	cab to airport	0	0	0	34	0
Total		0	0	0	68	123.71

Record: 1 of 1

Figure 8-17. Expense report records

Remember, you can only insert one expense report with a given ID. If you want to insert another expense report, either change the ID number in the spreadsheet, or delete the original record from the database.

Creating the Summary Web Page

Now that the information is stored in the database, you can allow users to access and modify that information in a number of ways. For example, you could create a custom application or an Excel spreadsheet that allows users to approve expense reports. In our next example, you'll build a simple ASP.NET page that extracts all the available information and displays it in an HTML page.

There are several ways that you could build this page. You could write custom logic to inspect the database values, format them, and then use ASP.NET web controls. In this example, you'll take a different approach and use nothing more than XML and XSLT.

To start with, load up Web Matrix and create a new web page named ExpenseSummary.aspx. Then, scroll to the bottom of the Toolbox and find the Xml web control. Drag this control onto the page, where it will become the gray box shown in Figure 8-18.

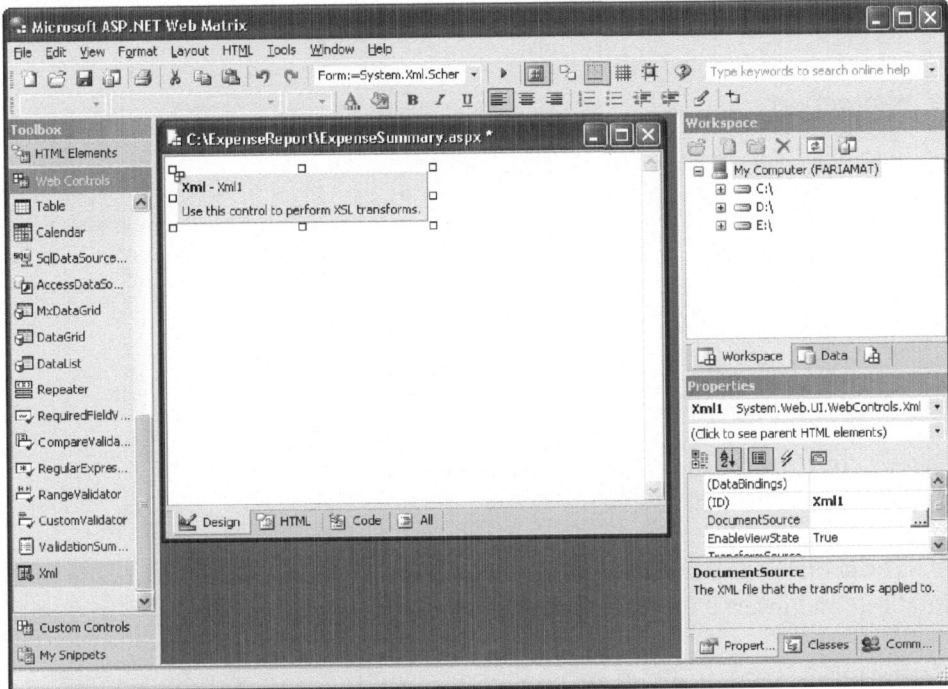

Figure 8-18. Adding the Xml web control

The Xml web control performs a single task: It converts XML into HTML based on an XSLT transform, and then inserts the results into the web page.

To make this work, you need to retrieve the data from the database when the page first loads. To create this code, select the Page object in the drop-down list of the Properties window (at the bottom right of the Web Matrix interface), click the lightning bolt to choose events, and then double-click in the space next to the word "Load" as shown in Figure 8-19.

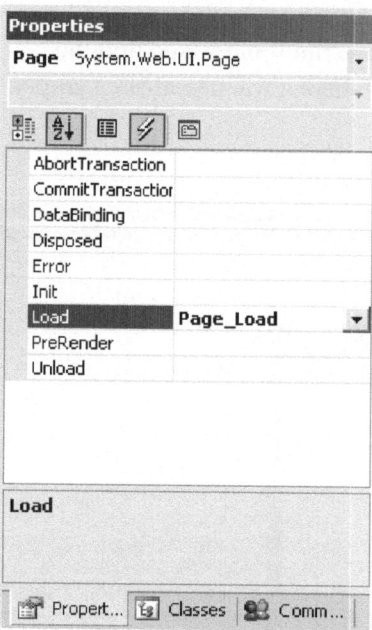

Figure 8-19. Creating code that runs when the page loads

The actual code you'll use will retrieve all the data from both tables in the database, and insert it into a special .NET object called the DataSet.

```
Dim ConnectionString As String = _
   "Provider=Microsoft.Jet.OLEDB.4.0;Data Source=c:\ExpenseReport\Expenses.mdb"
Dim Connection As New OleDbConnection(ConnectionString)
Dim SQL As String = "SELECT * FROM ExpenseReport"
Dim Adapter As New OleDbDataAdapter(SQL, Connection)

Dim DS As New DataSet("Expenses")
Adapter.Fill(DS, "ExpenseReport")
Adapter.SelectCommand.CommandText = "SELECT * FROM ExpenseItem"
Adapter.Fill(DS, "ExpenseItem")
```

The DataSet is an object that's designed to contain one or more tables for data. One of its unique features is its ability to support XML. Using the GetXml() method, you can extract an XML document that represents the data you've added. This XML document won't correspond to the ExpenseSchema.xsd. Instead, it follows its own system of organization, similar to that used when exporting data from Access. Element names are based on table names and column names. Here's an example of the XML that the DataSet will hold after being filled with the expense report data:

```
<Expenses>
  <ExpenseReport>
    <Name>Karen Archer</Name>
    <Email>karena</Email>
    <IDNumber>123987</IDNumber>
    <Purpose>Business trip to chicago</Purpose>
    <ExpenseItem>
      <Date>2002-05-01</Date>
      <Description>cab to hotel</Description>
      <Miles>0</Miles>
      <Rate>0</Rate>
      <AirFare>0</AirFare>
      <Other>34.0000</Other>
      <Meals>0</Meals>
      <Conference>0</Conference>
      <Misc>0</Misc>
      <MiscCode>0</MiscCode>
      <Total>34.0000</Total>
      <ExpenseReportID>123987</ExpenseReportID>
    </ExpenseItem>
    <ExpenseItem>...</ExpenseItem>
  <ExpenseReport>...</ExpenseReport>
  </ExpenseReport>
</Expenses>
```

It's fairly easy to write an XSLT that selects the elements you're interested in from this XML document, and formats them into HTML. The stylesheet you'll use, ExpenseSummary.xslt, is shown next. Note that it doesn't define the basic HTML starting tags like <html> and <body>, because this HTML will be inserted into a page that already has these tags.

```
<?xml version="1.0"?>
<xsl:stylesheet version="1.0" xmlns:xsl="http://www.w3.org/1999/XSL/Transform">
    <xsl:output method="html"/>

    <xsl:template match="/Expenses">
        <font face="Verdana">
        <h2>Expense Reports</h2>
        <xsl:apply-templates select="ExpenseReport"/>
        </font>
    </xsl:template>

    <xsl:template match="ExpenseReport">
        <hr/>
```

```
        <font size="4">Expenses - <xsl:value-of select="Name"/></font>
        <font size="1">
        <i><xsl:value-of select="IDNumber"/>:
          <xsl:value-of select="Purpose"/></i>
        </font>
        <table border="1" cellpadding="1" width="100%">
            <xsl:apply-templates select="ExpenseItem"/>
        </table>
        <br/><br/>
    </xsl:template>

    <xsl:template match="ExpenseItem">
       <tr>
           <td><font size="1"><xsl:value-of select="Date"/></font></td>
           <td><font size="1"><xsl:value-of select="Description"/></font></td>
           <td bgcolor="#FFCC33">
             <font size="1">$<xsl:value-of select="Total"/></font>
           </td>
       </tr>
    </xsl:template>


</xsl:stylesheet>
```

The final step is to set the XML and XSLT for the Xml web control. In this case, you extract the XML as a string, but submit the XSLT using the name of the file:

```
Xml1.DocumentContent = DS.GetXml()
Xml1.TransformSource = "ExpenseSummary.xslt"
```

The generated summary page is shown in Figure 8-20.

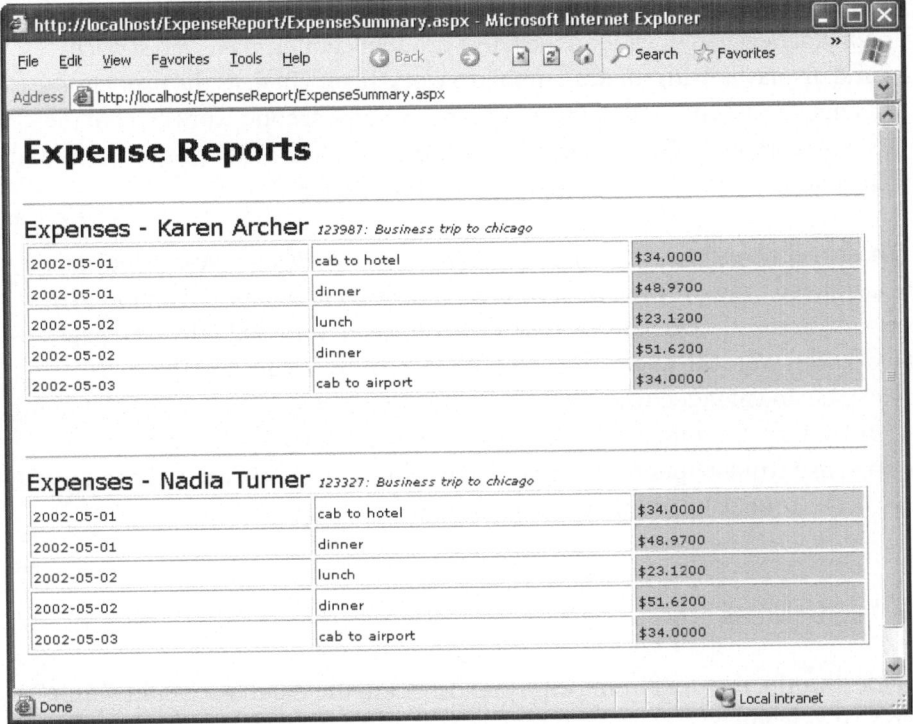

Figure 8-20. The summary page

Other Scenarios

In this chapter, you've seen one type of workflow with an expense report. A similar approach can be used to automate a number of different processes. Here are some examples:

- Use a mapped Word template to create news articles. Use a Word macro to submit the XML for the news article to a Web service, which stores it inside a server-side database. Display the news article in a web page using an XSLT transform.

- Use an Excel spreadsheet to analyze data from a sales database. The spreadsheet can retrieve data from a Web service, and insert it into a spreadsheet using a preestablished macro when a Retrieve button is clicked.

- Use an Excel spreadsheet to coordinate the entire ordering process. The spreadsheet can download the latest product catalog via a Web service, and display it using an XML map in a worksheet. Then, as the user chooses items, these can be added to an order form on a second worksheet in the same workbook. Finally, the XML for the completed order can be submitted to a different web method in the same Web service.

These tasks aren't easy, but they are finally possible. If you want to look at a more advanced example that incorporates the full version of Visual Studio .NET, download Microsoft's DocLibrary case study. It uses several ASP.NET web pages that work with WordML to generate and process insurance forms. This case study can be downloaded with the Microsoft Office System Content Development Kit (CDK) at http://msdn.microsoft.com/downloads/list/office2k3.asp, and is described in a white paper on Microsoft's web site at http://msdn.microsoft.com/library/en-us/dno2k3ta/html/odc_unlock.asp.

The Last Word

In an ideal world, the road from your spreadsheet to the database would require a single XML document. In fact, with today's XML hype, it often seems that everything supports XML, from databases to Web services to business documents. Unfortunately, just because one product or platform supports XML doesn't mean that it can be used with other XML-enabled tools seamlessly. It's still a challenge to connect different components with XML, and there are always several options.

In this chapter, you saw how you could feed XML generated from an XML document directly to an XML Web service. This still requires some thorny code, because data needs to jump between several different representations: as XML, as objects, as office data, and as tables in a database. In the future, other third-party products, like Microsoft's BizTalk server, might coordinate much of the work, routing and transforming XML documents so you don't need to wrestle with any code. Or, you might delve deeper into the code with .NET and SmartDocuments, which allow you to control the entire document editing process, but require a much greater developer investment. (For more information about using .NET and Office, you might want to check out Microsoft's Visual Studio Tools for Office at http://msdn.microsoft.com/vstudio/office/officetools.aspx.) Although there's still far to go, the transformation has definitely begun. Excel is now a full XML-enabled node, which means it can participate in an XML workflow for the first time.

InfoPath

THROUGHOUT THIS BOOK, you've witnessed the good and the bad of Office XML. At their best, the Office XML features allow you to link Office applications to other applications and business processes, broadening the reach of your documents and spreadsheets. At their worst, these features seem like difficult compromises welded onto existing formats, without the flexibility or ease of use most users demand.

Part of the problem is that Excel and Word are burdened with a long and illustrious history. Both products have existed for well over ten years in their Windows versions, which means they emerged long before XML was created. Although Office 2003 shows that both can use XML, neither one makes a perfect fit.

One solution to this problem might be to create a dedicated XML-based application that fills the wide gap between Excel and Word. This application wouldn't restrict users to rigid rectangular structures, like Excel, but it wouldn't allow the free-flowing freedom of Word. It would boast many of the rich Office features, like spell checking and validation, but it wouldn't require as much work to implement. Microsoft has taken its first shot at creating just such an application with InfoPath, a new addition to the Office 2003 family. InfoPath is an all-purpose tool for XML data entry. Using InfoPath, you can create attractive forms based on any XML schema. End-users can then create XML documents that match the schema by filling out the custom form. Best of all, you can link InfoPath directly to a Web service, allowing you to automate the process of collecting data in the enterprise.

In this chapter, you'll be introduced to InfoPath, and you'll learn about its advantages and shortcomings. By the end of this chapter, you'll see that although InfoPath may not be the perfect solution to XML headaches, it just might be the start of a new direction.

An Overview of InfoPath

Most of this book has concentrated on making the jump between rich Office documents and XML. I've assumed that the Office documents are the focus of your work. Other business processes might use the data in spreadsheets and documents, but the data is usually authored and analyzed using Word or Excel.

This focus makes sense, because it's the way of life in most organizations. However, it's not the only possibility. Sometimes, developers might start by creating custom applications or Web services that automate business processes. These applications might be completely new, and have no relationship to existing spreadsheets or documents. In this case, the focus is the custom applications, and the Office software is just another collection of tools. The new question is what's the easiest way to feed data into these applications? Is there a way that ordinary humans can submit the correct XML data?

One possibility is to leverage the XML export features in Word and Excel, and write custom macros like those shown in the last chapter. Another solution is to use InfoPath. With InfoPath, a user simply fills out a straightforward form, and submits the data. InfoPath converts the data to the appropriate type of XML, and either saves it to disk or sends it directly to a data source like a Web service.

You can perform exactly two tasks with InfoPath:

- *Design a rich form:* You can design this form by hand using controls like text boxes, checkboxes, and so on. However, it's much more likely that you'll quickly generate a new form based on an existing XML schema.

- *Fill out a form:* Once the form controls have been filled in, you can save the form as XML, or submit it directly to a Web service.

When to Use InfoPath

So when would it make sense to trade Excel and Word for an InfoPath solution? Here are some scenarios where InfoPath works best:

- You want to create a simple way to submit data to a centralized Web service or database, without needing to write any macro code.

- All of your data can be faithfully represented as XML.

- There is no need to retain a local copy of the data. The real task is just sending the data to the right server-side application.

On the other hand, there are a number of scenarios in which you would *not* want to use InfoPath:

- You need Office-specific functionality (like the ability to insert graphics, apply text formatting, create charts, perform calculations, and so on).

- The end user needs to keep a copy of the data to edit, reformat, incorporate into other documents, and so on.

- You don't have a central Web service or database where users can submit their data. Even though InfoPath data can be stored on local computers in XML files, this isn't the most useful approach.

As an example, InfoPath would work well for submitting expense report forms like those that were developed in the last chapter. On the other, InfoPath would be the wrong place to write a resume. Even though the resume contains useful data, it's far more flexible to create it with Word, and then export the details through the XML mapping features.

The Limits of InfoPath

InfoPath is an exciting way to convert user-submitted data into the rigid XML expected by another application. It holds great promise for automating information collection tasks. However, there are some gaps.

The key problem you'll find in InfoPath is that in order to fill out an InfoPath form, the client needs to have the InfoPath application. Other data-collection tools on the market leverage technologies like HTML web pages or the Adobe PDF format, ensuring that a wide range of users can create forms without installing any specialized software.[1] Unfortunately, these types of forms are more limited, awkward, or just slower to use.

The other key drawback is that InfoPath works best if you have somewhere to send the data. Usually, you'll create a centralized Web service to process the data or store it in a database. If you don't take this step, users will be forced to store the data in ordinary XML on their local computers. Though they can open this XML and edit it with InfoPath later on, they don't have nearly the same ability to analyze, format, or edit the information as they would in Word or Excel. In other

---

1. Two examples include Acrobat forms, which are a part of Adobe's Acrobat product, and the emerging XForms standard (see http://www.w3.org/TR/xforms), which aims to enhance HTML pages so they can better collect XML data.

words, InfoPath is a great tool for collecting data, but it doesn't give end users much ability to work with it on their own.

Designing InfoPath Forms

When you first launch InfoPath, an empty window will appear (see Figure 9-1), with several options in the Task pane:

- *Fill out a form:* This option allows you to enter data using an existing form. You choose the form template from a list of installed templates or recent files.

- *Open a form:* This option also allows you to enter data using an existing form. In this case, you choose the form by browsing to the template file. You can also use this option to open an XML file that contains partially completed form data. InfoPath will automatically find the linked form template, if it's available.

- *Design a form:* This option allows you to create a new form template.

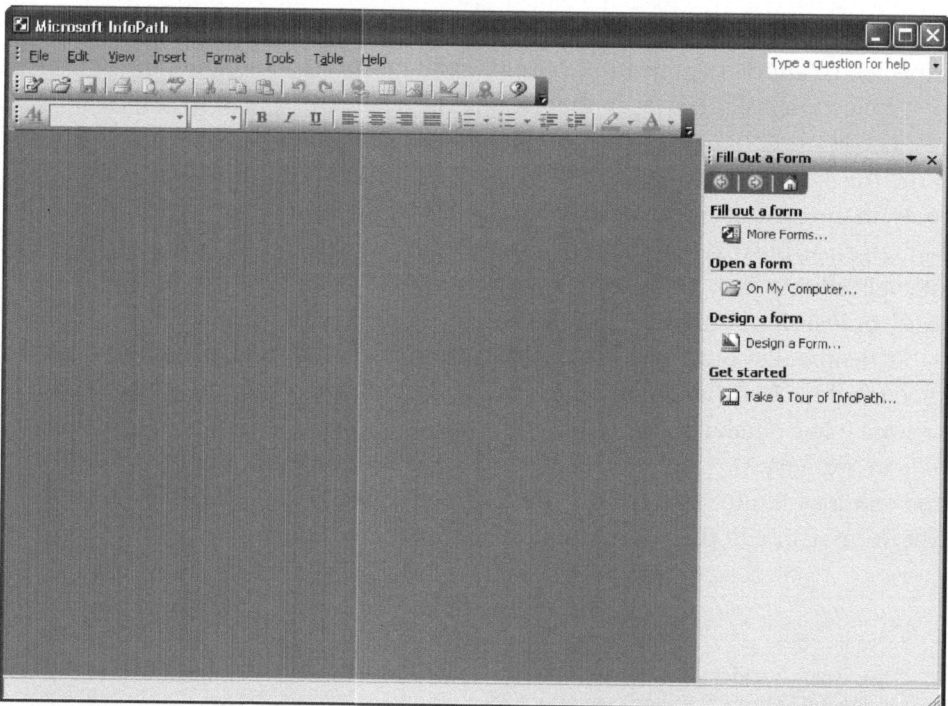

Figure 9-1. Launching InfoPath

To begin, click the "Design a form" option. Several new options will appear in the Task pane (see Figure 9-2). You have essentially three choices for creating a form:

- *New from Data Source:* This option allows you to create a form based on an XML schema, database, or Web service.

- *New Blank Form:* This option creates a new form that you can design by dragging and dropping the available controls.

- *Customize a Sample:* This option allows you to modify one of the sample forms included with InfoPath.

Figure 9-2. Options for designing a form

Usually, you'll design a form based on an existing schema or data source, and choose the first option. Although it's possible to design the form first in InfoPath and then generate the schema based on this form, this approach isn't as flexible as it should be. When you design a form by hand, InfoPath builds the corresponding schema based on the order that you place the form controls. You lose the ability to customize the schema according to your needs (unless you're willing to edit the automatically generated schema by hand outside of InfoPath).

In the next section, I'll walk you through the process of building a form using an XML schema.

Creating a Form Based on a Schema

The examples in this book have presented several sample schemas that you can use to try out InfoPath. To get started with a simple example, choose "New from Data Source" from the "Design a new form" options in the Task pane. The data source wizard will start (see Figure 9-3), which gives the three options. You can build a form based on an existing XML schema, a table in an Access or SQL Server database, or the definition of a Web service (an approach I'll discuss later in this chapter). Choose the first option to create a new InfoPath form based on an existing XML Schema, and click Next.

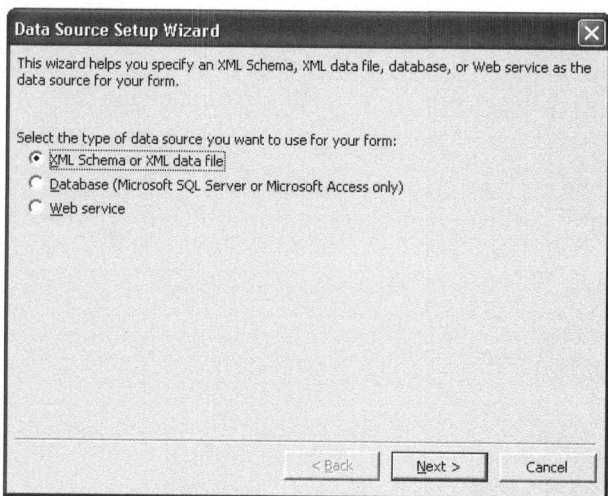

Figure 9-3. The data source wizard

Next, browse to the location where the schema file is stored. In this example, you'll use the FullQuotation.xsd schema file from Chapter 2, which defines <text>, <source>, and <category> elements inside a <quotation>, as shown here:

```
<?xml version="1.0"?>
<xsd:schema xmlns:xsd="http://www.w3.org/2001/XMLSchema"
 targetNamespace="http://www.prosetech.com/Schemas/QuotationList" >
    <xsd:element name="quotation">
        <xsd:complexType>
            <xsd:sequence>
                <xsd:element name="text" type="xsd:string"/>
                <xsd:element name="source" type="xsd:string"/>
                <xsd:element name="category" type="xsd:string"/>
            </xsd:sequence>
        </xsd:complexType>
    </xsd:element>
</xsd:schema>
```

> **TIP** *You can also design a form based on an XML document rather than a schema. In this case, InfoPath will attempt to infer the structure and rules of your markup language based on the example document. For better control, it's recommended that you always use a schema.*

Once you've chosen your schema file, click Finish to continue. A new, blank form will be created inside the InfoPath window, and the Task pane will change to show various layout options. Each layout option shows a different set of choices in the Task pane.

- *Layout:* Select this option to show a list of special layout controls like tables. You can insert these controls onto the form. Layout controls are designed to aid organization.

- *Controls:* Select this option to show the full list of basic controls, like test boxes, checkboxes, list boxes, and so on. This is where the user enters the form data. Typically, each control is bound to an element in the schema you're using.

- *Data Source:* Select this option to see an outline of elements in the corresponding schema. You can drag and drop these elements to the form, and InfoPath will generate the most suitable controls automatically.

By default, the Data Source option is selected. In Figure 9-4, you can see the outline of the FullQuotation.xsd schema, which includes four elements.

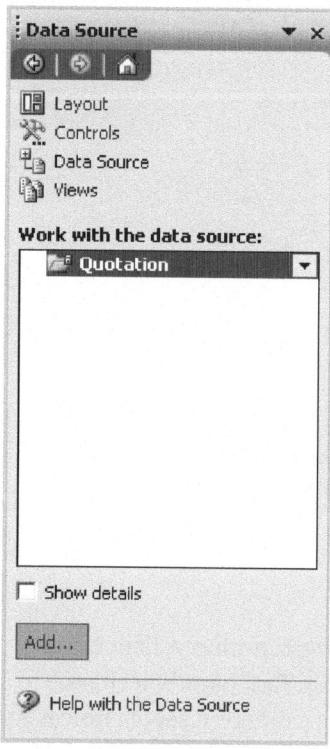

Figure 9-4. Designing with the FullQuotation.xsd schema

The easiest way to create a quotation form is to select the root <quotation> element from the Task pane, and drag it onto the form surface. When you release the mouse button, a menu will appear prompting you to choose how you want to generate controls for the quotation elements (see Figure 9-5).

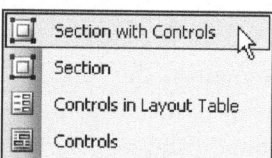

Figure 9-5. Inserting elements from the schema

Your choices include the following:

- *Section with Controls:* This inserts the controls for the <quotation> elements, and groups them into a section (which looks more or less like a box around the controls).

- *Section:* This inserts the section for the <quotation>, but it doesn't add any controls. You'll need to add those manually, or drag and drop the elements you want individually.

- *Controls in Layout Table:* This inserts the controls for the <quotation> elements in an invisible table, so that they are all aligned with one another.

- *Controls:* This inserts the controls for the <quotation> elements with no additional formatting.

Generally, the first option—Section with Controls—gives the nicest appearance for a form. But just in case you want to compare the different choices, Figure 9-6 shows what each one looks like when it's added to a form. You'll notice that the controls are always generated using ordinary text boxes, because the <quotation> elements use the simple string data type.

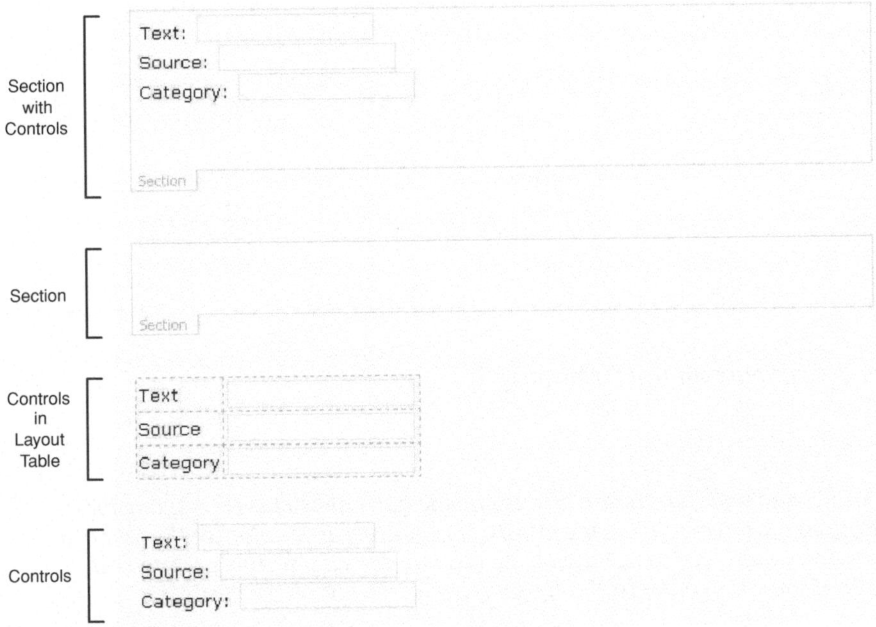

Figure 9-6. Different ways to insert form controls

Of course, once you've added the controls by dragging and dropping the schema elements, you're still able to change the text, rearrange the order by cutting and pasting, and change formatting details like fonts and colors. In fact, nothing could be easier. Just position your mouse over the control you want to change, at which point a special icon will appear indicating the XML element to which it's bound (see Figure 9-7).

Figure 9-7. Selecting an individual control

Next, click once on the element to select it. To change the font, apply style characteristics like bold or italic, or change the text or background color, and click the appropriate control on the formatting toolbar, which closely resembles the formatting toolbars of Word and Office. Some of the key ingredients are highlighted in Figure 9-8.

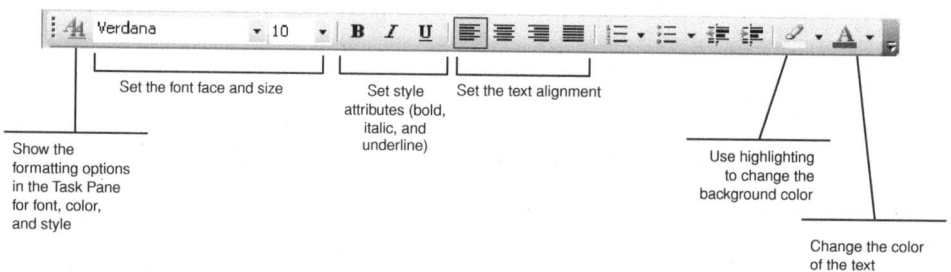

Figure 9-8. Configure control formatting

TIP *You'll also find that some controls provide quick shortcuts for copying formatting characteristics to other controls. For example, if you change the font of a text box, you only need to right-click the text box and choose Apply Font to All Text Box Controls in order to change all the other text boxes on the form.*

Many controls include some advanced formatting properties as well. These can be accessed by right-clicking the control. For example, if you right-click a text box and choose Text Box Properties, you can supply a default value; designate the field as read-only; enable text wrapping, auto-complete, and spell checking; and even configure tooltip text and a shortcut key. For advanced forms, you can even attach event handlers written with macro code that will react to certain change events, and perform the appropriate actions, like modifying a value or prompting the user for more information.

To see how your form looks, you can open a preview window at any time by clicking the Preview Form button on the toolbar, or choosing File ➤ Preview Form ➤ Default. This loads the form and allows you to enter data. You can also choose to open an existing XML file into your form for a preview. The only requirement is that the XML file must match the schema you used to design the form. In this example, you design a form based on the FullQuotation.xsd schema file, so you can launch a preview using the FullQuotation.xml data file. If you do, you'll see the window shown in Figure 9-9.

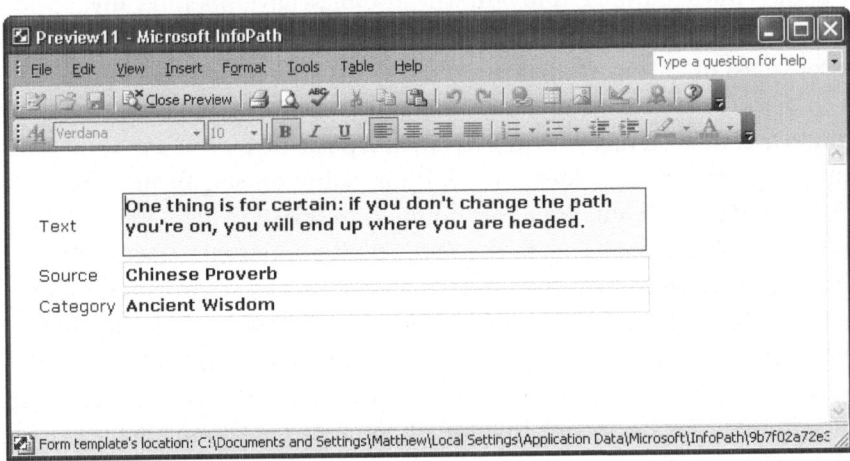

Figure 9-9. Previewing the FullQuotation.xml data file

When you've finished designing the form, you can save it to disk by choosing File ➤ Save from the menu. InfoPath will prompt you with a dialog box that asks whether you want to save or publish the form. Choose to save it to store the form template on your local hard drive. InfoPath template files are stored as .xsn files. Incidentally, InfoPath files use a proprietary binary standard, so you won't be able to use an XML reader to crack open a template file and see how it's designed. We'll consider how to publish forms a little later in this chapter.

Filling Out the Form

To fill out the form you've created, other users will need to open the .xsn template file using InfoPath. Simply choose the "Fill out a form" option from the Task pane when starting InfoPath, or select File ➤ Fill Out a Form from the menu.

> **TIP** *When you save an InfoPath template, it stores information about its current location. If you move the InfoPath form to another location, you won't be able to open it. This is to prevent users from saving modified versions of your templates, and using them to enter invalid data. However, it can be quite an annoyance when you copy a file from one location to another, and find out you can no longer open it! If you find yourself in this situation, there's an easy fix. First, open the form in design mode (which is allowed). Then, save or publish the form to its new location. Publishing is discussed in detail later in this chapter.*

While editing the document, InfoPath will automatically underline any schema errors. If you've configured spell checking (the default for text fields), you'll also see questionable words being underlined. A simple right-click gives the user a choice of alternatives, as shown in Figure 9-10. You'll also find the ability to undo and redo changes, as well as cut and paste text.

The simple quotation form doesn't provide any submit mechanism, so once users have finished filling it out, their only option is to save it to disk. All form data is saved as ordinary XML, according to the XML schema you used to design the form. The only additional detail is the insertion of two processing instructions at the beginning of the XML document. These processing instructions specify that InfoPath was used to create the document, and indicate the location of the corresponding .xsn template file. If the user double-clicks to open the XML file at a later time, it will automatically be opened in InfoPath, provided the template file can be found in the same location.

Here's what an XML document authored with the quotation template might look like:

```
<?xml version="1.0" encoding="UTF-8"?>
<?mso-infoPathSolution solutionVersion="1.0.0.4"
 productVersion="11.0.4920" PIVersion="0.9.0.0"
 href="file:///C:\FullQuoteTemplate.xsn"
 language="en-us" ?>
<?mso-application progid="InfoPath.Document"?>
<ns1:quotation xmlns:ns1="http://www.prosetech.com/Schemas/QuotationList">
    <ns1:text>I know nothing except the fact of my own ignorence </ns1:text>
```

```
    <ns1:source>Socrates</ns1:source>
    <ns1:category>Ancient Wisdom</ns1:category>
</ns1:quotation>
```

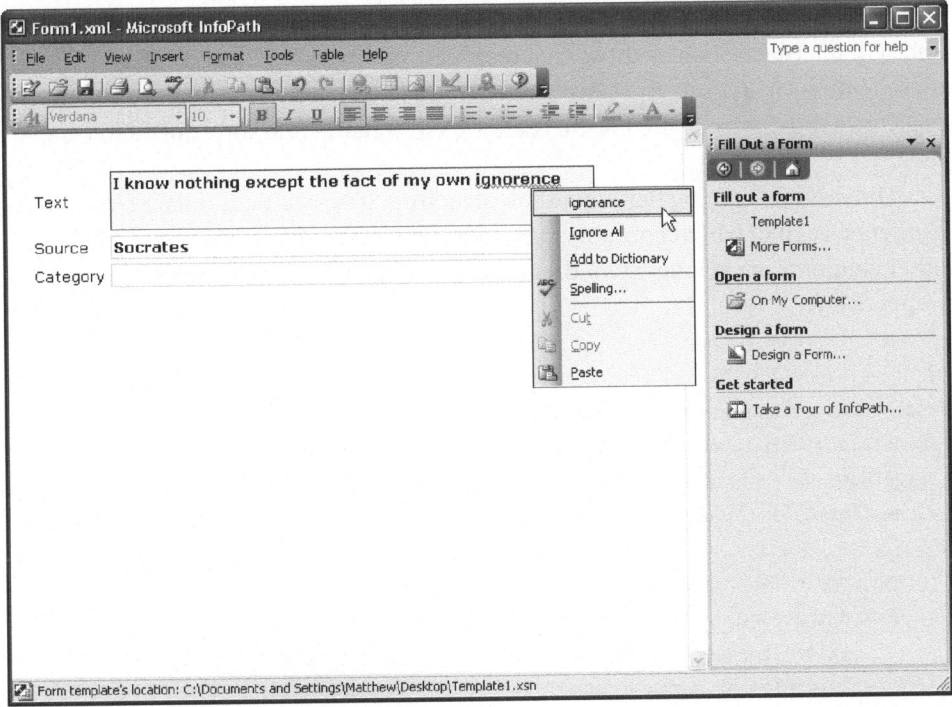

Figure 9-10. Filling out a form

Once the file is saved, users can take additional steps like e-mailing the file to a specific user or copying it to a network drive. Ideally, you'll have a Web service ready to receive the data directly—an approach I'll discuss later in this chapter. Users also have the ability to print forms by selecting File ➤ Print.

> **NOTE** *Users who open your form will be able to not only fill out copies of the form, but also change the design of your form. You can prevent this in the same way that you stop users from modifying Word documents or Excel spreadsheets: by protecting the document. In InfoPath, select Tools ➤ Form Options. Next, in the General tab, choose "Enable protection". This prevents the user from accidentally switching into design mode by disabling these options in the menu when filling out a form. However, it won't prevent the user who chooses to explicitly open the form in design mode from making changes. The best way to prevent this sort of tampering is to store your form template in a secure shared location (like a write-protected network drive), so that it can't be overwritten by ordinary users.*

Complex Forms

InfoPath really shines when you design forms for more complex schemas. Because InfoPath has been designed from the ground up to understand the XML Schema standard, it can easily handle details like special data types, variable-length lists, and schema rules (such as those that restrict text length or allowed values). To see these features in action, you simply need to work with a more advanced schema file. One good choice is the ProductCatalog.xsd schema first introduced in Chapter 2.

The product catalog has a two-part structure. It's essentially a list of <product> elements, each of which contains four additional pieces of information. These other elements are strongly typed as a string, Boolean, decimal, and integer, respectively.

```xml
<?xml version="1.0"?>
<xsd:schema xmlns:xsd="http://www.w3.org/2001/XMLSchema"
 xmlns:prod="http://www.prosetech.com/Schemas/ProductCatalog"
 targetNamespace="http://www.prosetech.com/Schemas/ProductCatalog"
 elementFormDefault="qualified">

    <xsd:complexType name="product">
        <xsd:sequence>
            <xsd:element name="productName" type="xsd:string"/>
            <xsd:element name="productPrice" type="xsd:decimal"/>
            <xsd:element name="inStock" type="xsd:boolean"/>
        </xsd:sequence>
        <xsd:attribute name="id" type="xsd:integer"/>
    </xsd:complexType>

    <xsd:element name="productCatalog">
        <xsd:complexType>
            <xsd:sequence>
                <xsd:element name="catalogName" type="xsd:string"/>
                <xsd:element name="expiryDate" type="xsd:date"/>

                <xsd:element name="products">
                    <xsd:complexType>
                        <xsd:sequence>
                            <xsd:element name="product" type="prod:product"
                              maxOccurs="unbounded" />
                        </xsd:sequence>
                    </xsd:complexType>
```

```
                </xsd:element>
              </xsd:sequence>
            </xsd:complexType>
          </xsd:element>

</xsd:schema>
```

You can build a form for this schema in InfoPath in the same way that you did for the quotation schema. Simply choose the New from Data Source option in the Task pane, and select XML Schema in the data source wizard. When the wizard is finished, the structure of your schema will appear in the Task pane (as shown in Figure 9-11). Select the "Show details" checkbox under the schema tree to see the details about the type of content stored in each element and attribute. Elements that are marked with an asterisk aren't allowed to contain empty values.

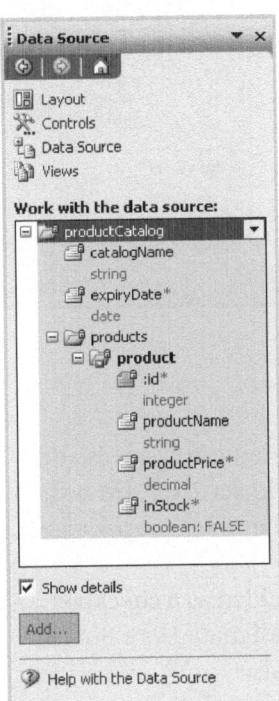

Figure 9-11. The ProductCatalog.xsd schema

Once again, you have several choices for adding these controls to your form. For maximum control, you can drag and configure each element one by one. However, an easier approach is to select the entire structure by clicking the root

<productCatalog> element, and then dragging it onto the form surface. Choose Section with Controls from the context menu. InfoPath will generate the controls shown in Figure 9-12.

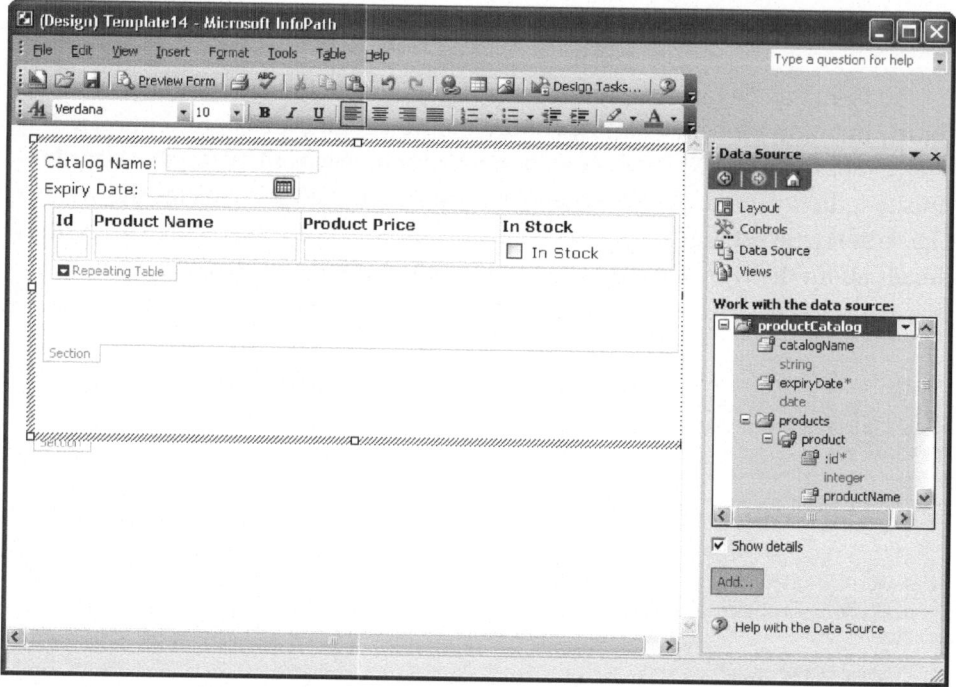

Figure 9-12. The product catalog controls

Already, there are a few differences you'll notice between these controls and those used for the quotation schema. The Expiry Date field looks like a text box, but it sports a calendar icon. When users fill out this data, they have the assistance of the integrated calendar picker shown in Figure 9-13.

Another difference is the <inStock> element, which is added as a checkbox control. InfoPath makes this choice because <inStock> is designated as a Boolean data type, which means it can only take the values true or false.

The most important change, however, is the way that the <product> elements are treated using a special repeating table layout control. Though you only see one empty item, the user filling out the form can add as many items as required, and the list will grow dynamically. To test it out, preview the ProductCatalog.xml data file. When you right-click the list, you can insert new items into the table in any position, as shown in Figure 9-14.

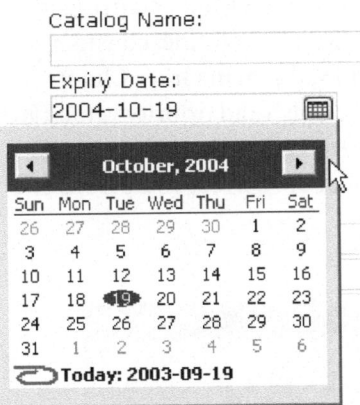

Figure 9-13. The calendar control

Products

ID	Product Name	Product Price	In Stock
1,001	Magic Ring	$342.10	☑ In Stock
		$982.99	☑ In Stock

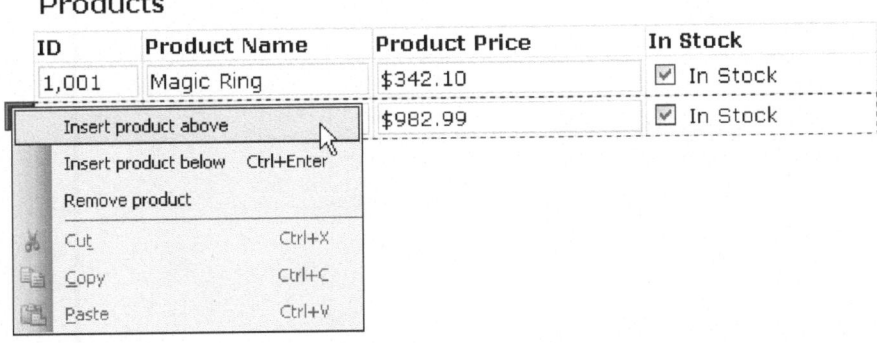

Figure 9-14. A dynamic list control

> **TIP** *One customization is so subtle you probably missed it completely. InfoPath automatically generated the correct headings for all your controls, even though these headings don't match the element names. For example, for the <product-Price> element, it created the heading "Product Price". Clearly, InfoPath has some built-in intelligence that helps it to break compound terms down into their individual words.*

It goes without saying that InfoPath enforces the schema rules. If you break them, the offending input will be flagged with a red outline. You'll be able to save the form to XML, but you won't be able to submit it. In this example, the form doesn't have submit capabilities, so you won't notice this limitation.

Of course, the best way to solve errors is to prevent them from occurring in the first place. InfoPath does this where it makes sense. For example, consider Figure 9-15, which shows a form based on the Memo.xsd schema from Chapter 4. This schema uses an enumeration to specify that the only valid priority values are High, Low, and Medium. Rather than forcing the user to guess this information and type it in correctly, InfoPath asks the user to select the correct value from one of the options in a drop-down list box.

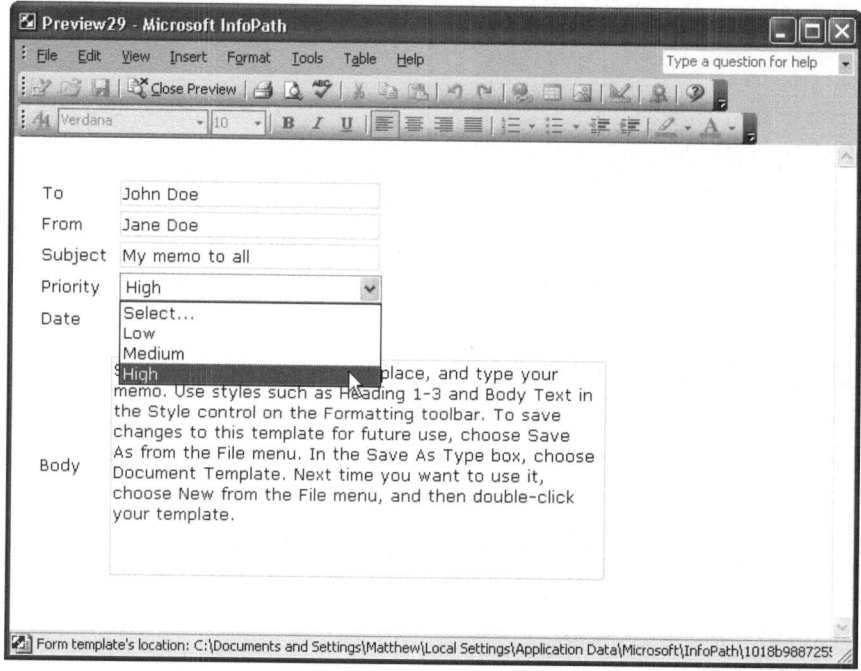

Figure 9-15. Selecting a value from an enumeration

This underscores two key benefits of InfoPath. First of all, InfoPath allows you to design forms quickly by dragging and dropping schema elements. This is a refreshing improvement over the often tedious process of mapping XML in Word and Excel. Secondly, InfoPath includes controls that are tailored to the different schema data types, and flags any discrepancies immediately with descriptive tooltip text. In Word and Excel, users are free to enter any text, possibly violating schema rules. Excel is the worst offender—it doesn't even validate schema rules until the XML is exported. It's these differences that make InfoPath a more natural companion for XML data.

Publishing Forms

In order to fill out an InfoPath form, the user needs to be able to access the .xsn template file. You can't simply distribute it by e-mailing it or copying it onto a disk, because it must be opened from the same location where it was created. The solution is to use InfoPath's publishing feature.

Publishing is a special form of template deployment that minimizes version problems. When you publish a template, you copy it to a shared location, like a shared network drive, a SharePoint form library, or a virtual directory on a web server. Users who want to fill out the template must open it using the exact same location path that you use to publish it. This ensures that only one version of the template will exist. If a user copies the template (for example, to his or her local computer), the user won't be able to open the template and fill out forms. What's more, whenever a user opens an XML file that was created with a template, InfoPath will load the template from the published location, ensuring that the latest version of the form is being used to edit the data.

Publishing a form template is quite easy. All you need to do is follow these steps:

1. Open a form in InfoPath in design mode, and select File ➤ Publish from the menu. This starts the publishing wizard.

2. Click Next to get started with the wizard.

3. The wizard allows you to publish the form to one of three types of locations: a shared network folder, a SharePoint form library (which requires the SharePoint Services available in Windows Server 2003), or a web server. These options are shown in Figure 9-16. The simplest form of deployment is the first option—to use a shared folder.

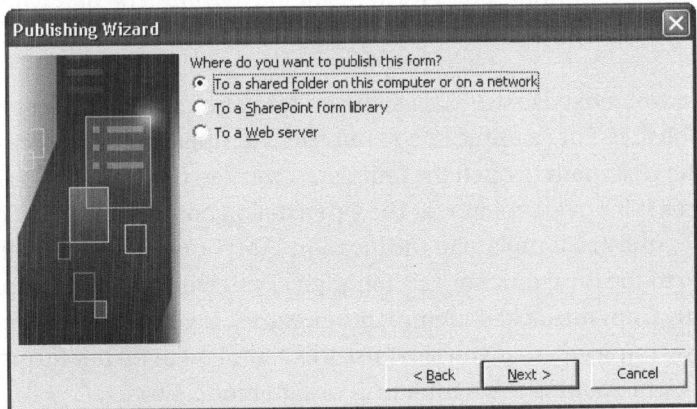

Figure 9-16. Choosing a location type

4. The next window prompts you to specify the shared location you want to use (see Figure 9-17). Keep in mind that all users will need to use this location path. Thus, if you use the path h:\Templates\MyTemplate.xsn, all users must have the same drive mapping and be able to access the Templates folder on drive h.

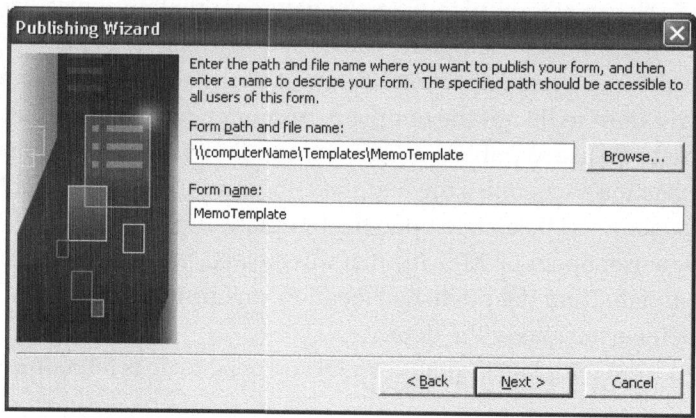

Figure 9-17. Specifying a location as a UNC path

> **TIP** *In many cases, it's better to use a UNC path than a drive-letter path. UNC paths incorporate the name of the computer, and follow the format \\[ComputerName]\[ShareName]\[FileNameOrPath]. As long as the computer is accessible, the UNC path will work, even if the drive mappings aren't the same.*

5. Click Next to continue, and Finish to end the wizard. The files will be copied.

Remember, you must use the exact same path to open the file as the one you used to publish it. For example, if you publish a template using a UNC path, you must use the UNC path to open the template. (You can type the UNC path into Internet Explorer, Windows Explorer, or the Open dialog box in InfoPath.) For example, if you publish a template to the location \\MyComputer\Templates, and this share maps to the local directory c:\Templates, you won't be able to open the template directly from the local c:\Templates directory. If you do, you'll receive an error message warning you that you can't use this template to fill out forms. This won't stop you from opening the template in design mode, however.

> **NOTE** *Make sure you don't save over a published template. Instead, make changes to a separate copy, and then publish it to the same location when it's complete. Ideally, you should use a new template name. Otherwise, users who have stored partially completed forms might not be able to edit them, depending on the changes you've made.*

InfoPath and Web Services

XML isn't terribly useful on its own. It becomes far more useful when it's combined with a business application that can make decisions or perform other tasks based on the data it contains. Likewise, InfoPath becomes a much more compelling solution when you decide to plug it into a live Web service.

In the previous chapter, you saw how you could build an XML workflow from scratch. InfoPath allows you to create the same system but skip many of the more painstaking steps. Instead of writing custom macro code, for example, you can build a form based on the Web service you want to use.

InfoPath can plug into a Web service in these ways:

- You can create a form that displays the XML data retrieved from a Web service. This might be useful if you just need a way to show summary information, or the most recent version of the company product catalog.

- You can create a form that accepts user input and submits the data to a Web service. This allows you to collect XML data without jumping through any extra programming hurdles.

As an example, consider the expense report service demonstrated in the previous chapter. It provided a single web method, called SubmitReport(), that takes expense report data and stores it in an Access database. To build an InfoPath for this Web service, follow these steps:

1. Choose the New from Data Source option in the Task pane.

2. When the data source wizard appears, select "Web service" and click Next.

3. The data source wizard will prompt you for information about how the form will interact with the Web service (see Figure 9-18). The quickest way to design this form is to choose the third option ("Receive data"). Once you choose the SubmitReport() method, InfoPath will recognize that it not only returns a confirmation message, but also requires you to submit an expense report, and it will allow you to generate the forms for both tasks with a minimum of confusion. You could also select the "Receive and submit data" option, but you'll be forced to walk through more steps in the wizard.

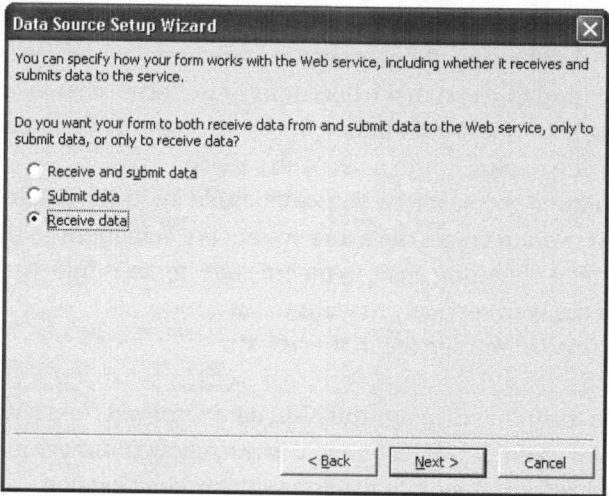

Figure 9-18. Specifying how a form interacts with a Web service

4. Next, the data source wizard will request the location of the Web service you want to use (see Figure 9-19). You must supply the complete virtual directory path, with ?WSDL appended at the end. That means you'll use a path like http://localhost/ExpenseReport/ExpenseReportService.asmx?WSDL. Enter this path and click Next to continue. (You can also click the Search UDDI button, which allows you to locate a Web service by searching the catalog on a Universal Description, Discovery, and Integration (UDDI) server. UDDI is still an emerging standard, but Microsoft provides a reference implementation and information at http://uddi.microsoft.com.)

5. The next window shows the available web methods defined in the Web service (see Figure 9-20). Choose the only one available (SubmitMethod), and click Next to continue.

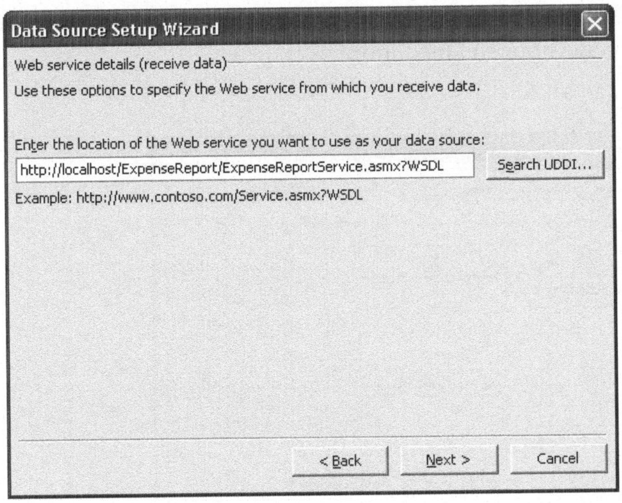

Figure 9-19. Specifying the Web service

> **NOTE** *Remember, the ?WSDL requests the Web service's WSDL (Web Services Description Language) document. This document describes the service and the methods it provides, and it provides the XML schema for all the messages that are sent to and received from the Web service. Using this schema, InfoPath can construct a form that will generate the right SOAP message for your web method. Technically, you don't need to add the ?WSDL portion—InfoPath will add this automatically if you leave it out of the URL.*

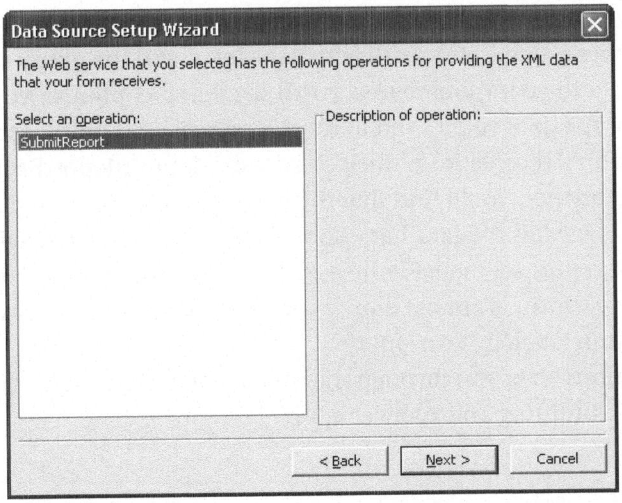

Figure 9-20. Choosing a web method from the Web service

6. Finally, InfoPath shows a summary window that lists the Web service and method you have chosen (see Figure 9-21).

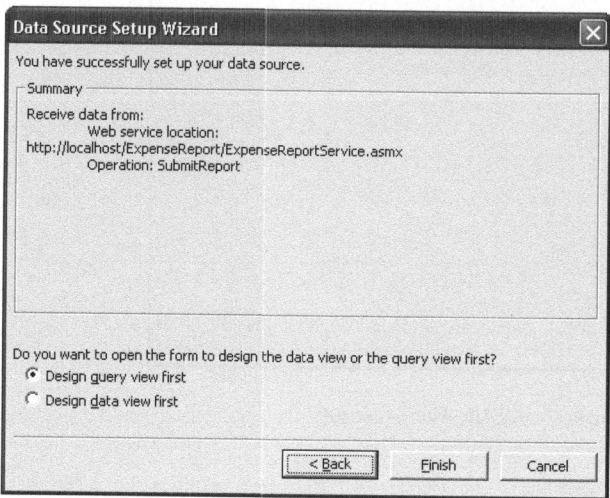

Figure 9-21. The Web service summary

7. Because this web method both requires and returns information, you'll actually design two separate forms. One form (the query form) allows the user to input an expense report, while the other form (the data form) displays the returned confirmation message. At the bottom of the window, choose to design the query form first, and then click Finish.

A new form will be created in InfoPath with two views, and the query view will be shown. If you look at the data source tree, you'll see that it contains two separate branches: one for the data you'll send to the Web service (SubmitResponse), and one for the data you'll receive from the Web service (SubmitReportResponse). If you expand these branches, you'll find that the response contains a single string, while the request message has the familiar <Root>, <Meta>, and <ExpenseItem> tags from the expense report schema. Figure 9-22 shows the full InfoPath window. Note that the query view form is almost empty—it begins with some descriptive text and a submit button labeled "Run Query".

The next few sections walk you through the process of designing the query and data forms, and submitting an expense report.

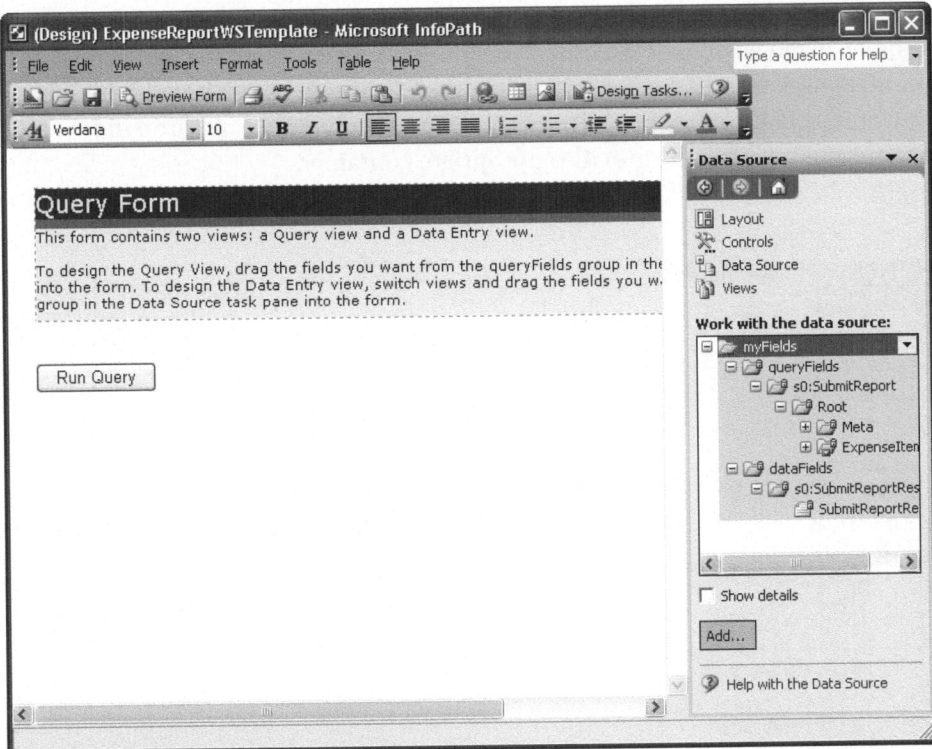

Figure 9-22. InfoPath with the Web service query form

Designing a Query Form

Using the query form, the end user will enter the expense report data, and submit it to the Web service. Creating this form is just as easy as the previous examples, because you can generate it automatically using the Web service schema.

To create the expense report controls, simply select the <Root> tag in the element tree, as shown in Figure 9-23. Drag the elements onto the form, and select Section with Controls from the context menu. For the best appearance, try to drop the controls into the blue query section. If you want to customize the look a little more, you can insert the <Meta> and <ExpenseItem> elements separately. That way, you can put each group into its own formatted table.

No matter which approach you take, you'll end up with a form like the one shown in Figure 9-24. You'll notice here that only one expense item is shown at a time. However, you can add new expense items in the same way as you added product items in the product catalog example—just click the arrow on the left and choose one of the insert options from the menu. The only difference is that the

<ExpenseItem> elements are in a repeating section control, rather than a repeating table. If you want to dive a little deeper into InfoPath, you can change this around completely. All you'll need to do is add the layout controls you want manually from the controls section of the Task pane, and then drag and drop the <ExpenseItem> elements into the appropriate container.

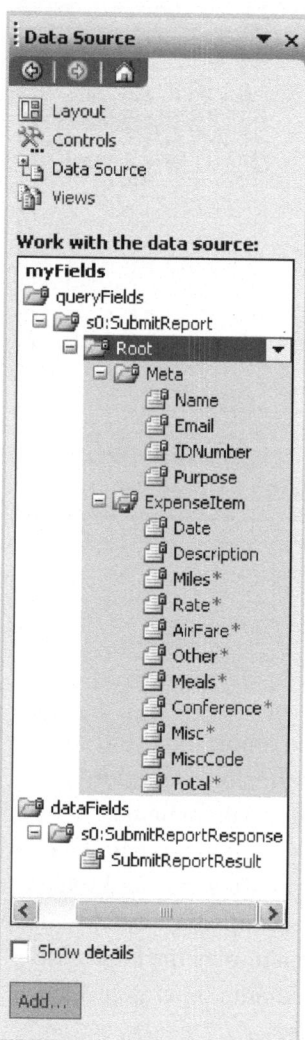

Figure 9-23. The expense report elements

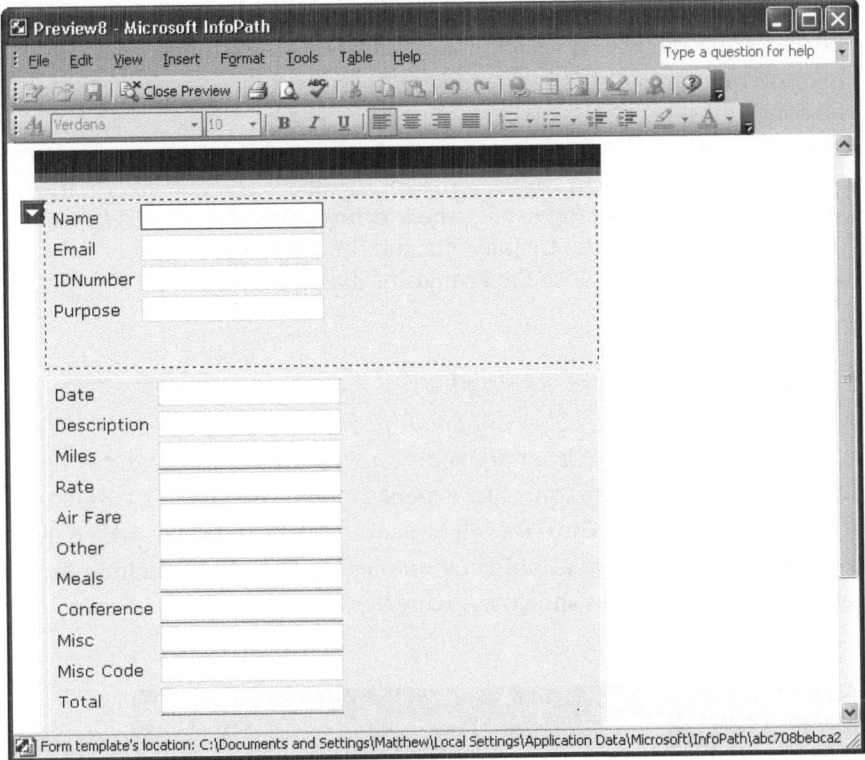

Figure 9-24. The expense report query form

Designing a Data Form

The next step is to design the form that will display the confirmation message you receive from the SubmitReport() web method. You'll need to follow these steps:

1. To change views, click the Views option in the Task pane.

2. Right-click the Query view and select Set as Default. This way, the user will start with the expense report form.

3. Select the Data Entry view. This opens a new blank form.

4. Next, choose the Data Source option in the Task pane to show the schema tree.

5. Scroll down to the <SubmitReportResponse> element, and drag it onto the data entry page. This will contain the text response that's received from the web service after it's invoked. Choose Section with Controls from the context menu.

6. In this situation, it doesn't make sense for the user to be able to edit the confirmation message. Right-click the text box control, and select Text Box Properties. Select the Display tab, and then select the Read-only checkbox. Click OK to close the Properties dialog box.

Submitting an Expense Report

You can now test the InfoPath Web service solution. Preview the form, and enter the required expense report data (only one expense item is needed). Then, click Run Query to submit the data. The data will be sent to the Web service, which will add it to the database and return a confirmation message. The confirmation message appears in the data view, as shown in Figure 9-25.

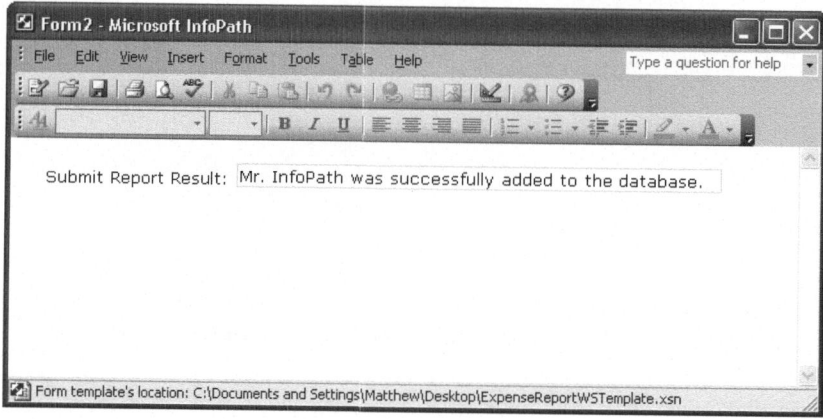

Figure 9-25. The Web service confirmation message

This highlights InfoPath's greatest benefits. To create the end-to-end solution in the previous chapter, you need to write custom macro code, and rely on other components like the SOAP Toolkit. With InfoPath, however, the form data can be submitted to an XML Web service with no extra work. Alternatively, you can submit data to a database (including Access or SQL Server), or to a SharePoint form library. SharePoint is a collaboration technology integrated into Windows Server 2003. For more information, surf to http://www.microsoft.com/sharepoint.

The Last Word

In this chapter you had a lightning tour of the latest addition to the Office family: InfoPath, a tool for generating and filling out XML-based forms. InfoPath is somewhere in between the extremes of raw XML and rich Office applications. It won't replace Word or Excel, or remove the need for their XML mapping features, but it does present an interesting alternative when all you need to do is collect data, convert it to XML, and submit it to a business process in the fastest and most convenient way possible.

INDEX